UNDERSTANDING
MANAGEMENT

UNDERSTANDING MANAGEMENT

edited by

*Stephen Linstead, Robert Grafton Small
and Paul Jeffcutt*

SAGE Publications

London · Thousand Oaks · New Delhi

First published 1996

SAGE Publications Ltd
6 Bonhill Street
London EC2A 4PU

SAGE Publications Inc
2455 Teller Road
Thousand Oaks, California 91320

SAGE Publications India Pvt Ltd
32, M-Block Market
Greater Kailash - I
New Delhi 110 048

British Library Cataloguing in Publication data

A catalogue record for this book is
available from the British Library

ISBN 0 8039 8912-1
ISBN 0 8039 8913-X (pbk)

Library of Congress catalog card number 95-072171

Typeset by Type Study, Scarborough, North Yorkshire
Printed in Great Britain by The Cromwell Press Ltd,
Broughton Gifford, Melksham, Wiltshire

To the memory of Dan Gowler (1931–1992); and Keith Turner (1949–1993), an indefatigable ally, innovative agitator, inimitable critic, irrepressible spirit, and irreplaceable friend.

Contents

Acknowledgements

Certain of the chapters of this book have appeared previously in a different form in other places. We are grateful to the following for permission to reproduce them, in revised form, here:

Blackwell Publishers for Chapters 5 and 7; the editors of *Sociological Review* for Chapter 3; MCB Publications for Chapter 9; and Oxford University Press for Chapter 2.

Chapter 2 appeared as 'The Meaning of Management and the Management of Meaning: a view from social anthropology', in Michael J. Earl, (ed.) *Perspectives on Management: A Multidisciplinary Analysis*. Oxford: Oxford University Press 197–233 (1983).

Chapter 3 appeared as 'Establishing Blissful Clarity in Organizational Life: Managers', in *Sociological Review*, 28(4): 763–82 (1980).

Chapter 5 appeared as 'Some Everyday Rituals in Management Control', *Journal of Management Studies* 28(6): 569–83 (1991).

Chapter 7 appeared as 'Management in Context: an essay on the relevance of culture to understanding organizational change', *Journal of Management Studies* 23(6): 587–607 (1985).

Chapter 9 appeared as 'Marketing, or the Anthropology of Consumption', *European Journal of Marketing*, 21(9): 66–71 (1985).

Contributors

Omar Aktouf is full Professor of Management at the École des Hautes Études Commerciales (HEC), Montréal, Québec, Canada.

Barbara Czarniawska-Joerges is Professor of Management in the School of Economics and Management, University of Lund, Sweden.

Steven P. Feldman is Associate Professor of Management Policy, Weatherhead School of Management, Case Western Reserve University, Cleveland, Ohio, USA.

David Golding is Senior Research Fellow in the Institute for Organisational Analysis, University of Hull, UK, and Visiting Professor of Management at Sheffield Business School, Sheffield Hallam University, UK.

The late **Dan Gowler** (1931–1992) was a Fellow of Templeton College and University Lecturer in Organizational Behaviour, University of Oxford, UK.

Robert Grafton Small was formerly Lecturer in Marketing and Organizational Symbolism in the department of Management at the University of St. Andrews, Fife, Scotland.

Paul Jeffcutt is Director of the Institute for Organisational Analysis, University of Hull, UK.

Karen Legge is Professor of Organizational Behaviour in the Department of Behaviour in Organizations, The Management School, University of Lancaster, UK.

Hugo Letiche is Visiting Professor of International Business and Research Methodology at the University of Keele, UK, and lectures in qualitative research methodology at Erasmus University, Rotterdam, The Netherlands.

Stephen Linstead is Professor of Management at the University of Wollongong, New South Wales, Australia.

Thomas P. Mullen is Managing Director of the Park Li Group Ltd., Broadway, New York, USA.

Michael L. Rosen is President of Sundered Ground Inc., Broadway, New York, USA.

Stephen Lloyd Smith is Senior Lecturer in Sociology in the School of Social Science at Kingston University, Surrey, UK

Barry Wilkinson is Professor of Management at the University of Bath, UK.

Editors' Introduction

The present book has its origins in a number of puzzlements which we have shared over a period which spans three decades. Bob and Steve shared an office as researchers in Sheffield, and later in Hull, and along with David Golding were influenced, helped, inspired and challenged by Dan Gowler into taking social anthropology even more seriously than they already did. Paul left his initial training as an adult educator to move into social anthropology, and needed no persuading to embrace the arena of organizational analysis. We met at various conferences of the Standing Conference on Organizational Symbolism, where over the years we discovered several others who shared our concerns – on walks through summer-leafy Swedish lanes, on rolling night-rail journeys from the sparkling Midi to the crisp and breathtaking Dolomites, across flaming sambucas in smoky Milanese corner bars, umbrella-less on rainy but royal Danish cobbles or huddled over warm creamy ales in fire-flickering pubs which light and the Lune flood with spring tides. We (and our students) delighted in incongruous papers quarried like gems from the dull but bursting seams of mainstream journals; conference papers which sang to us but could never be sufficiently domesticated for journal publication, and ideas which drew us like an aura but never became concrete enough for the pale and empty page. Finally, over aromatic espressos in Vienna and cosy cappuccinos in Kelvinside, we formed the idea for a book which would combine some of the best published work, some of the most innovative unpublished work, and work which constituted a realization of those mendicant ideas which had wandered the world to find a form. The final shaping of the volume took place in Lancaster, Glasgow, Hong Kong and New South Wales. It emerged with an international flavour which reflects some of the conditions of its creation, with contributions from Australia, Britain, Canada, Holland, Sweden and the USA. However, whenever a significant step in its development has been taken, no matter where in the world, it has always, always rained.

The other purpose of this book is to bring together contributions which develop and and advance our understanding of management by taking up concepts, theories or methods developed in social anthropology and applying them to the analysis of managerial talk, thought and action. As such our contributions range from the epistemological to the empirical. All, however, are critical in their intent; all depart in some way from, and reinscribe, tradition in both organizational analysis and social anthropology; all take unaccustomed theoretical directions; and all set themselves to improve either analysis or praxis.

We have divided the book into five sections in order to emphasize what we feel are the most important, but not the only significant features of the chapters. Part 1: 'Making the Meaning of Management' looks at rhetorical and symbolic features of the construction of management as a concept. Stephen Linstead, in a chapter which is both a conceptual overview of the field where social anthropology and management meet and an agenda for development, argues that social anthropology offers concepts and methods which contribute directly to the understanding of management as a cultural activity. While developing our conceptual understanding of culture, it also provides new grounds for developing critique, and new ways of understanding and managing processes of change and development through pedagogical adaptations of ethnographic method. This is illustrated by a case study of part of a management development programme.

In Chapter 2, Dan Gowler and Karen Legge, in a more focused rewriting of a classic paper, illustrate the power of interpretative anthropology to expose the ideological infrastructure of management. Although their data are published fragments from letters to professional journals they apply key concepts – ritual, myth, totem, taboo – rigorously within a model of the working of the rhetoric of bureaucratic control, to expose the formative ideas and 'charter myths' which sustain them. Management is seen to be constituted around the central themes of *hierarchy*, *accountability* and *achievement* so that arrangements which are merely a technical necessity for the efficient control of production become a moral necessity, and hence a means of social control. In Chapter 3, David Golding, drawing on the early work of Roland Barthes, takes this further. In a discussion of examples drawn from extensive participant observation in two organizations, he demonstrates how control is preserved through 'blissful clarity' – the depoliticized, apparent naturalness of everyday interaction in management settings – which is only achieved by the artful, artificial, yet tacit suppression of unacknowledged alternatives of action and argument.

Part 2: 'Defamiliarizing Management Practice' contains three chapters which actively disrupt comfortable understandings and assumptions of the actual objectives 'managers' realize and the means by which they achieve them. In the first, drawing on comparative fieldwork in capitalist and communist systems in Canada and Algeria, Omar Aktouf discovers great similarities in management processes and a common paradox. That is, managers consistently reward and promote people who display exactly the opposite 'competences' to those which they themselves espouse as being criteria for promotion. Aktouf's close observation of the micro-practices of shopfloor management is extended into the boardroom in a second chapter by David Golding which examines interactive (as distinct from formal) rituals in managerial behaviour. The idea of a chain of command, and hence a deference order, is actively maintained and kept in place by secrecy rituals; rituals of distinctiveness, degradation and intimidation; and rituals of oppression. The essence of this activity is a subtle and complex manipulation of ambiguity which goes far beyond the level of its current appreciation in the organizational culture literature. In the third chapter in this section, Michael Rosen and Thomas Mullen deconstruct ideas of work, play and control through examinations of the work of a cocaine dealer, a result of a year-long participant observation. Their argument reveals a paradox – although the dealer traversed from a 'normal' nine to five existence to escape structure, control and to embrace more fully the stimulation-saturated world of play, his 'play' world became more controlled, more structured and less 'fun' as the pressures to 'professionalize' his life increased. The chapter is unusual both in style, as Rosen and Mullen exhilaratingly attempt to capture the pace and atmosphere of the dealer's argot and habitus, and in structure. The authors in fact interweave different accounts that they produced at different points in time, revealing a complicated intertext of truth and falsehood, fantasy and reality; and through their own radical reflexivity raise important questions about the nature of social scientific knowledge.

Part 3: 'Rethinking Symbolic Management' contains two chapters which through intensive and prolonged field studies confront some of the fondest and most widespread arguments in the current literature on corporate culture and its management. Steven Feldman directly challenges the distinction between *symbolic* and *substantive* management. Through a discussion of meetings of the transition team in part of the AT&T organization, he demonstrates that managers cannot choose whether to be substantive or symbolic, as all human action is symbolic to a degree. The best managers can do is to be aware of the potential symbolic import of their actions, for to do more would require culture to be a *cause* of action, which it is not – it can only ever be a *context* for action, a disposition to action. Steve Smith and Barry Wilkinson, through a study of part of a hugely successful multinational, present a case where symbolic management would appear to have been successful against Feldman's arguments. In a company which cares for its employees, its community, its customers, its suppliers and even its competitors, Marx's worst nightmare seems to have been realized – capitalism *without* conflict, which deals with its own contradictions. Managers discuss everything openly, even the managing director sharing the same open plan office area as everyone else. Everyone pulls together in the interests of getting things done, and subordinates can even demote their superior if the task demands it. Smith and Wilkinson, however, make a powerful argument that this is no more than an extremely subtle form of control, and use the managers' own Orwellian words – 'we are our own policemen' – to make a chilling point.

Part 4: 'Consuming and Constructing Identity' moves our developing critique of existing understandings towards more emergent fields of concern. In fact, the social constitution of subjectivity and the tension between this and the individual's tattered but increasingly nostalgic sense of a 'modern' identity are the substance of postmodernist arguments about 'fragmentation of the self'. These arguments emerge more fully in the final two parts. Robert Grafton Small argues that traditional theories of marketing have tended to separate the processes of production and consumption and have overemphasized the importance of exchange values. This constructs production as nothing more than the precipitate of enlightened rationality and an objectively achieved economic structure, rather than, as he argues, the social and cultural design of persons and goods. However, this latter process is far more complex in its organizational and societal realities than commentators have acknowledged, partly because the *solitary* consumer as the basis of economic decision making is swamped by *communal* processes; partly because consumption goes on before and long after the market-place *transaction* has finished. Recognizing that the meaning or value of a product is *inherently unstable* and difficult to grasp entails the recognition that these meanings, including the meanings of such commodities as time, space, structure and values, are socially negotiated and culturally embedded. Grafton Small goes on to discuss, through an interpretative anthropology of several examples, methods by which these tacit understandings and the ways in which they are developed and re-evaluated through the processes of seduction, repression and *bricolage* can be addressed. His final point is a telling one: 'we as consumers can neither escape the ambiguities of our own culture nor take any active part in it without exercising forms of moral power and judgement over each other, forms which surely demand we each be responsible for the ethics of our communal exchange'.

Barbara Czarniawska-Joerges develops some aspects of this argument in examining how identity is produced in one organization, a 'constellation' of offices in the Swedish public sector dealing with social insurance. Beginning by examining the concept of identity as being non-essential but achieved through *actual performances*, she goes on to claim that the main means of 'performing' identity is through the creation of *narrative*. Arguing that the phenomenon of 'modern identity' appears to have emerged alongside the development of the literary form 'autobiography', she observes that 'a societal institution, individual identity, is similar to, but also facilitated by, a literary institution – a genre called autobiography'. Extending this into an analogy between individual and organizational identity, she contends that storytelling attempts to write or rewrite the history of an organization in part or in whole, and can be fruitfully (but not exclusively) considered as an autobiographical act – an endeavour to constitute the self-identity of the organization *in the present* through the reconstruction of the past. Recounting and justification become inseparable in this process. Czarniawska-Joerges examines the detailed process involved in this form of knowledge-production through textual and interview data obtained from an organization which was experiencing an identity crisis, and where competing versions of the history of social insurance were struggling for supremacy on a very public stage. Finally, she offers the metaphor of 'quest' as a more appropriate one to capture the negotiated uncertainties and emergent self-knowledge of this process than the dominant metaphor of 'search' (for solutions) in the organizational sciences.

Part 5: 'Changing Identities' takes the theme of change introduced in the previous chapter further with two extensive participant case studies, culminating in Letiche's ground-breaking attempt to assess how post-modernism can be used to shape organizational intervention. First, however, is Paul Jeffcutt's own partially autobiographical attempt to deal with organizational change as a transitional process in which the boundaries between individuals, groups and the organization were extremely fluid, and, similar to Rosen and Mullen, the analyses produced at different times came to be seen as highly divergent. Jeffcutt points out that although the subdiscipline of 'symbolic anthropology' is perhaps equally dominated by two major figures, Clifford Geertz and Victor Turner, only the work of Geertz has been taken up (most frequently inappropriately) by writers on 'organizational culture', despite the great relevance of Turner's work. A major theme of Turner's work is the process of transition, especially an extension of Van Gennep's concept of liminality into a more detailed understanding of phases of change, and a more fluid reconceptualization of the ambiguous and contested processes of identity emergence. Jeffcutt takes up Turner's ideas in an ethnography of a training organization which was contracted by the government to provide programmes for women intending to return to work after a career break or unemployment. These training programmes were intended to achieve a modification in the participants' sense of identity, but the participants experienced this change at a far more profound level as their domestic, social and gender-based constructions of self were all being dislocated. Importantly, the training organization itself was temporary and depended on successful performance for renewed or continued contracts, but was also hostage to any change in government policy and had no assured future even in the short term. Furthermore, the researcher himself was also going through a turbulent passage, both in his academic identity and through a personal tragedy. Using Turner's concept of 'social drama' and an examination of the ways in which metaphors were used in understanding and motivating transition through its four phases, Jeffcutt reveals the extent to which change was a contradictory and paradoxical struggle for all concerned. The various transitions which occurred were not coterminous but were connected through certain passages and diverged through others. The outcomes of transition in this case were much dissatisfaction, recrimination, scapegoating and debili-tation, but at the same time this process also provided sustenance. Jeffcutt finally argues that the understanding of transition requires that 'the processes of organizing become manifest as text and characterized by tension and transformation in the transactional constitution of subjectivity'. What is entailed, then, is a letting go of the assumptions common in much mainstream literature (that is, *shared* meaning manifest in a setting characterized by unity, the assumption of meaning as relatively stable and predictable over time, and the detachment of the researcher producing relatively fixed descriptions and analyses) and the embrace of a far more problematic position (that is, meaning as ambiguous or paradoxical in a setting characterized by division, meaning as in a state of flux and transformation, and the researcher as inextricably 'involved' in the processes of production of readings and accounts which are transient). In short, organization development here becomes organizational deconstruction.

Jeffcutt clearly opens the door for not only a fuller recognition of the contribution that Turner is able to make to organizational analysis, but also for the combination of his consideration of subjectivity with that of Foucault as an avenue for further research. Hugo Letiche takes an even more active approach to the question of the practical implications of the acceptance of the postmodern demolition of modernist epistemology. Letiche's work flies directly in the face of oppositional readings of postmodernism exemplified by Parker (1993) who argues that the consequences of taking Lyotard and Baudrillard seriously in the realm of organization studies are the inability to take any moral, ethical or political position, resulting in an inability to undertake the 'rigorous analysis of organizational changes' in order 'to critique it in the hope of changing it' (*sic*.). It is interesting that, despite a clear staking of a claim to the moral high ground on the basis of a superior 'ontological foundation' here (which is in fact nothing more than implied empirical supporting evidence, an unacknowledged aesthetics itself in part a by-product of a particular epistemology), the focus of Parker's argument is optimistic rather than pragmatic and is couched in terms of the level of changes in 'global capitalism' rather than those of specific organizations. Letiche clearly demonstrates that, although it is not the only possible interpretation, the profound disillusion with the conditions of postmodern society which is apparent in the work of Lyotard and Baudrillard can easily be read to *require* and *entail* moral, ethical and political commitment as a response, although no such position has an automatic foundational warrant. Letiche illustrates this through a study of a multinational design company with several offices in Europe which attempted to develop a new corporate identity, concentrating in particular on the difficulties encountered between the Dutch head office and the Paris subsidiary.

Letiche deploys references frugally in trying to 'leave theory behind and . . . do something with postmodernism' in a user-friendly manner. Nevertheless, the complexity of his argument is not compromised. Letiche sees the choice for the field of organizational behaviour/studies as being that between *techne* and *praxis*. *Techne* is the language of the engineer, appropriate to the solving of design problems, which denies the specificity of situations. *Praxis* involves a specific situation in which practice is guided by social ethics, and a balance must be found between principles, goals and possibilities. Baudrillard's *hyperreal* is a world where the denial of existential consciousness makes management systems more real than individual choice, packaging more significant than actual use. The *protest* which postmodernism makes about postmodern society (a dimension which is completely lost to such commentators as Parker (1993) and Thompson (1993), and arguably Tsoukas (1992)) is 'rooted in the realization that contemporary choices and actions are not grounded in defensible decisions and that the warrants needed to ground decision-making are not at all easily earned'. Although modernist organizational science is animated by the will to produce a *Grande Histoire* or metanarrative of organizational existence, it has fragmented issues politically and impoverished action ethically through over-reliance on research techniques. Alternatively, organizational behaviour/studies can exemplify openness to the other and allow itself to *encounter the hyperreal* (which is very different from *adopting* it as a way of life, which is what Parker et al. seem to imply). This produces *Petites Histoires* – micro-narratives where the relationship between the real and the imaginary dissolves, and none of the crucial terms of identity are certain.

Letiche's study of the case of Source reveals an organization where modernist rhetoric, which promised a utopian organizational ideal which would have earned plaudits from the 'excellence' theorists, created a model which was simply unworkable. Everyone admired the rhetoric, the vision, the publicity, the corporate ads, but no one could translate them into practice – the customers could not see how they could be helped, the designers did not see how they could produce or develop the necessary skills to deliver new services, and no one knew how to develop the relationships that would lead to the projected new business. *Hyperreality* needed to be replaced by *performativity*: mission statements by cash flow. Managers' need to control and personnel's need to know became lost in a simulacrum of participatory management which was out of touch with the harsh reality that the organization was only six months away from going out of business. The parallels with other recently-changed service organizations, particularly in the higher education sectors, are readily discerned.

The postmodern approach to consulting enabled the director of the agency to recognize the unacknowledged role which his managerial 'I' had played in the situation. The manager was faced with a choice, as are many other managers: either to break with the 'I'-centred *logos* of modernist managerial ideology, to let go of control, admit failure and respond to circumstance; or to preserve the 'I' at all costs, at the risk of becoming increasingly institutionally ineffective (this 'I' is often only preserved by leaving the organization and retrospectively blaming it). Although such an abandonment of control can be liberating in practice, Letiche notes the problem that 'if the client is overmastered by a sense of inadequacy when stripped of the modernist ideology, ineffective practice can be replaced with the total disintegration of practice. If the commitment to circumstance and to concrete action is strong enough, the client will develop a new repertoire of activity grounded in a newly-won perceptual realism.'

This finally raises a paradox for the title of our book. Letiche argues that modernism privileges *understanding* at the expense of *seeing*. In effect, explanations and interpretative schemes inculcate blindness to concrete existence. Modernism as a will to understand (or control) becomes a refusal to see (or be open to influence). Even optimistic ideologies, in this argument as in the case study, become pessimistic as they are a *refusal to see human existence as it is*, or at least a refusal to accept it as it appears, and to commit to the capacities of human agents to respond to it *in and on their own terms*. This echoes some of the concerns of Smith and Wilkinson with the 'is' and the 'ought' of Sherwoods, although in this case the company was successful against criteria which Source could not have met.

In fact, the contributors to this book all address the concept of understanding in order to both extend and problematize it in some way. The idea of openness to concrete experience is close to the heart of the arguments of all of our authors, although not all of them would see this as an imperative to abandon modernist argumentation entirely. Nevertheless, without pretending closure or indulging in a form of authorial control ritual, we think that something distinctive is presented here which represents both the debt which our contributors owe to social anthropology, and the contribution they have made to its ongoing conversation.

Finally, a few words about one of our authors, who passed away suddenly while this book was in preparation. Dan Gowler was born on 4 January 1931, and spent his early working life as a manager in the oil industry. Reading economics and social anthropology as a mature student at Cambridge, he never forgot that early experience and became a champion of and inspiration to those who came to intellectual work by non-standard roots. Work at Manchester Business School in the 1960s with Tom Lupton and Enid Mumford, led to appointment in the 1970s as a Professorial Fellow at the MRC Research Unit on Occupational Psychology at the University of Sheffield, with Nigel Nicholson, Roy Payne and, Dan's long-standing collaborator and marriage partner, Karen Legge. Although Dan moved to Templeton College, Oxford, as Fellow and University Lecturer in Organizational Behaviour in the early 1980s while Karen became Reader at Imperial College, London, their collaboration continued to produce important papers, especially some of the earliest attempts to incorporate deconstruction into organization theory.

Dan's influence on this book is hard to measure. He served as examiner for three of the authors, PhD supervisor for two, and his work influenced others. However, it was his enthusiasm for ideas, his coruscating abandonment to the *jouissance* of an argument, that elevated and inspired almost everyone who came into contact with him (certain positivists perhaps excepted!). Although intellectually he enjoyed a battle and was never one to compromise intellectual rigour, his immense kindness and personal generosity meant that he could never be one to take advantage of a superior position. The experience of a doctoral supervision tutorial with Dan was stuff to dine out on – this tiny, gentle, genial figure sparkling with wit, wisdom and insight literally whirled around his study delighting in the generation of figures and bibliographical references with breathtaking speed (and, of course, accuracy), all in *interaction* – none of it was apparently prepared and yet all of it was sustained under later reflection and critique. The only problem ever was to decide which of the exciting vistas opened up would have to be denied in the interests of on-target completion. Dan had the gift of being able to take your work apart critically but incorporate your own thinking so much in the process that you felt, at the end of it, both brilliant and confident although your efforts had, in fact, been demolished. Dan's refusal to be confined by disciplinary limits frequently collapsed the boundaries of work and leisure, and he gave of himself to his students – for whom he cared enormously – unremittingly, regardless of what else was being asked of him. In the process, he built up an international family of former students and protégés to whom he remained immensely loyal. That this loyalty was returned was illustrated by the attendance at his memorial service. But, again in Dan's spirit, this relation extended horizontally and made 'Dan's People' something of a family – certainly we have had a high degree of success in spotting other members of the family from just a few minutes of a conference presentation or even a snatch of conversation! Ironically, the first signs of Dan's short illness emerged just before his death during the first brief sabbatical of his long academic life. Two of the most important of Dan's intellectual concerns – social anthropology and post-modernism – have animated our work over the past decades, and this volume is rightly seen as a culmination of that influence and, as such, a true labour of love.

Dan and Karen were, although in perpetual motion, the perfect couple. When they were together their happiness was glowing and tangible. On the 21 February 1992, Dan died, tragically but peacefully, in good spirits, with Karen at his side. Fittingly, his last words were humorous. Dan always taught us not to seek approval for our ideas but to believe in them. In this spirit, in dedicating this volume to him, our hope is that had he lived to see it, he would have had something to say about it. We could ask for no greater honour than it should prove to be a collection that would have been worthy of his attention.

Stephen Linstead, Robert Grafton Small and Paul Jeffcutt
Wollongong and Glasgow
January 1995

References

Parker, M. (1993) 'Life after Jean-Francois', in J. Hassard and M. Parker (eds), *Postmodernism and Organizations*. London: Sage. pp. 204–12.

Thompson, P. (1993) 'Postmodernism: Fatal distraction', in J. Hassard and M. Parker (eds), *Postmodernism and Organizations*. London: Sage. pp. 183–203.

Tsoukas, H. (1992) 'Postmodernism, Reflective Rationalism and Organizational Studies: A Reply to Martin Parker', *Organization Studies*, 13(4): 641–9.

PART 1

MAKING THE MEANING OF MANAGEMENT

1

Understanding Management: Culture, Critique and Change

Stephen Linstead

Some years ago I worked in a large manufacturing bakery which specialized in the production of dessert products – fruit pies, cakes, tarts, swiss rolls, madeleines and the like for national and even international consumption. Among my several jobs in the factory was one as a member of the fruit and dough mixing team on the mini-pie plant. Suspended above the line on a mezzanine floor, we mixed the ingredients at just the right time and to just the right consistency for them to be gravity fed into the hoppers of the machines below which stamped the dough into familiar shapes, filled it with sugary fruit mix, topped it off with a pastry lid and whisked it away to a huge oven, two storeys high and some 30–40 metres long. The fruit mixes took about 20 minutes to prepare but did not deteriorate rapidly so it was customary to produce ahead and store the mixes in mobile stainless steel containers about one and a half metres high. As Christmas approached, the international demand for traditional British fruit mince pies was strong, and the containers in storage were especially numerous as this mix had to be purchased externally, partly pre-mixed, and brought to us in bulk.

This led to an interesting problem. This mix, unlike others, thickened as it stood and it had to be thinned with sugar syrup before it became usable. However, the sugar already in the mix often crystallized with time and temperature variation, and formed itself into large hard lumps in the mix which could not be broken up and had to be removed. Unfortunately, these lumps frequently sank to the bottom of the mix and became lodged in the outlet pipe, which was designed so as to make it impossible to remove them by access through the pipe itself. No, you had to get them the same way they went in – through 200 kilos of rapidly-thickening fruit mix. If you're wondering how thick, cast your mind back to the days of school Christmas dinners and the feel of sticky fruit, propelled across the refectory from the end of a fifth-form ruler and into a soft, pink ear-hole – remember how your little fingers struggled to remove the cloying blob and you thought a sultana had penetrated your tympanum? Yes, that thick.

One member of the team, in order to remedy this situation, was forced to strip to the waist, and, holding his breath while a colleague held his ankles, fumbled in the fruit until, lungs bursting, he once more breached the surface with the crystal bauble. It was a time of drama, a time of triumph, a time to shower, but most of all a time when you discovered who your friends were. It was, of course, a job which usually fell to me as I had a Master's degree in literature.

At the time, I was also immersed in preparatory reading for a course in management. I was fascinated by the silences in the literature – how little there was to say about the motivation of people in situations like the one I have just described, about the relations which sustained the group at such times; about the ways in which our capacity to solve problems in such a way was used to negotiate the everyday circumstances of our work; about the divergences of meaning and perception between the guy with his head in the fruit and the planner with his head in the figures, and the managers who managed as though the figures were all that mattered. My breath was literally taken away by the subtleties, the paradoxes, the ambiguities of my working life: the moments when you recoiled in horror or doubled up with laughter, or were stopped in your tracks not knowing which was the appropriate reaction. It was this struggle to understand the processes of working life which gave rise to, admittedly fluid, sense making which constituted the texture of organizational life but to which management texts and managers in practice appeared blind.

I first began to find some recognition of the richness of these processes of understanding through reading in social anthropology and some of its relatives, and later adopting some of its methodology of immersion (in which, as we have seen, I was already trained and was particularly adept at dealing with sticky situations) for my own investigations into management processes and practice (see, for example, Linstead 1983, 1984, 1985a, 1985b). In this chapter I advance the idea that social anthropology as a field science has great potential for enhancing our insight into the process of management, both conceptually and methodologically more systematically. Taking as its objectives both accurate *description* of context and accurate *understanding* of how those contexts are interpreted and experienced by participants, social anthropology proceeds by a methodology of 'ethnographic immersion'. This is essential for the appreciation of elusive, ambiguous and tacit aspects of the flow of management activity, but also can allow grounded theory to be generated from 'thick' or 'rich' data. In this chapter I will take recent developments in postmodern and critical anthropology and outline the potential contributions of such an approach to the study, practice and teaching of management terms of three categories: culture, critique and change. In *culture*, new theoretical lines of enquiry can be developed, reassessing the significance of 'shared' meaning and conflicting interests in specific settings; the concept of the symbolic in management can be critically extended; and modes of representation of management can be deconstructed to open up possibilities for critical self-reflexivity. In *critique*, ethnography can be used to defamiliarize customary and taken-for-granted circumstances and reveal suppressed and alternative possibilities; new or unheard voices and forms of information can be resuscitated and used to sensitize managerial processes; and cognitive, affective, epistemological, ideological and ethical considerations can be linked within the same site or event framework. In *change*, anthropological ideas and concepts can be used to shape and reflect change processes and help resolve unproductive dilemmas; and managerial learning can be enhanced by promoting the ethnographic consciousness as a way of apprehending the world, a way of investigation and understanding, and a process of reflexive critique that develops an attitude of openness to otherness.

So my argument is that, thoughtfully approached and applied with care, ideas and methods drawn from social anthropology offer insights into three significant areas of management interest. These are the understanding of cultural processes at work inside organizations, including symbolic understanding and communication; the critical appraisal of managerial practices, initiatives and ways of knowing in wider social, structural and economic contexts; and the nature of organizational change and its management. Further, and more generally, social anthropology not only offers a method for research in its use of ethnography, but ethnographic processes can become the foundation of an interpretative pedagogy of management. I will discuss an example of this later in the chapter. Finally, of all the social sciences, anthropology is clearly the furthest advanced in contributing to the development of postmodern thought about the representation of truth and knowledge and, in fact, it has been argued that ethnography is *the* methodology of postmodernism (Tyler 1986; Woolgar 1989).[1]

Management studies is arguably the most doggedly resistant discipline to postmodernism, still dominated – as perhaps no other branch of the social sciences – by positivist epistemology and methods. Where such postmodern approaches as deconstruction are introduced into management thought, they tend to be applied as mere techniques for mounting critiques of 'classic' texts (Calàs and Smircich 1989; Kilduff 1993) or they are used as an excuse for extemporization which is perhaps only tenuously supported by the text.[2] This chapter is not the place to expand on these arguments, merely to note that there is a tendency among mainstream organizational and management theorists to incorporate the postmodern turn by treating it as either a technical analytic option or an epistemological footnote. I will avoid both of these directions.

Before outlining the key contributions to be made to management studies by a social-anthropological perspective, it is necessary briefly to outline three things. First, my understanding of the 'multidisciplinary' nature of both social anthropology and management research; second, what characterization of 'management' I assume; and, finally, what I consider the field of the social anthropology of management to look like.

Multi- and Interdisciplinary Research in Management

In recent years, concepts have been borrowed from the social sciences and applied to management practice, after a fashion, at an alarming rate. There has been too little critical reflection as to whether the conceptual base of the particular branch of social science was in fact sound enough (Blackler and Brown 1980). Social anthropology, however, remained relatively uncolonized by the managerialists until the 1980s, when the often crude appropriation of the concept of culture spawned a mass of borrowings of terminologies – rituals, rites, myth, taboo, shamanism, etc. – which perhaps made social anthropology the most widely utilized and least understood of any of the social sciences in management (Alvesson 1993: 60–6; Gregory 1983; Helmers 1991, 1993; Kluckhohn 1985; Sinclair 1994). At best, borrowings were drawn predominantly from one tradition within social anthropology only (Meek 1988), and failed to reflect the debates and controversies which surrounded the use of the deployed concepts within the discipline (Thomas 1993).[3]

The point of this chapter is not to present social anthropology as another discipline which offers an imperialistic master metaphor for the analysis of management (see Buckley and Casson 1993).[4] Social anthropology is a *field* science – it depends for its material not on the output of databases, or the carefully controlled results of laboratory experiments, but on the outcome of *experience* of the studied group, society or organization through immersion in the everyday life of the group, even to the extent of participation as a member of such a group. The point is not simply to explain as an external observer what is happening, but to understand *what the group members think is happening* as an insider (Geertz 1983; Rosen 1991a, 1991b; Schwartzman 1993). The essential rigour of ethnography comes from this constant exposure to the 'other', the constant revalidation of descriptions and accounts against the perceptions of the studied group, the constant reflexive scrutiny of the anthropologist/author's role in relation to the accounts generated. The specific methods employed, beyond this exposure, may embrace a broad range of disciplinary orientations.[5] The anthropologist may (and in most cases will) need to become a linguist, or at the very least develop a linguist's ear for nuance, argot and jargon. He or she may need to apply quantitative techniques if they seem appropriate for the range and quality of information with which he or she has to come to terms, and for comparative purposes. He or she may need to develop specific skills, such as husbandry or engineering, depending on the nature of the community studied and this may involve an extensive period of learning; they may use field notes, tape recorders or video cameras, but will need to develop a way of recording information which allows it to be responsive and accurate descriptively, yet also sufficiently systematic to render it amenable to other forms of analysis. The anthropologist has many techniques at his or her disposal, but these techniques will not be fully determined in advance; they will always, to some considerable degree, be shaped by the experiences of the target group. Thus social anthropology remains always reflexively open at a methodological level and is, potentially, always multidisciplinary.[6]

Characterizing Management

Why, then, is management a suitable field for this kind of research approach? Surely the nature of management as an organizational practice has been well studied and established over the years? In order to answer this question, I will have to clarify what characterization I am using of 'management', with a hint of how it may differ from some more conventional accounts.

In presenting this view I am drawing in particular on classical studies of management (for example, Fayol 1949; Urwick 1952; Carroll and Gillen 1987); studies of managerial work and behaviour and reviews of such studies (for example, Mintzberg 1973; Reed 1989; Stewart 1983, 1989; Whitley 1989; Willmott 1984); and recent broader studies of management considering empirical and analytical approaches (for example, Hales 1993; Thomas 1993). Of course, some of these studies have themselves been influenced in some ways by ideas drawn from anthropological work and work done along anthropological lines. However, what I am arguing for here is not a recognition of the slippage of the double hermeneutic – whether it be between anthropology and sociology, or sociology and management studies – but a more considered reconstruction of the conceptual terrain and the 'object' of exploration.

Management is a *social process*, involving negotiation and construction of meaning to get things done (Mangham 1986; Reed 1989; Strauss 1978). It is, although a central part of formal organizations, also a part of organizing any sort of activity, information or informal group, so most people have experience and insight into some part of the management process even if it is incomplete. (Alvesson and Willmott 1992; Drucker 1989; Carter and Jackson 1990). Even 'managers' may not have a complete view, as hierarchies limit discretion, authority, and exposure. Therefore, management is differentially defined at the operational level. This implies the need to study management closely in the field with sensitivity to both actions performed and the intersubjective meanings given by the actors to those actions.

Management is *embedded in socio-economic contexts* which reside outside the organization, and it also impacts on those situations. It is formed by and grounded in, reproduces and transforms socio-political, economic and cultural contexts (see, for example, Alvesson and Willmott 1992; Thompson and McHugh 1990). Management can also be seen as a *function*, performed mainly by managers (that is, management is what managers ought to do as well as what they actually do), but capable of performance by any member of the organization. In networks, and under conditions of 'empowerment', the 'management' function may be dispersed among the members and may even extend outside the organization. It is also seen as a *process*: not simply a set of tasks to be performed but an ongoing set of relations – changing and emerging, affected by communication, perception, behavioural problems and styles – which need to be nurtured, treated, developed or changed on a continuing basis. The first style is said to involve *substantive* management, the second *symbolic* management (Johnson 1990; Pfeffer 1981). However, as Feldman (1985 and Chapter 7 in this volume) argues, these types are not actually separable if considered in terms of the context of management, and management can be seen as a series of 'events' occurring within such a context. *Event studies* need to be investigated by immersion methods to pursue the ambiguous relationship between the symbolic and the substantive and the meanings which members attribute to the events. A consideration of symbolic artefacts and their deployment (Gagliardi 1990) also links management into the wider processes of the social anthropology of goods and consumption (Douglas and Ishwerwood 1980).

Finally, management involves thought *and* emotion (Fineman 1993). It involves substantive and symbolic activity which overlap, expressed through symbols and rhetoric often with layers of meaning accessible only to 'insiders'. It involves overt and covert power struggles and political infighting. Management is also involved in the production and consumption of both goods *and* identities, or subjectivities (Knights and Morgan 1991), and as such takes the form of what Foucault calls a 'discourse' (Knights 1992). It reflects ideologies and beliefs which may lead to the suppression of alternatives, and therefore can be seen as central to the continued domination of particular classes in capitalism, and requiring critique. However, critique does not have to be oppositional, and a critical capacity in managers is just as necessary for the pursuit of change from within.

All of these characteristics argue that ambiguities, symbolic dimensions, covert informal practices, real conditions rather than ideal conditions, and informal arrangements and networks rather than formal rules and organizational charts, need to be studied by an approach which immerses itself closely in the detail of managerial life. It also needs to emphasize description, and concentrate on accessing meaning – both shared and unshared – unearthing conflict and paradox, and observing how this is dealt with and accounted for by organizational members (see, for example, Czarniawska-Joerges 1992, 1993, and Chapter 10 in this volume). Thus it attempts to describe and explain situations in ways which are deemed adequate by members, and therefore has to open itself to information from this source without neglecting objectively-observable characteristics. It needs reflexively to consider the investigator's own role in knowledge production, as well as being a participant in ideological frames. In its more postmodern guise, this extends to the consideration of the tacit, the implicit and the unsaid, but includes that which seems to be unsayable and unpresentable, including silence and spacing as well as talk (Tyler, 1987). This aesthetic dimension has been especially emphasized in recent social anthropology (Jones 1987).[7] Finally the process of investigation must also produce some theorizing which is both adequate to explain the situation and allows comparison and argument with other contexts.

Why Social Anthropology?

So what exactly has social anthropology contributed so far to the study of management which makes it worth our continuing attention? Recent accounts can be found in Smircich (1983), Allaire and Firsirotu (1984) and Meek (1988) covering, in particular, the development of functionalist and structural functionalist approaches and derivatives. Rosen (1991a, 1991b) discusses ethnography in organizations in some detail, and Jones et al. (1988) offer some useful examples of the approach taken so far.[8]

Much of this innovative recent work, and some of the earlier work, have great significance for the understanding of management as a critical function within organizations; as a fundamental process which extends far beyond its functional importance; as a key factor in the manufacture of meaning in organizations; and as a central focus for understanding the symbolic processes of production and exchange which constitute the 'culture' of organizations. In particular, the majority of recently published work on organizational culture has lacked any critical edge as it has tended to take at face value the symbolic constitution of organizations (Turner 1990a, 1990b) – unable to distinguish between the significant and the insignificant, the rite and the not-rite (Alvesson 1993). The work which offers the most interesting line of development investigates the process by which this 'symbolic' dimension is constituted, consumed, exchanged and revalued – treating the process as problematic and meaning as an emergent property, while focusing on managers and managing in its broadest sense.

Let me give some examples of the sort of work which has been taking place. A powerful line of critique developed from the work of Claude Lévi-Strauss (1977), who argued that social scientists should explore the underlying 'grammars' of symbolic systems, languages, stories, and so on to identify how human consciousness was 'patterned'. Human problems and our way of responding to them are not, he argued on the basis of an analysis of myths around the world, radically different. Myths, however, conceal their own origins in human dilemmas and contingency, and act to present absolute guidance which – because of its ambiguity – is both flexible and timeless. Roland Barthes (1973) took Lévi-Strauss' exposure of mythology into contemporary society, arguing that modern myths are consistently being produced in speech, in visual discourse, in art, in advertising, and in media and communications, and the task of the modern 'mythologist' is to expose the underlying contingent and political (that is, related to power) basis of such speech. Ideology in an everyday, and critical, sense became more significant at this point. Foucault (1977, 1980) recognized not only that meaning construction is central to the sense we have of ourselves as individuals, but that that sense of 'subjectivity' is created as much outside the individual as inside. It is *socially* constructed and negotiated; it is *symbolically* constructed; and it is *historically* constructed through style or genre, and through its place in a *narrative* of the past and future sustained in specific accounts or more distributed discourses in the present.

When social anthropologists applied some of these perspectives to their existing interests, in myth, ritual and symbolism for example, new critical concerns with the relationships of language, power and knowledge emerged.[9] This is not the direction that most studies of symbolism and culture took in organizational settings, preferring to emphasize shared meaning, cohesion, functionality, socialization and 'social glue'.

Critical management anthropologists working in an alternative direction have two main approaches. The first is *defamiliarization by epistemological critique*. This begins by recognizing the nature both of native knowledge and their own as problematic, and proceeds to defamiliarize assumptions about management and organizing by applying concepts and thought processes acquired from studies of other societies to our contemporary situation. The second, *defamiliarization by cross-cultural critique*, proceeds by using social structures and arrangements of other societies as a comparator or metaphor for understanding managerial and organizational structures of our own. This often entails a reduction of focus from elaborate and protracted rituals to rituals found in the everyday, which itself should remind us that the mundanity of the everyday is an illusion (Young 1989). However, the two lines of critique are generally inseparable. The critical anthropologist works simultaneously in two areas often felt to be analytically exclusive (see Parker 1992a, 1992b; Thompson 1993) – the *epistemological* and the *ethnographically empirical*, that is working on 'thick' theory as well as 'thick' description. Additionally, the temptation to be drawn into fragmented and diverse empirical (or theoretical) backwaters needs to be resisted by a constant attempt (however provisional) to take a holistic perspective on wider conditions of integration (Burrell 1990; Linstead 1993a: 112). Gowler and Legge (1983), in an early paper, are able to illustrate how managerial discourse draws upon non-rational thought – myth, ritual, totem, taboo – to construct rhetorics which 'manage the meaning of management' and enhance its public authority. Stephen Turner (1977) makes an early attempt to consider complex organizations as savage tribes, and also draws on Lévi-Strauss. However, his case study analysis tends to trivialize Lévi-Strauss' approach to binary thinking and, particularly, misrepresents Derrida's deconstruction (S. Turner 1983). Golding (1979, 1980a, 1980b) uses Barthes' discussion of myth as a starting point to reveal the grounding of myths relating to managerial authority, sovereignty, and the right to manage in the everyday discourse (including its silences and suppressions) of managers in a steel company and a public utility.[10] In a later development

(Golding 1991 and Chapters 3 and 5 in this volume), he analyses how the uses of apparently minor everyday rituals in the same companies become an essential element in re-creating and maintaining structures of control and dominance. What these treatments are doing is raising important points about the nature of knowledge while simultaneously emphasizing the dynamic nature of both culture and structure, especially in the need for 'customary relations' and structures of dominance to be constantly re-created, re-enacted, reinforced, resisted and subverted on a daily basis.

Grafton-Small and Linstead (1985) discuss professional groups in terms of quasi-kinship relations, maintaining their symbolic boundaries on a daily basis in ways which are socially rather than technically based, in direct contrast to Abbott's (1981) functionalist analysis. Linstead and Grafton-Small (1990a, 1990b) also observe how symbolic processes involving improvization ('bricolage') and evocation are part of both everyday and academic understanding. Grafton Small (1991 and Chapter 9 in this volume) develops and broadens this analysis of symbolic consumption and production of individual subjectivity and kinship group identity to argue that marketing itself is, or should be, the social anthropology of consumption. Again, the holistic approach enables ethnography to demystify as well as defamiliarize the taken for granted. If the postmodern concept of fragmentation is to be at all useful in the analysis of management, then it must be constantly and reciprocally focused on conditions and structures of social and organizational integration (Burrell 1990; Ulin 1991). If thought in general, as Rabinow (1986: 239) argues, is 'nothing more and nothing less than a historically locatable set of practices', then the devices which *connect management thought and organized society* must feel the focus of this attention.

In summary, the particular social anthropological style I am recommending has relevance because of its:

- emphasis on mind, interpretation and understanding (unconscious assumptions, implicit structures, common sense, myth)
- recognition of the importance of the symbolic process to knowledge formation
- introduction of existing concepts facilitating epistemological critique, for example ritual, rites, totemism, taboo, kinship, shamanism
- analysis of 'native' formal and informal methods of organizing both practically and conceptually
- recognition of the value of objects, artefacts, visual and material symbols, and their consumption, production and exchange
- emphasis on the importance of textual constructions of life-worlds, and the recognition of oral tradition (including self-reflexive consideration of its own constructions of those worlds)
- stress on the importance of communicative media in the reproduction, transmission, obstruction of and resistance to social values and structures (talk, stories, rhetoric, humour, style, ideology, public and private modes of communicating)

- concern with formative processes of socializing, learning, relationships, continuity and change.

New Directions for Management Theory, Practice and Development

Specifically, then, how can such a social anthropology contribute to management research? What profitable lines of development does it offer? I see immediate possibilities for the study of management and organization in three areas: culture, critique and change.

Culture – New Theoretical Lines of Enquiry

Developing Theory from Ethnographic Data   The first contribution is to redirect the focus of much 'culture' work from its obsession with often superficial manifestations of what is taken to be 'shared meaning' towards building theory from specific circumstances, with a particular eye for the problems and paradoxes (explicit or implicit) the 'culture' seems to face. Symbolic forms are invariably related to problems and dilemmas in specific circumstances (Hampden-Turner 1990) and often indicate the presence of schism, division and conflict where they express shared identity (Young 1989; Linstead and Grafton Small 1992). This more holistic approach will bring into focus 'marginal' issues often overlooked or de-emphasized by other studies, but which are often important to management in managing boundaries and tensions.

Critically Extending the Concept of the Symbolic in Management   'Culture' covers both the *working of cultural processes in organizational settings* and the *emergence of specific cultural forms and practices in those settings* which may or may not be expressive outputs of the former. What is necessary here is closer attention to the underlying nature of the symbolic process, and the way it connects individual understanding, identity and subjectivity to wider power relations through language. We are immersed in power – steeped in it in our everyday lives – and an understanding of its fluid workings needs to be based on close attention to its 'microphysics' and 'micropolitics' (De Certeau 1984). Symbolic processes also work alongside conceptual and rational processes (all of which are cultural processes anyway), which interweave in particular sets of circumstances. Alvesson (1993: 61–5) argues that culture researchers have exhibited a tendency to be seduced by the obvious, to be enthralled by surface resemblances to anthropological phenomena, and to fail to distinguish significant symbolic phenomena from trivia. The answer to this problem is only to be found within specific investigations, where the process is as much the topic as is the symbolic 'product' itself.

Examining Modes of Representation of Management   Following from our preceding argument, this entails looking at the ways in which our knowledge of management is constructed, produced and presented (Jeffcutt 1994; Woolgar 1989). Deconstruction and reconstitution of the identities of both researcher (author) and research subject (other), can reveal ideological dimensions and open up possibilities for a critically self-reflexive social science of management.

Critique – Developing Critical Praxis

Using Ethnography as a Deconstructive Practice as well as a Reconstitutive One   Although ethnography is based on description, as discussed earlier it can also expose new possibilities and suppressed alternatives by giving attention to the ways in which suppression takes place. Bringing ethnographic techniques and analytical frames close to home can reveal unacknowledged dimensions of the already familiar and often taken for granted, demystifying them.

Examining Possibilities for New Forms of Organization based on Greater Variety of Inputs to the Managerial Process   Recent ethnographic works have emphasized the narrative approach, suggesting that ethnographic texts should incorporate more than one authorial voice as real experience is an interweaving of several 'voices'. Ethnography can open up silenced areas and amplify unheard voices in organizations, both for more sophisticated analysis and for shaping change. These voices do not have to be constructed as 'collective' and politicized voices, and may not necessarily be those of individuals (for example, as one might speak of the voice of reason, the voice of compassion, and so on). These voices can be resuscitated and can sensitize individual managers in a powerful way to the importance of neglected issues or forgotten dimensions (Höpfl and Linstead 1993). These topics can similarly be rediscovered for organizational analysis.

Linking Cognitive, Epistemological, Affective, Ideological and Ethical Considerations within the Same Frame   The concentration of ethnography on *site* and *event* serves naturally to break down traditional disciplinary fragmentations. Where action and interpretation of those involved is the focus, disciplines are better able to inform each other and loosely couple previously closed disciplines and – with some cautions as expressed earlier – even paradigms.

Change – Management Learning, Development and Education

Using Anthropological Ideas to Shape and Reflect Change Processes   Although social anthropology is often presented in its structural-functionalist guise as being preoccupied with stability, this is misleading. Culture has always been recognized as being in flux, and the tensions between change and continuity have always been an important focus to all approaches. Jeffcutt (Chapter 11 in this volume) uses the unjustly neglected work of Victor Turner (1983) to examine the stages in the processes of learning and change in a training organization that produce differing states of liminality, attachment and resistance. As Jeffcutt argues, current models of the stages of change lack theoretical depth, while Turner's discussions offer a greater sophistication in understanding the complexities of duration and varieties of response, and potentially link to broader sociological interrogations of subjectivity. On a more applied note, Hampden-Turner has used a basically Lévi-Straussian model of myth, or dilemma, to help companies like British Airways to think their way out of unproductive stand-offs and into positive resolutions of difficulties. Jim Olila (1991), president of the Corporate Anthropology Foundation, argues that corporations need to improve their own self-knowledge and anthropologists can help them to take a long, hard and often uncomfortable look at themselves. Roger McConochie and Anthony Gianni, of Corporate Research International, have developed a systematic programme designed to assist companies in this process. Olila's approach is intended for even greater depth data-gathering, involving participant observation on and off the job (with confidential protection for individuals and feedback of data to all involved) and is in use in several major corporations, particularly those working to resolve problems of cultural diversity in their workforces. Slipy (1990) offers a client's perspective on this activity and Laabs (1992) discusses the use of internal staff anthropologists by Arthur Andersen & Co. in cross-cultural learning situations to redesign management development programmes.

Developing a Pedagogy which Seeks to Develop the Manager as Anthropologist, Using Ethnography as: a mode of apprehension (becoming receptive to others and otherness, developing a negative capability to absorb rather than construct data); a means of learning and understanding (by actively seeking to take the perspectives of others and test those views); a process of self-critique (becoming aware of alternative knowledge and practices, and one's own role in the construction of truth).

Using Ethnographic Skills in Management Development Programme

Let me offer a final example of a small project which emerged out of a much larger one but which helped the development of the ideas expressed above. Some aspects of the project are reported in Höpfl and Linstead (1993).[11] The programme itself was a management development course, leading to a graduate diploma. The whole programme consisted of 10 weeks of delivered content spread over 18 months, with work-based assignments in the intervening periods. I will concentrate particularly on two of the ten sessions which occurred in the middle of the programme, the first dealing with managing the employment relationship, the second with managing in the organization (with a particular focus on culture). In the first we took the approach that management, as the management of relationships, depended on managers developing sensitivity to a wide variety of forms of 'information', including legal, technical, statistical, anecdotal and emotional forms. Through a series of theoretical and practical exercises we moved towards an objective that, at the end of the first week, the participants would be able to bring a problem they had experienced or were close to into their learning set of six people, who would then co-consult on the matter. This would lead into an assignment in which they would pair up with someone from a different part of the organization to investigate and prepare a cultural diagnosis of that part of the organization, which they would feed back to its members. They would then report on the whole exercise in writing up their diagnosis.

We were aware that what we had planned depended on a high degree of mutual support and sensitivity, but also a considerable degree of ethnographic awareness coupled with some methodological technique. We were also fortunate that the company had a powerful and very visible 'corporate culture' which acted as a benchmark for our activities at all times. One of the very significant features of this company was a high reliance on 'emotional labour' (Hochschild 1983) in part of its activities, and the final part of the workshop involved a session on this issue. We began by identifying a small group of those in jobs which had clear dimensions of 'emotional labour': high visibility, high levels of contact with the public, the need to maintain a particular 'face', and the need to manage one's self. We then adopted a method which was a modified ethnographic interview, asking the core group to imagine that they were briefing an actor on how to get inside their role (the objective of knowing how to go on, how to perform as a 'member' was, of course, also the anthropologist's). Their responsibility was to present not just the visible, easily verbalized parts of that role, but the intangibles – the tensions, the strains, the moments of stress, the exhilarations of success – which could only be effectively conveyed by examples and stories illustrating their lives. We asked them to consider what made them 'tick' in their job and to try to give the 'actor' everything necessary to achieve empathy, to don their uniform and 'feel' right in the role. The sharing of information and experiences in the core group actually proved a powerful learning experience for them, but that is not the subject of this chapter.[12] We then subdivided the group and sent them into other groups who had the 'actor's' brief – to allow the 'actors' to talk, question and converse with the core members sufficiently for them to feel they were 'inside the skin' of the role and knew how to be a member of that occupational group. The powerful recollections and re-creations of emotional situations sensitized the group as a whole, and released a great deal of energy which continued to produce discussion and insight outside the boundaries of the session.[13] We were able to roll on this heightened awareness and go straight into the co-consulting sessions, which were in many cases very powerful learning experiences and went on, voluntarily, well past the scheduled ending of the session.

On the strength of this exercise, the pairs were able to move into the part of the exercise that featured more traditional ethnographic skills, producing an account of a subculture and exchanging that account with the natives (which allowed us to lead into issues of resistance and change in the following workshops). The first session of the following workshop involved sharing the results of the exercise, in which, despite the strong overarching culture, several significant subgroups were seen to have radically different ways of relating to it – even remaining untouched by it. The participants were surprised, even shocked, at the unacknowledged degree of cultural diversity in their company, and the extent to which that which they had assumed they knew – even their own departments – was revealed as unfamiliar to them. This enabled us to move into a range of discussions of change management, critique of current practice, generation of new ideas, and made the later strategic planning and implementation module far richer in its exploration of implementation issues. Apart from academic benefits and dramatic personal insights, the approach had a concentrating effect on the attentions of the group, coupled with a stimulus to a gradual but sustained increase in their energy levels – with sessions constantly running over because of discussion and interaction, and working conversations often running late into the night. We ran several subsequent groups in the same manner, with similar effects. On the basis of these experiences of a limited pilot application of the method, and the strength and coherence of the supporting theory to which it relates, there is good reason to believe that the more extensive application I am advocating is justified.

In terms of our three categories, how did this exercise advance the argument? In *culture*, clearly the participants became newly aware of *conflicting interests in specific settings*, and this helped them to *reassess the significance of 'shared' meaning* within departments and across the company. Typically, managers sharing insights about the difficulty of transferring successful practices from one department to another prompted them to rethink the extent and significance of 'corporate culture'. This enabled them to reassess the theoretical literature on the company, and helped us to develop our own *new theoretical line of enquiry* (Höpfl and Linstead 1993). We were able to follow up this work with further research on different visual languages in the company, and this enabled us to develop our critique of *the concept of the symbolic in management*; and we were able to *generate critical self-reflection on modes of representation of management*. In terms of *critique*, the emotional labour exercise brought out *previously unheard voices* and injected a new sensitivity into our proceedings; the diagnostic exchange extended this and introduced the *defamiliarization* process; and, although it was not our purpose to develop it theoretically, at a practical level the material generated clearly interleaved *cognitive, affective, epistemological, ideological and ethical considerations*. In *change*, we were able to use some of the anthropological ideas and concepts which had emerged diagnostically to *identify possibilities and obstacles to change and reflect on change processes* (following, for example, Cohen 1975, 1985; Johnson 1987 and V. Turner 1983), and help resolve unproductive dilemmas (following, for example, Hampden-Turner 1990). In terms of a longer process of self-development, many of our participants began to embrace our arguments on management learning: that it can be enhanced by promoting *ethnographic consciousness as a way of apprehending, investigating and understanding the world* through reflexive critique and openness. This very process demands the crossing, and ultimately the dissolution, of disciplinary boundaries.

Managers are constantly embedded in fruitful research settings in their own everyday working lives, yet they only very infrequently take advantage of this situation. They find it difficult to interrogate that which surrounds them. Similarly, they all have ethnographic skills to some extent and all are capable – with the right support – of developing them, though not all with the same degree of success. I have found no one who was unable to improve these skills, though for some it proved a challenge. This improvement inevitably impacts on their practice as a manager, especially on their ability to handle difficult, sensitive or ambiguous situations. It also develops a healthy critical attitude towards both theory and practice. Management studies and management practice will benefit immensely if these managerial resources can be fully explored. Social anthropology offers both methodological and theoretical frameworks to enable this to happen, without the inevitability of paradigmatic, disciplinary or epistemological constriction.

References

Abbott, A. (1981) 'Status and Status Strain in the Professions', *American Journal of Sociology*, 86(1): 819–35.

Allaire, Y. and Firsirotu, M. (1984) 'Theories of Organizational Culture', *Organization Studies*, 5(3): 193–226.

Alvesson, M. (1993) *Cultural Perspectives on Organizations*. Cambridge: Cambridge University Press.

Alvesson, M. and Willmott, H. (1992) *Critical Management Studies*. London: Sage.

Atkinson, P. (1990) *The Ethnographic Imagination: Textual Constructions of Reality*. London: Routledge.

Babcock, B. (ed.) (1978) *The Reversible World: symbolic inversion in art and society*. London: Cornell University Press.

Bailey, F.G. (1977) *Morality and Expediency: The Folklore of Academic Politics*. Oxford: Blackwell.

Barthes, R. (1973) *Mythologies*. London: Paladin.

Blackler, F. and Brown, C. (1980) *Whatever Happened to Shell's New Philosophy of Management?* London: Saxon House.

Buckley, P.J. and Casson, M. (1993) 'Economics as Imperialist Social Science', *Human Relations*, 46(9): 1035–52.

Burrell, G. (1990) 'Fragmented Labours', in D. Knights and H. Willmott (eds), *Labour Process Theory*. London: Macmillan. pp. 274–96.

Calàs, M. and Smircich, L. (1989) 'Voicing Seduction to Silence Leadership'. Paper presented to conference, *The Symbolism of Leadership*. SCOS, INSEAD, Fontainebleau, France, June.

Carroll, S.J. and Gillen, D.J. (1987) 'Are the Classical Management Functions Useful in Describing Managerial Work?', *Academy of Management Review*, 12(1): 38–51.

Carter, P. and Jackson N. (1990) 'The Emergence of Postmodern Management?', *Management Education and Development*, 21(3): 219–28.

Cleverley, G. (1973) *Managers and Magic*. London: Pelican.

Clifford, J. and Marcus, G. (eds) (1986) *Writing Culture: the Poetics and Politics of Ethnography*. Berkeley: University of California Press.

Cohen, A.P. (1975) *The Management of Myths*. Manchester: Manchester University Press.

Cohen, A.P. (1985) *The Symbolic Construction of Community*. London: Tavistock.

Collinson, D. (1992) *Managing the Shopfloor*. Berlin: De Gruyter.

Czarniawska-Joerges, B. (1992) *Exploring Complex Organizations: A Cultural Perspective*. London: Sage.

Czarniawska-Joerges, B. (1993) *The Three Dimensional Organization: A Constructionist View*. Lund: Studentlitteratur.

Dalton, M. (1959) *Men Who Manage*. New York: Wiley.

De Certeau, M. (1984) *The Practice of Everyday Life*. Berkeley: University of California.

Ditton, J. (1977) *Part-Time Crime: An Ethnography of Fiddling and Pilferage*. London: Macmillan.

Douglas, M. (1966) *Purity and Danger*. London: Routledge and Kegan Paul.

Douglas, M. (1980) *Evans-Pritchard*. London and Glasgow: Fontana.

Douglas, M. and Isherwood, B. (1980) *The World of Goods*. Harmondsworth: Penguin.

Drucker, P. (1989) *The Practice of Management*. London: Heinemann.

Duncan, H.D. (1967) *Symbols in Society*. Oxford: Oxford University Press.

Fayol, H. (1949) *General and Industrial Management*. London: Pitman.

Feldman, S. (1985) 'Management in Context: an essay on the relevance of culture to the understanding of organizational change', *Journal of Management Studies*, 23(6): 587–607.

Fineman, S. (ed.) (1993) *Emotion in Organizations*. London: Sage.

Firth, R. (1973) *Symbols Public and Private*. London: Allen and Unwin.

Foster, M.L. and Brandes, S.H. (1980) *Symbols as Sense: Approaches to the Analysis of Meaning*. London: Academic Press.

Foucault, M. (1977) *Discipline and Punish*. London: Allen Lane.

Foucault, M. (1980) *Power/Knowledge*. Brighton: Harvester.

Frost, P.J., Moore, L., Louis, M.R., Lundberg, C. and Martin, J. (eds) (1985) *Organizational Culture*. London and Newbury Park: Sage.

Frost, P.J., Moore, L., Louis, M.R., Lundberg, C. and Martin, J. (eds) (1991) *Reframing Organizational Culture*. London and Newbury Park: Sage.

Gadamer, H.-G. (1975) *Truth and Method*. London: Sheed-Ward.

Gagliardi, P. (1990) *Symbols and Artefacts: Views of the Corporate Landscape*. Berlin: De Gruyter.

Geertz, C. (1973) *The Interpretation of Cultures*. New York: Basic Books.

Geertz, C. (1983) *Local Knowledge*. New York: Basic Books.

Golding, D. (1979) 'Symbolism, Sovereignty and Domination in an Industrial Hierarchical Organization', *Sociological Review*, 27(1): 169–97.

Golding, D. (1980a) 'Authority, Legitimacy, and the Right to Manage at Wenslow Manufacturing Co.', *Personnel Review*, 9(1): 43–8.

Golding, D. (1980b) 'Establishing Blissful Clarity in Organizational Life: Managers', *Sociological Review*, 28(4): 763–82.

Golding, D. (1991) 'Some Everyday Rituals in Management Control', *Journal of Management Studies*, 28(6): 569–83.

Gowler, D. and Legge, K. (1981) 'Negation, abomination and synthesis in rhetoric', in C. Antaki (ed.), *The Psychology of Ordinary Explanations of Social Behaviour*. London: Academic Press. pp. 243–69.

Gowler, D. and Legge, K. (1983) 'The Meaning of Management, the Management of Meaning: a view from Social Anthropology', in M.J. Earl (ed.), *Perspectives on Management*. Oxford: Oxford University Press. pp. 99–233.

Grafton-Small, R. (1991) 'Marketing, or the Social Anthropology of Consumption', *European Journal of Marketing*, 21(9): 66–71.

Grafton-Small, R. and Linstead, S.A. (1985) 'The Everyday Professional: Skill in the Symbolic Management of Occupational Kinship', in A. Strati (ed.), *The Symbolics of Skill*. Trento: Quaderno (5/6): 53–67.

Gregory, K. (1983) 'Native-view Paradigms: Multiple Cultures and Culture Conflicts in Organisations', *Administrative Science Quarterly*, 28(3): 359–76.

Hales, C. (1993) *Management through Organization*. London: Routledge.

Hampden-Turner, C. (1990) *Corporate Cultures: From Vicious to Virtuous Circles?* London: Hutchinson/Economist Books.

Hammersley, M. (1990) 'What's Wrong with Ethnography? The Myth of Theoretical Description', *Sociology*, 24(4): 597–615.

Hassard, J. (1990) 'An alternative to paradigm incommensurability in organization theory', in J. Hassard and D. Pym (eds), *The Theory and Philosophy of Organizations*. London: Routledge. pp. 219–30.

Hassard, J. (1991) 'Ethnomethodology and Organization: an Introduction', in N. Craig Smith and P. Dainty (eds), *The Management Research Handbook*. London: Routledge. pp. 132–44.

Heidegger, M. (1971) *Poetry, Language, Thought*. New York: Harper and Row.

Helmers, S. (1991) 'Anthropological Contributions to Organizational Culture', *SCOS Notework*, 10(1): 60–72.

Helmers, S. (1993) 'The Occurrence of Exoticism in Organizational Literature'. Paper presented to 11th EGOS Colloquium, *The Production and Diffusion of Managerial Knowledge*. Paris, July.

Hochschild, A.R. (1983) *The Managed Heart*. Berkeley: University of California Press.

Höpfl, H.J. and Linstead, S.A. (1993) 'Passion and Performance: Suffering and the Carrying of Organizational Roles', in S. Fineman (ed.), *Emotion in Organizations*. London: Sage. pp. 76–93.

Jackson, N. and Carter, P. (1991) 'In Defence of Paradigm Incommensurability', *Organization Studies*, 12(1): 109–28.

Jackson, N and Carter, P. (1993) 'Paradigm Wars: A response to Hugh Willmott', *Organization Studies*, 14(5): 721–6.

Jackson, N. and Willmott, H. (1987) 'Beyond Epistemology and Reflective Conversation: Towards Human Relations', *Human Relations*, 40(6): 361–80.

Jeffcutt, P.S. (1993) 'From Interpretation to Representation', in J. Hassard and M. Parker (eds), *Postmodernism and Organizations*. London: Sage. pp. 25–48.

Jeffcutt, P.S. (1994) 'The Interpretation of Organization: a Contemporary Analysis and Critique', *Journal of Management Studies*, 30(2): 225–50.

Johnson, G. (1987) *Strategic Change and the Management Process*. Oxford: Blackwell.

Johnson, G. (1990) 'Managing Strategic Change: the Role of Symbolic Action', *British Journal of Management*, 1(4): 183–200.

Jones, M.O. (1987) 'Aesthetics at Work: Art and Ambience in an Organization', in M.O. Jones (ed.), *Exploring Folk Art: Twenty Years on Craft, Work and Aesthetics*. Ann Arbor, MI: UMI Press. pp. 133–57.

Jones, M.O. (1990) 'Emotions in Work: A Folklore Approach', *American Behavioural Scientist*, 33:278–86.

Jones, M.O., Moore, M.D. and Snyder, R.C. (eds) (1988) *Inside Organizations: Understanding the Human Dimension*. Newbury Park: Sage.

Kilduff, M. (1993) 'Deconstructing Organizations', *Academy of Management Review*, 18(1): 13–31.

Kluckhohn, C. (1985) *Mirror for Man: the Relation of Anthropology to Modern Life*. Tucson: University of Arizona Press.

Knights, D. (1992) 'Changing Spaces: Towards a New Epistemological Location for the Study of Management', *Academy of Management Review*, 17(3): 514–36.

Knights, D. and Morgan, G. (1991) 'Corporate Strategy, Organizations and Subjectivity: A Critique', *Organization Studies*, 12(2): 251–73.

Kunda, G. (1992) *Engineering Culture*. Philadelphia: Temple University Press.

Laabs, Jennifer, J. (1992) 'Corporate Anthropologists', *Personnel Journal*, 71(1): 81–91.

Lash, S. (1990) *Sociology of Postmodernism*. London: Routledge.

Lash, S. (1993) 'Reflexive Modernization: The Aesthetic Dimension', *Theory, Culture and Society*, 10(1): 1–23.

Leach, E. (1970) *Levi-Strauss*. London: Fontana.

Lévi-Strauss, C. (1977) *Structural Anthropology*. London: Peregrine.

Linstead, S.A. (1983) 'The Sorcerer's Apprentice: Problems in Establishing Student/ Researcher Credibility as Consultant', *Personnel Review*, 12(4): 3–9.

Linstead, S.A. (1984) 'The Bloody Worm: Problems in the Production of a Consulting Report', *Personnel Review*, 13(1): 21–6.

Linstead, S.A. (1985a) 'Organizational Induction: The Re-creation of Order and Re-reading of Discourse, *Personnel Review*, 14(1): 3–11.

Linstead, S.A. (1985b) 'Breaking the Purity Rule: Industrial Sabotage and the Symbolic Process', *Personnel Review*, 14(3): 12–19.

Linstead, S.A. (1993a) 'Deconstruction in the Study of Organizations', in J. Hassard and M. Parker (eds), *Postmodernism and Organizations*. London: Sage. pp. 49–70.

Linstead, S.A. (1993b) 'From Postmodern Anthropology to Deconstructive Ethnography', *Human Relations*, 46(1): 97–120.

Linstead, S.A. (1994) 'Objectivity, Reflexivity and Fiction: Humanity, Inhumanity and Social Science', *Human Relations*, 47(11): 1321–46.

Linstead, S.A. and Grafton Small, R. (1990a) 'Organizational Bricolage', in B. Turner (ed.), *Organizational Symbolism*. Berlin: De Gruyter. pp. 291–309.

Linstead, S.A. and Grafton Small, R. (1990b) 'Theory as Artefact: Artefact as Theory', in P. Gagliardi (ed.), *Symbols and Artefacts: Views of the Corporate Landscape*. Berlin: De Gruyter. pp. 387–419.

Linstead, S.A. and Grafton Small, R. (1992) 'On Reading Organizational Culture', *Organization Studies*, 13(3): 331–55.

Mangham, I. (1986) *Power and Performance in Organizations*. Oxford: Basil Blackwell.

Marcus, G. and Fischer, M. (1986) *Anthropology as Cultural Critique*. Chicago: Chicago University Press.

Mars, G. (1982) *Cheats at Work: An Anthropology of Workplace Crime*. London: Allen and Unwin.

Mars, G. and Nicod, M. (1984) *The World of Waiters*. London: Allen and Unwin.

Martin, J. (1992) *Cultures in Organizations*. Oxford: Blackwell.

Mauss, M. (1967) *The Gift*. New York: Norton.

Meek, V.L. (1988) 'Organizational Culture: Origins and Weaknesses', *Organization Studies*, 9(4): 453–73.

Mintzberg, H. (1973) *The Nature of Managerial Work*. New York: Harper and Row.

Nietzsche, F. (1974) *The Gay Science*. New York: Vintage Books.

Norris, C. (1991) *What's Wrong with Post-Modernism?* London: Harvester Wheatsheaf.

Norris, C. (1993) *The Truth about Post-Modernism*. Oxford: Blackwell.

Olila, J. (1991) 'Corporate Anthropology', *Corporate Anthropology Newsletter*, 1(1): 6–9.

Parker, M. (1992a) 'Post-modern organizations or Postmodern organization theory?', *Organization Studies*, 13(1): 1–18.

Parker, M. (1992b) 'Getting Down from the Fence: A Reply to Haridimos Tsoukas', *Organization Studies*, 13(4): 651–3.

Parker, M. (1993) 'Life after Jean-Francois', in J. Hassard and M. Parker (eds), *Postmodernism and Organizations*. London: Sage. pp. 204–12.

Pfeffer, J. (1981) 'Management as Symbolic Action: The Creation and Maintenance of Organizational Paradigms', in L.L. Cummings and B. Staw (eds), *Research in Organizational Behaviour*, Vol 3. Greenwich, Conn.: JAI Press. pp. 1–52.

Pondy, L., Frost, P.J., Morgan, G. and Dandridge, T. (1983) *Organizational Symbolism*. Greenwich, Conn.: JAI.

Poster, M. (1988) 'Introduction', in M. Poster (ed.), *Jean Baudrillard: Selected Writings*. Cambridge: Polity.

Rabinow, P. (1986) 'Representations are Social Facts: Modernity and Post-modernity in

Anthropology', in J. Clifford and G. Marcus (eds), *Writing Culture*. Berkeley: University of California Press. pp. 234–61.

Reed, M. (1989) *The Sociology of Management*. Hemel Hempstead: Harvester Wheatsheaf.

Reed, M. (1993) 'Organizations and Modernity: Continuity and Discontinuity in Organization Theory', in J. Hassard and M. Parker (eds), *Postmodernism and Organizations*. London: Sage. pp. 163–82.

Richardson, M. (1994) *Georges Bataille*. London: Routledge.

Rorty, R. (1980) *Philosophy and the Mirror of Nature*. Oxford: Basil Blackwell.

Rorty, R. (1991) *Essays on Heidegger and Others: Philosophical Papers Volume 2*. Cambridge: Cambridge University Press.

Rosen, M. (1991a) 'Coming to Terms with the Field: Understanding and Doing Organizational Ethnography', *Journal of Management Studies*, 28(1): 1–24.

Rosen, M. (1991b) 'Scholars, Travellers and Thieves: On Concept, Cunning and Method in Organizational Ethnography', in P. Frost, L. Moore, M.R. Louis, C. Lundberg and J. Martin (eds), *Reframing Organizational Culture*. Newbury Park: Sage.

Sackmann, S. (1992) *Cultural Knowledge in Organizations*. Newbury Park: Sage.

Sahlins, M. (1976) *Culture and Practical Reason*. Chicago: University of Chicago Press.

Schwartzman, H. (1993) *Ethnography in Organizations*. London: Sage.

Sinclair, J. (1994) 'Reacting to What?', *Journal of Organizational Change Management*, 7(5): 32–40.

Slipy, D. (1990) 'Anthropologist Uncovers Real Workplace Attitudes', *HRM Magazine*, October, 76–9.

Smircich, L. (1983) 'Concepts of Culture and Organizational Analysis', *Administrative Science Quarterly*, 28(3): 339–58.

Smircich, L. and Morgan, G. (1983) 'Leadership: the Management of Meaning', *Journal of Applied Behavioural Science*, 18(2): 257–73.

Sperber, D. (1975) *Rethinking Symbolism*. Cambridge: Cambridge University Press.

Stanley, L. (1990) 'Doing Ethnography: Writing Ethnography – A Comment on Hammersley', *Sociology*, 24(4): 617–27.

Stewart, R. (1983) 'Managerial Behaviour: How Research has Changed the Traditional Picture', in M.J. Earl (ed.), *Perspectives on Management*. London: Oxford University Press. pp. 82–9.

Stewart, R. (1989) 'Studies of Managerial Jobs and Behaviour: the Ways Forward', *Journal of Management Studies*, 26(1): 1–9.

Strauss, A. (1978) *Negotiations*. San Francisco: Jossey-Bass.

Thomas, A.B. (1993) *Controversies in Management*. London: Routledge.

Thompson, P. (1993) 'Postmodernism: Fatal Distraction', in J. Hassard and M. Parker (eds), *Postmodernism and Organizations*. London: Sage. pp. 183–203.

Thompson, P. and McHugh, D. (1990) *Work Organizations: A Critical Introduction*. London: Macmillan.

Trice, H. (1991) 'Comments and Discussion', in Frost et al. (eds), *Reframing Organizational Culture*. Newbury Park: Sage. pp. 298–309.

Trice, H. and Beyer, J. (1993) *The Cultures of Work Organizations*. Englewood Cliffs: Prentice-Hall.

Turner, B.A. (1971) *Exploring the Industrial Sub-Culture*. London: Macmillan.

Turner, B.A. (1990a) *Organizational Symbolism*. Berlin: De Gruyter.

Turner, B.A. (1990b) 'The rise of organizational symbolism', in J. Hassard and D. Pym (eds), *The Theory and Philosophy of Organizations*. London: Routledge. pp. 83–96.

Turner, B.A. (1992) 'The symbolic understanding of organizations', in M. Reed and M. Hughes (eds), *Rethinking Organization*. London: Sage. pp. 46–66.

Turner, S. (1977) 'Complex Organizations as Savage Tribes', *Journal for the Theory of Social Behaviour*, 7(1): 99–125.

Turner, S. (1983) 'Studying Organization through Lévi-Strauss's Structuralism', in G. Morgan (ed.), *Beyond Method: Strategies for Social Research*. London: Sage. pp. 189–201.

Turner, V. (1967) *The Forest of Symbols*. Ithaca, NY: Cornell University Press.

Turner, V. (1974) *Drama, Fields and Metaphors: Symbolic Action in Human Society*. Ithaca, NY: Cornell University Press.

Turner, V. (1983) *From Ritual to Theatre*. New York: Performing Arts Journal Publications.

Turner, V. (1986) *Anthropology of Performance*. New York: Performing Arts Journal Publications.

Tyler, S. (1986) 'Post-modern Ethnography: from Document of the Occult to Occult Document', on J. Clifford and G.E. Marcus (eds), *Writing Culture*. Berkeley: University of California Press. pp. 122–40.

Tyler, S. (1987) *The Unspeakable*. Madison: University of Wisconsin Press.

Ulin, R.C. (1991) 'Critical Anthropology Twenty Years Later: Modernism and Postmodernism in Anthropology', *Critique of Anthropology*, 11(1): 63–89.

Urwick, L. (1952) *Notes on the Theory of Organization*. New York: American Management Association.

Van Gennep, A. (1960) *The Rites of Passage*. London: Routledge.

Vattimo, G. (1988) *The End of Modernity*. Cambridge: Polity.

Wallman, S. (ed.) (1979) *The Social Anthropology of Work*. London: Academic Press.

Watson, T.J. (1994) *In Search of Management*. London: Routledge.

Whitley, R.D. (1989) 'On the Nature of Managerial Tasks and Skills: Their Distinguishing Characteristics and Organization', *Journal of Management Studies*, 26(2): 209–24.

Willmott, H.C. (1984) 'Images and Ideals of Managerial Work: a Critical Examination of Conceptual and Empirical Accounts', *Journal of Management Studies*, 2(3): 349–68.

Willmott, H.C. (1993) 'Breaking the Paradigm, *Organization Studies*, 14(5): 681–719.

Woolgar, S. (1989) 'Reflexivity is the Ethnographer of the Text', in S. Woolgar (ed.), *Knowledge and Reflexivity*. London: Sage. pp. 14–36.

Wright, S. (ed.) (1994) *The Anthropology of Organizations*. London: Routledge.

Wuthnow, R., Hunter, J.D., Bergesen, A. and Kurzweil, E. (1984) *Cultural Analysis: The Work of Berger, Douglas, Foucault and Habermas*. London: Routledge and Kegan Paul.

Young, E. (1989) 'On the Naming of the Rose: interests and multiple meanings as elements of organizational culture', *Organization Studies*, 10(2): 187–206.

Notes

1   Although I will not adopt the sort of language commonly deployed in 'postmodern' pieces, the unwary reader should not be misled into reading the concepts I deploy as having a positivistic or objectivist acceptation. I do discuss in some detail the relationships of ethnography with forms of postmodern thought, truth and objectivity in Linstead (1993a, 1993b, 1994), where the interested reader will find sources fully detailed. Important discussions of these issues can be found in Geertz (1983) particularly the chapter 'Blurring Genres', and also (though not in the same context) in Norris (1991, 1993).

2   A counter to this approach in applying deconstruction to organizational action is explored in Linstead and Grafton-Small (1990a, 1990b, 1992) and in organizational analysis and ethnography by Jeffcutt (1993, 1994) and Linstead (1993a, 1993b, 1994).

3   For a more sophisticated example of this unacknowledged epistemological base, see Trice (1991) and Trice and Beyer (1993: ch. 1, particularly the discussion of 'metaphor' on p. 21).

4   Nor have I any wish to ignore the extensive tradition of participant observation which developed out of anthropological practice into other areas of the social sciences. That the boundaries of social anthropology are permeable in both directions is testimony to its interdisciplinarity. The impact of organizational and occupational participant observation studies has been considerable. In Britain, the community ethnographies of Malinowski, Radcliffe-Brown, Evans-Pritchard, Leach and Lienhardt influenced the development of work by Mary Douglas and Andrew Cohen, the more sociological studies of Gluckmann and Frankenberg, and the occupational ethnographies of Ditton, Lupton and Mars (for example, Ditton 1977, Mars 1982, Mars and Nicod, 1984). In the United States – from the 'Chicago'

ethnographies of Donald Roy and William H. Whyte (revisited by ethnographers in Frost et al. 1991), the work of Goffman, the symbolic interactionism of Becker, the reflexive sociology of Alvin Gouldner, through the development of ethnomethodology, the urban ethnographies of Spradley and into the variety of ethnographies, critical and uncritical, of organizations and 'organizational culture' of the 1980s – social anthropology has had a significant theoretical and methodological impact. Related collections include Wallman (1979) on the social anthropology of work, and Wright (1994) with a rather conservative view of the anthropology of organizations. However, if we are in search of studies which focus on management, rather than touch on it as a part of a broader organizational study, we find far fewer examples. If we apply rigorously the criterion of *participant* observation, and not just observation, the number dwindles even further. If we then want to look for full-length studies, Rosen (himself the author of several valuable shorter studies) observed in 1991 that full-length ethnographies of organizations were few in number, and although since then some interesting examples of organizationally-based ethnographic work have been produced – Collinson (1992), Kunda (1992 the richest example), Martin (1992), and a rather data-impoverished Sackmann (1992) – only Watson (1994) focuses specifically on management. Schein in his review of Watson calls it the best study of management since Dalton (1959); it is virtually the only one. Work by Mangham (e.g. 1986) critically develops the interactionist tradition but takes a micro focus on process. Cleverley (1973) is an insightful and accessible full length exposition of why it makes sense to treat managers as a 'tribe' but the anthropological concepts used are quite basic and the illustrations anecdotal. Many writers since the 1970s have misapplied these concepts and trivialized them. There is no extensive tradition of sociological participant observation in *management* research. Where the participation is total the involvement with management is usually partial, and where the involvement with management is total the participation is partial. This differs significantly from the method as applied in the social anthropological tradition. You cannot investigate the Nuer or the Azande two days a week.

5   The sociological development of participant methods, and the way in which the resulting accounts are treated, has differed from the social anthropological approach, although the boundaries are somewhat blurred. The relevant debate here is between Hammersley (1990) and Stanley (1990). Stanley's argument is that sociological accounts have failed to treat their descriptions as accounts, and have continued to build their arguments as though their methods were transparent. They talk, basically, about objects of study as objects. Stanley argues that ethnomethodology, taking 'talk' as the basic medium for the construction of meaning, makes such descriptive processes central. Social anthropologists, at the risk of oversimplification, work within an expanded symbolic field recognizing the importance of 'accounting' for phenomena and behaviour in establishing 'knowledge', actively reflecting on the epistemological grounding of the knowledge their various techniques produce (Douglas 1980: 49–73). This is probably why anthropology has been the first field thoroughly to explore the consequences of treating its researches as representations rather than taken for granted truisms (Atkinson 1990; Clifford and Marcus 1986; Hammersley 1990; Linstead 1993a; Marcus and Fischer 1986; Rabinow 1986; Ulin 1991).

6   This reflexive capacity also provides a means of coming to terms with the problem of paradigm incommensurability (Hassard 1990; Jackson and Carter 1991, 1993; Jackson and Willmott 1987; Willmott 1993). The heart of the debate seems to be that one group of commentators believe that all world-views or 'paradigms' are tied to a specific way of knowing, a set of methods by which knowledge may be produced. Some commentators believe that these paradigms can be mixed in particular investigations, others argue that they are incommensurable because they have opposing views of how knowledge is produced and can only co-exist by a failure to address such problems in sufficient depth. Further, Jackson and Willmott (1987) in particular argue that paradigms are also incommensurable in terms of non-epistemological issues, i.e. they pursue knowledge in particular ways that are acceptable[1] ideologically, politically and socially to particular subcommunities of the social scientific world, and are a matter of beliefs which are non-negotiable. Jackson at this point parts company with Willmott in terms of what can be done about this, but Jackson and Carter (1991) do observe that all paradigms interpenetrate; they share an intertext of partially common terms and articulations.

What becomes important then is to focus on where and how these paradigms articulate with each other, and where inevitably they clash and fall silent. Social anthropology has no easy answers to this question, but it does offer the orientation of self-reflexivity as a part of its most recent methodological advances, and focuses its attentions very much on the articulations between discourses, accounts, texts, rhetoric, and symbols in an interdiscursive field. As a result, it becomes a very good place in which to explore the possibilities and limitations of multidisciplinarity and their underpinnings.

7 Jones approaches the issue as a field anthropologist in several works (for example 1987, 1990) but the intersection of aesthetics and anthropology is also felt in the work of several recent philosophers of the social sciences. It is, in fact, especially characteristic of those commentators who attempt to interpret later Nietzsche (e.g. *The Gay Science* [1974]) and Heidegger (e.g. *Poetry, Language, Thought* [1971]). Foucault and Habermas both engage in this expanded idea of 'cultural anthropology' (Wuthnow et al. 1984); Rorty (1980: 381), in challenging the 'empiricism' of Habermas, argues that 'cultural anthropology (in a large sense which includes intellectual history) is all we need'. Gadamer's *Truth and Method* (1975), in resuscitating the idea of 'hermeneutics' for the human sciences, sets out to bridge the gap between the 'truth' of art and the 'truth' addressed through social scientific methods. Rorty engages sympathetically with Gadamer (Rorty 1980) and Heidegger (Rorty 1991) particularly on science as metaphor and politics, philosophy as a literary genre, language and pragmatic action; and Vattimo (1988) argues somewhat against these readings (see especially the essay 'Hermeneutics and Anthropology') in pursuit of a postmodern hermeneutic. The essence of this critique is that Gadamer and Rorty read Heidegger in terms of a tradition – dialectics or pragmatism – which overemphasizes the idea of 'play' between positions and interpretations in a ludic sense and the idea of 'radical alterity' (an artificial extension of the challenge of otherness *within*). Vattimo (1988: 161) comments that we must 'keep in mind the experience of anthropology and the condition of the primitive as ghetto and as margin. . . . The world of hermeneutic ontology . . . is instead the world of an active nihilism.' His 'weak thought' entails the recognition of the ironic essence of history in which 'interpretation and distortion, or dis-location, characterize not only the relation of thought to the messages of the past, but also the relation of one "epoch" to the others' (1988: 180). This seems to me to be an important recognition characteristic of postmodernism which commentators in organization studies rather oddly view as an argument against it (e.g. Parker 1992a, 1992b, 1993; Reed 1993; Thompson 1993). The importance of 'vision', 'perspective' and 'margin' also run through Bataille's extensive reworking of Durkheim into a symbolic anthropology/political economy of waste and abundance, which heavily influenced Baudrillard's 'excremental culture' of consumption, simulacra and symbolic exchange (see Richardson 1994 and Poster 1988 for relevant discussion). Finally, Scott Lash (1990) exemplifies the extent to which aesthetics and cultural anthropology blend in his *Sociology of Postmodernism* which, perhaps surprisingly but illuminatingly, includes an extended treatment of the French 'structuralist' social anthropologist/sociologist Pierre Bourdieu. See also Lash (1993) on aesthetics and modernization.

8 Discussion of more recent developments in postmodern anthropology and political economy as related to critical anthropology can be found in Ulin (1991); the possible relationships of these to organization studies are explored by Jeffcutt (1993; 1994) and Linstead (1993a, 1993b, 1994).

9 Social anthropologists had already been long concerned with the nature of the symbolic and its role in communication and production of meaning. Mary Douglas (1980) points out the proximity of Evans-Pritchard's approach to accountability with that of the ethnomethodologists; Leach (1970) gives a thorough and sympathetic assessment of the impact of Lévi-Strauss' structuralism on traditional structural-functionalism; and Sperber (1975) comes closest to developing a theory of symbolism which links the said with the unsaid and potentially articulates with post-structuralist approaches to language. Across the Atlantic, Duncan (1968) and Firth (1973) opened up the study of symbolism for Babcock (1978) and Foster and Brandes (1980) to develop our understanding of reversibility and inversion; Geertz (1973, 1983) and V. Turner (1967, 1974, 1983, 1986) developed symbolic anthropology as a subdiscipline with particular reference to ritual, performance, cultural forms and change. The work of Van

Gennep (1960) on liminality, and Mauss (1967) on reciprocation, though from an earlier period, has been revivified through this work. Geertz in particular is invariably, and frequently irresponsibly, cited as a major influence on the development of an interpretative school of organizational culture studies (see Pondy et al. 1983; Frost et al. 1985, 1991), and the range of theoretical influences on organizational culture studies from social anthropology has been indicated by Smircich (1983) and Allaire and Firsirotu (1984). B.A. Turner (1971) was an early attempt to apply anthropological approaches to the industrial subculture, beginning work which developed into explicitly symbolic analysis (B.A. Turner 1990a, 1990b, 1992). Bailey's (1977) work on negation and abomination in academic politics was taken up by Gowler and Legge (1981). Sahlins (1976) was also a critical and often dissenting influence. Cohen (1975, 1985) prefigures work on the 'management of meaning' (Gowler and Legge 1983; Smircich and Morgan 1983) and incremental v. revolutionary change (Johnson 1987). More recently postmodern philosophy and social theory have begun to influence modern ethnography as a mode of representation, a means of 'writing' the cultures observed (Clifford and Marcus 1986; Marcus and Fischer 1986; Tyler 1987). This has also raised crucial questions for ethnographic method and objectivity, in the light of its challenge to, or deconstruction of, the dominant Western conceptualization of the self and individuality.

10   I could add here early papers of my own in which ideas of accountability drawn from Evans-Pritchard, performance and mythic structure from Levi-Strauss, and ritual and group identity from Mary Douglas are used to analyse field data on consultancy, induction, and sabotage (Linstead 1983, 1984, 1985a, 1985b).

11   Detailed examples of the sort of data generated are given in the paper.

12   The exercise was illuminating for those participants who were the source of data for two reasons – first, they had never thought through the common dimensions of their roles with others from similar positions, and were often amazed at the degree of commonality; second, they had never attempted to present this 'identity' to others who were completely unfamiliar with it. Additionally, we were supported by able facilitators who stayed with each group throughout the exercise.

13   The most important aspect of this was the demonstration of differences in the way in which others carve up their world, and construct and negotiate their reality. One example given by a steward who turned the fire extinguishers on two recalcitrant smokers in a non-smoking compartment brought out for him – for the first time, as he was telling it – the extent to which it had been a socially-structured performance. Another example was of the '221 divorce' – the debriefing room which marked the boundaries between airborne 'reality', where intensive relations were formed quickly, and 'normality', where crews dispersed and were unlikely ever to meet again and had to readjust to the everyday world of others who were unfamiliar with their work.

2

The Meaning of Management and the Management of Meaning

Dan Gowler and Karen Legge

Rhetoric, like ritual, may be more than a symbolic reaffirmation of social relations. Through rhetoric people have licence . . . to explain and evaluate the causes and consequences of social relations, sometimes to the point of distortion. Rhetoric is thereby dynamically involved in their organisation and perpetuation. (Parkin 1975: 119)

In this chapter, 'management' is treated as that segment of the semantic order (subculture) of contemporary English-speaking societies which is characterized by the language of efficiency and control. This relatively broad perspective is more narrowly focused on a proposition, derived from social anthropology, that management may be viewed essentially as an oral tradition. The significance of this perspective is that it highlights how this oral tradition simultaneously accomplishes the meaning of management and the management of meaning by the use of plain speaking and rhetoric (see Figure 2.1).

One justification for taking this position is that empirical research on managerial roles and work (Mintzberg 1973, Stewart 1976, Davis and Luthans 1980) has repeatedly shown that managerial activity has a high oral communication content. For example, Stewart (1976: 92) reports that 'management is a verbal world where people are usually instructed, assisted, and persuaded by personal contact rather than on paper'. Davis and Luthans (1980: 65) comment that:

Observational studies by researchers indicate that most managers operate at a very high activity level and spend . . . two-thirds to three-fourths of their time communicating with others . . . *the modern manager's world is a verbal – specifically, oral – one*. Much time is spent in persuading, justifying, and legitimizing past, present, and future courses of action. [emphasis added]

We go beyond this relatively uncontroversial assertion to contend that such verbal activity frequently involves the use of rhetoric, that is, *the use of a form of word-delivery* (Parkin 1975: 114) *which is lavish in symbolism and, as such, involves several layers or textures of meaning* (Gowler and Legge 1981). This view of management is explored in four sections, each of which deals with a theme in *the rhetoric of bureaucratic control*, that is, highly expressive language that constructs and legitimizes managerial prerogatives in terms of a rational, goal-directed image of organizational effectiveness. The first section describes our general model, with particular reference to the distinction between plain speaking and rhetoric. The second, third, and fourth sections discuss the interrelated themes of hierarchy, accountability, and achievement respectively. Each of these themes has been selected to illustrate how *the rhetoric of bureaucratic control conflates management as a moral order with management as a technical-scientific order, while submerging the former*. They also demonstrate how, *through the management of meaning, the rhetoric of bureaucratic control contributes to management as a political activity* concerned with the creation, maintenance, and manipulation of power and exchange relations in formal work organizations. As Cohen and Comaroff (1976: 102) comment: 'a crucial variable in the construction of reality lies in the *management* of meaning: actors compete to contrive and propagate interpretations of social behavior and relationships. . . . The management of meaning is an expression of power, and the meanings so managed a crucial aspect of political relations.'

Golding (1980a: 43) reports that the management of meaning, with explicit and implicit appeals to 'the right to manage', becomes particularly evident in situations where those concerned perceive their managerial authority to be continually eroded and undermined. Accordingly we are presenting a view which constructs management as a *subculture* – a social collectivity whose members share a set of implicit and explicit meanings acquired through innumerable communicative exchanges. Furthermore, the possession of these shared meanings 'can only be demonstrated or utilised in communication, or in acts related to communication. Further, it is only by usage that the set of meanings, and the system of symbols to which they are attached within the subculture, can change, develop and extend' (Turner 1971: 61).

Thus, we present 'management' not only as an oral tradition in its *literal* sense, that is that managers spend most of their time talking, but also in its *anthropological* sense, that is as a means by which culture is generated, maintained, and transmitted from one generation to another. This emphasis on language also stems from a commitment to the idea that 'semantic powers make human beings members of a self-defining species' (Crick 1976: 3). In other words, human beings are fundamentally creatures who use language to make and communicate meanings, and who, as such, are rhetoricians and 'partly creations of their own talk and other social practices' (Harré 1980: 205).

We develop this 'semantic' approach to illustrate how, in the managerial subculture, meaning may be created through rituals, myths, magic, totemism, and taboo. Social anthropologists use these concepts to make sense of a wide range of cultural phenomena but they remain relatively little used in the *serious* description and interpretation of managerial constructions of reality. For it appears that, even when such ideas are put to 'serious' use, they often have negative connotations. Douglas (1970: 1–2), for example, points out that ritual has become 'a bad word signifying empty conformity' and a 'despised form of communication'. Similarly, Pym (1975a: 677) complains that 'industrial man gives precious little credibility to ritual. For him it belongs to Church, Army, and the Sepik River tribes, lesser societies than his own' – no doubt an observation which would also apply to contemporary lay views about myth, magic, totemism, taboo, and so on.

Plain Speaking and Rhetoric

When managers express views about their speech acts, they tend to emphasize the unambiguous articulation of aims, means, outcomes, and achievements. Indeed, that such plain speaking is necessary for the clear communication of managerial purposes is often asserted in the correspondence columns of professional and trade journals. While managers often espouse the virtues of, and a commitment to, plain speaking, they frequently adopt a type of speech that is highly ambiguous – rhetoric. Furthermore, they employ a form of rhetoric that associates two distinct orders of meaning in such a way as to preserve the appearance of plain speaking.

To convey this point, and following Parkin (1975), we represent plain speaking and rhetoric as two ends of a continuum (see Figure 2.1). With an increase in the symbolic content of a verbal or written statement, one moves from plain speaking to rhetoric. Parkin states that rhetoric is:

> a type of ritual: it says something about the speaker, the spoken-to, and the situation, which goes beyond what is contained in the surface message. At the other end of the continuum we have plain speaking. Moving constantly around the half-way mark between these poles of flowery speech and stark statement we have the styles of delivery used by most of us, but with sometimes significant cultural, as well as situational differences as to the precise position on the continuum. (Parkin 1975: 114)

Parkin (1975: 116) goes on to emphasize the point that, since rhetoric is lavish in symbolism, it has the power to engage attention and arouse emotion. Furthermore, as symbols both reveal and conceal, they increase the degree and variety of ambiguity in any act of communication (Lewis 1977). Managers are able, within the same statement, to use the ambiguity of rhetoric to arouse emotion and the clarity of plain speaking to direct behaviour. Rapid shifts between plain speaking and rhetoric permit managers, *ceteris paribus*, to generate motivation – that is, the arousal and direction of behaviour.

This essentially 'flip-flop' model of shifts between plain speaking and rhetoric, by varying the degree and variety of symbols and meanings, however, is too simple a view of the complexities of communication. This is because it emphasizes the *content* (degree and variety of symbols and meanings used) at the expense of the *structure* of statements (the relations between the symbols and meanings used). Paradoxically, when the structure

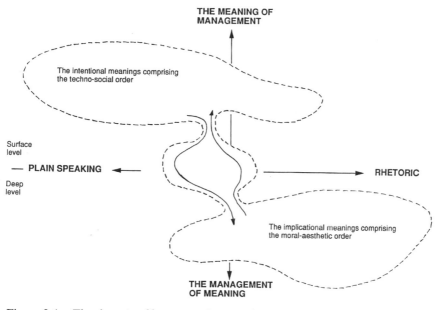

Figure 2.1 *The rhetoric of bureaucratic control*
Source: Gowler and Legge (1983)

of a statement is examined, what might appear on the surface as plain speaking emerges from this deeper level of analysis as rhetoric.

Hanson (1975) draws attention to the distinction between *intentional meanings* (for example, the reasons given for variations in the turnover of retail stock in high street stores), and *implicational meanings* (for example, the traditions and values of Christmas) which enrich and embellish them. For Hanson (1975: 10), implicational meanings raise sociocultural issues, since they involve a whole network of values, beliefs, norms, and so on. In Figure 2.1, we identify meanings as comprising either the techno-social or moral-aesthetic order. The techno-social order is defined by Peacock (1975: 5) as those meanings which 'connect events, roles, groups, tools, and resources in causal/functional relationships'. Briefly, the meanings comprising this order invoke ideas about achievement and agency, for example 'getting things done' by 'rational decision-making' and 'effective managerial controls'. Indeed, the plain speaking of managers and management theorists is replete with references to, and admonitions about, goals, objectives, intentions, plans, outcomes, and effectiveness. What is more, many definitions of 'management' and 'managers' make direct use of these techno-social meanings.

A manager, in the first place, sets objectives. He determines what the objectives should be. He determines what the goals in each area of objectives should be. He decides what has to be done to reach these objectives. He makes the objectives effective by communicating them to the people whose performance is needed to attain them. (Drucker 1974: 400)

By contrast, the moral-aesthetic order is comprised of the implicational meanings referred to by Hanson (1975: 10):

> the moral order and the knowledge which sustains it are created by social conventions. If their man-made origins were not hidden, they would be stripped of some of their authority. Therefore the conventions are not merely tacit, but extremely inaccessible to investigation. (Douglas 1973: 15)

However, the tacit, ambiguous meanings comprising the moral-aesthetic order are emergent and constructed through social interaction, especially through such forms of talk as gossip and humour. Managers consistently invoke moral-aesthetic meanings, particularly in those situations where questions of control arise. They surface when the issue of 'responsibility' emerges. While the meanings of this rather slippery term vary in the context concerned, for many managers it refers to a hierarchically-organized set of priorities. When asked about their jobs, managers will often draw attention to their responsibility for profits, productivity, people, quality, service, and so on. But, when questioned about their organizations, they frequently refer to the roles and personalities of those to whom they claim to be responsible. In both instances, though, there emerges a hierarchy of duties, which also operates as a set of moral-aesthetic imperatives. In other words, the rhetoric of bureaucratic control relates the 'positive' field of rational purpose, that is the techno-social order, to the 'normative' field of ethical justification, that is the moral-aesthetic order.

While we elaborate upon the nature of this complex relationship in the following sections, at this point it is necessary to comment further upon the concept of an 'order of meaning' (see Figure 2.1). First, the abstract character of this concept is suggested by an indeterminable, amoeba-like shape. The dotted line defining this form represents the idea that orders of meaning do not have the concrete boundaries usually accredited to objects in the physical world. Second, the dotted line is also intended to make the point that these orders or provinces of meaning have been arbitrarily chosen from among the many others with which they are interwoven. As evidence of this point, the reverse arrows located in the 'waist' of the figure, represent the idea that orders of meaning may exercise an influence upon one another. As Douglas (1973: 13) puts it, 'There is a tendency for meaning to overflow and for distinct provinces to interpenetrate.' It is this fluidity of meaning that is central to the perspective being developed here. In other words, it is from this ability to stimulate flows of meaning from one order to another that rhetoric derives its evocative and directive powers. But it should be noted that the exercise of these powers requires that the rhetorician and his audience be 'on the same wavelength'. Consequently, like gossip, rhetoric is a parochial business by which, through language and social interaction, those involved participate in the creation and maintenance of shared meanings.

To recapitulate, then, the solid lines in Figure 2.1 represent an attempt to frame the indistinct and 'messy' processes described above in terms of a formal analysis. Thus, the solid horizontal line indicates how a move from plain speaking to rhetoric increases the level of symbolic complexity. Furthermore, the solid reverse arrows within the waist of Figure 2.1 suggest that, with an increase in symbolic complexity, there is an increase in the flows of meaning from one order of meaning to another. Finally, the solid vertical line illustrates the idea that, in the special case of the rhetoric of bureaucratic control, the flows of meaning bring into association the surface intentional and the deep implicational meanings of management. It also is intended to suggest that these associations, conflations, and inter-penetrations of meaning not only accomplish our everyday, taken-for-granted understanding of management, but simultaneously achieve the covert manipulation of these understandings in the flux of complex social interactions and contexts.

The following sections discuss examples of these processes and consider three distinct though interrelated themes in the rhetoric of bureaucratic control: management-as-hierarchy, management-as-accountability, and management-as-achievement.

The Management-as-Hierarchy Theme

Hierarchical control, in one form or another, is a universal feature of organization and it therefore provides the basis for comparative research (Tannenbaum and Cooke 1979: 183).

The 'sovereignty of management' is generally regarded as in some way given (deriving inexorably from the 'essence' of hierarchy), and the fatalistic acceptance of this by 'actors', has led to the idea that the 'sovereignty of management' in an industrial hierarchical organization is some kind of truism. The truism perspective is a teleological confusion originating from the failure to consider the elements of 'sovereignty' and 'hierarchy' which derive from the structuring of the actors' social worlds (Golding 179: 169).

Overall, 'academic' commentators tend to treat hierarchy in a more explicit manner than managers. For example, until very recently, academic commentators have been inclined to highlight the origins, functions, and malleability of social and organizational hierarchies. On the other hand, like other laymen, managers tend to allude to hierarchy in a more oblique and implicit fashion, for example when referring to such issues as delegation, participation, leadership, motivation, responsibility, and performance. For instance, the following quotations have been taken from two letters appearing in the same correspondence column of a monthly, professional journal:

> The art of delegation as I see it is to know the strengths and weaknesses of subordinates and to delegate those jobs which the subordinates can perform. Not because they do them better but for the reason that, because you can complete the task anyway there is no need for you to do it. By thoroughly understanding all

aspects of his department's work in this way, the manager should be free for more important tasks which his subordinates cannot yet do.

Under this system, continual delegation of work should allow the department to grow and expand its capabilities. Delegation can only come from the top and must be completely controlled from the top. (Clark 1979: 51)

It is nonsense to suggest that officials delegate to their staff because they feel the latter can do a better job or because they wish to get rid of unwanted tasks. Officials delegate certain tasks because in their opinion such tasks are better suited to a subordinate because such work does not require the higher ability and experience of themselves. To undertake such work themselves would be wasting their own time, the company's money and reducing their own efficiency. An experienced departmental head needs no authority to delegate: it is a matter of personnel [*sic*] judgement.

Departmental heads in general are fully aware of the ability of their subordinates and selection for delegation of work is an easy task. They normally treat their staff as human beings and at times praise their efforts but under no circumstances do they treat them as equals in the running of a department. (Fleet 1979: 51)

At first glance, these letters might appear to be pieces of plain speaking about the efficient allocation of work in formal organizations. However, when viewed in terms of the perspective being developed here, it is possible to offer alternative interpretations. First, as suggested above, comments about 'subordinates', 'heads of departments', 'officials', and so on imply the existence of a hierarchy of roles and controls. Second, in both letters it is explicitly stated that such structures are, or should be, hierarchies of abilities and expertise. Indeed, in the first letter the correspondent concludes that, if this is not the case 'it is a sad reflection of [*sic*] business organisations'. Third, these letters explicitly refer to the delegation of tasks as opposed, for example, to the delegation of powers and responsibilities. Finally, they clearly attribute departmental and organizational efficiency to these bureaucratic arrangements.

When analysed in this way, the rhetoric of bureaucratic control becomes more apparent. For example, these letters fail to draw the distinction between what might be termed the normative and positive approaches to delegation. In other words, one is not sure whether delegation does, or should, take the form these correspondents describe. In the light of this, we suggest that the generation of such ambiguity is a major characteristic of rhetoric, where the rhetorician conflates the intentional meanings associated with *actual* causes and effects in the world with the implicational meanings associated with *proper* causes and effects in the world. Thus, like ritual, rhetoric expresses what *is* as what *should be*.

This becomes more significant when one examines the empirical evidence on managerial behaviour. Despite the claims and strictures of the correspondence quoted above, observations of managerial activities reveal a somewhat 'informal' state of affairs Pym (1975b: 140–1). Consequently, it seems reasonable to suggest that the blurring of 'real' and 'preferred' states of affairs is partially accomplished by backgrounding informal and lateral interaction, while foregrounding formal and vertical interaction.

To summarize, we can see how an implied hierarchy of roles positively relates control to efficiency. Moreover, by conflating a hierarchy of power relationships with a hierarchy of expertise, this link between control and efficiency reinforces 'the right to manage', that is, it helps to legitimate managerial prerogatives. Finally, the hierarchy theme in the rhetoric of bureaucratic control is interwoven with those of accountability and achievement, and, as such, contributes to the creation and maintenance of the meaning of management in a highly uncertain world.

The Management-as-Accountability Theme

> The *foundation of meaning*, according to my reconstruction upon his [Evans-Pritchard] work, is the *system of accountability*. As people decide to hold others accountable and as they allow the same principles to extend universally, even to apply to themselves, they set up a particular kind of moral environment for each other. (Douglas 1980: 71) [emphasis added]

In this section, we examine this 'foundation of meaning' and discuss how the rhetoric of bureaucratic control uses 'accountability' to present a rational, goal-oriented image of managerial action as 'a particular kind of moral environment'. Furthermore, we define 'accountability' as a form of moral and technical reckoning, where the careful husbandry of scarce resources is treated not only as a sign of *managerial competence* but also of *moral superiority*.

This approach to the management-as-accountability theme is influenced too by the observation that the rhetoric of bureaucratic control is permeated by the logic and language of accounting. This reflects the increasing significance that accountants and accounting practices have in contemporary market-oriented societies.

> What is accounted for can shape organizational participants' view of what is important, with the categories of dominant economic discourse and organizational functioning that are implicit within the accounting framework helping to create a particular conception of organizational reality. (Burchell et al. 1980: 5)

When looked at in terms of the model developed in Figure 2.1, two issues come into high relief. First, the computational practices that comprise accounting rest upon a system of symbolic classification, that is a number of plausible binary distinctions – for example debits and credits, expenditure and revenue, profits and losses, assets and liabilities – which go beyond a mere description of objective conditions in the world. This is because when such terms are used in everyday conversation, apart from their doubtful specificity, they involve moral-aesthetic judgements about the proper order of things:

> talking and acting is the very stuff of organizations and it is my contention that we would know more about the behavioural implications of accounting in organizations if research were directed to listening to such talk and observing such acting . . . it may be possible to discern the organizational scripts which facilitate the

talking and acting and to see the role accounting plays in such a process. (Colville 1981: 131)

Second, it is central to our argument that not only has accounting terminology become part of organizational language – for example, people are said to be 'written off' or labelled 'a liability' – but, when incorporated in the rhetoric of bureaucratic control, it also appears to clarify results and resolve problems by reducing individuals, things, acts, and events to a common denominator: money. Then, by the use of a variety of polarities such as costs and benefits (Chambers, 1980), it interprets the past, forecasts trends, determines ends, means, and the relationships between them. As suggested above, such modes of transformation – turning the intangible into the tangible and the normative into the positive – help managers to evoke a sense of 'blissful clarity' in their world (Barthes, 1972: 143), Through such reification, simplification, abstraction and rhetorical manipulation, managers (like the rest of us) construct a relatively-concrete world. However, it has been argued that such achievements are not without their dangers (see Golding, 1980b and Chapter 3 in this volume).

The rhetoric of bureaucratic control uses the language of accountability and accounting to help construct a 'moral environment', where the hierarchical ordering of roles and relationships is equated with the responsible conduct of human affairs, and where 'the right to manage' is extended to become 'the right to manage power and exchange relationships'. However, as discussed in the following section, this fusing of the themes of hierarchy and accountability is reinforced by the theme of achievement.

The Management-as-Achievement Theme

One of the first things a newcomer to a work organization is likely to be told is: 'In this place you will be judged by your results'. What is more, this prediction is likely to be accompanied by some sharp observations about how results might be related to rewards. Indeed, several managers have told us that this is what management is really about: 'Getting the right results through the use of the right incentives'. Hence, in this section, we take the question of the achievement of results first and then discuss issues about the preferred and supposed relationships between achievement, status, reward, effort, and so on. A characteristic view about management-as-achievement is stated in the following extract from a letter, where the correspondent asserts that:

> Managers are, or should be, employed by organizations to achieve results and should be evaluated on those results, rather than on how they are achieved.
> If those results are not being achieved then, yes, we need to know which specific behaviour patterns need to be changed. (Binnie 1981: 52)

Similarly, Heller writes:

> The objective and justification of management lie [*sic*] only in the achievement of results. It follows that any abstract theories of management, and any attempts to

describe management in terms other than those of effectiveness, create myths – and that the good manager is a mythical beast. (Heller, 1972: 3)

Heller comes to the conclusion that, despite popular opinion:

> There is no absolute criterion of managerial achievement. A manager is good, and a company efficient, only because others consider the results of their work good: and the so-called goodness endures only as long as this good opinion – which can be for an indefensible length of time. (ibid.)

We take up the issue of the idealization of achievement below, but if management is actually the maintenance of the good opinion of others, then the prudent manager would be well advised to improve his or her rhetorical skills. Managers are sometimes 'offered' the opportunity to attend 'social skills' training courses. These are often justified on the grounds that, among other things, they will improve managers' powers of communication and persuasion which will result in 'personal development' and/or 'the achievement of better results'. But insofar as such training (sometimes termed 'development' or the acquisition of 'competencies') does improve a manager's powers of persuasion, and taking Heller's view, it might be argued that it may also improve the manager's ability to create the illusion of achievement, that is other peoples' 'good opinions'.

Talk about achievement, however, is frequently cloaked in the vocabulary of economic exchange and contracts of employment, for example 'effort', 'reward', the 'wage-work bargain', 'pay and productivity', 'incentives', and so on, which ensures a regular supply of semantic grist for the rhetorical mill. Indeed, not only does the rhetoric of bureaucratic control utilize ideas about rewards, motivation, performance, and so on, but this usage again illustrates the conflation of the two orders of meaning represented in Figure 2.1. The following example, which has been taken from the correspondence columns of a professional journal, helps to illustrate this point. Here the correspondent asserts that:

> Getting a weekly pay-packet stuffed with cash is enjoyable. It represents the work that you've done during the past week, and is a reminder, either consciously or subconsciously, of the reason that you are there – you supply the effort and the firm supplies the wages.
>
> Getting a monthly pay slip on the other hand, is one of the biggest anticlimaxes going. . . . This type of situation leaves the employee with precious little incentive for the next month's work. So before a firm switches to cashless pay in order to save £30 p.a. per employee administration costs, I would suggest that it also considers the longer term loss due to lower productivity resulting from the disappearance of that weekly incentive. (Paige 1981: 37)

The surface message of this letter makes the plausible suggestion that 'cashless pay' removes the concrete representation of the relationship between effort and reward. Perhaps more controversially, this correspondent goes on to claim that, in some way or another, this change damages the incentive to work and, consequently, productivity.

There is certainly something in this assertion, since it has been argued that such changes are manifestations of the reality that we live in an increasingly abstract and alienating society. Zijderveld (1982: 6) writes: 'the more abstract a society grows, the larger the chance will be that various groups of people begin to long for re-enchantment'. This is not to say that an increase in the use of the weekly wage packet would result in a 're-enchantment' with the world. But for many people it is a condensation symbol that seems to evoke a wide range of thoughts and feelings, for instance about social status, equity, 'a fair day's pay', economic security and, possibly, individual and collective achievements. Indeed, in his analysis of wage forms, shopfloor culture and conflict, Willis (1979: 198) draws attention to the power of the 'fetishized brown wage packet'. Put briefly, the whole issue of reward (and punishment) is awash with moral sentiment, much of which is directly concerned with ideas about acceptable goal-directed behaviours and their outcomes, that is, achievement. It is also relevant to note in Paige's letter there is the assumption that, whatever the means, effort/performance should be related to reward. Thus, what on the surface may appear as a piece of rational plain speaking about incentives, at a deeper level is a vehicle for polyvalent meanings summoned up from the moral-aesthetic domain.

White (1981) has made the point that not only are methods of salary and wage payment systems of economic exchange, but they are also instruments of authority.

> Over and above the economic significance of the pay system both for the organisation and for the employee there is a symbolic significance in the pay system. The condition of the pay system reflects the ascendancy of management or of workers, or the relative importance of various groups of workers . . . much effort is invested in the struggle around the pay system, irrespective of the direct economic returns . . . the pay system is a particular focus for managerial and worker ideologies. (White 1981: 45)

Now, given this 'functionalist' frame of reference, it is reasonable to consider the relationship between status, effort, and reward (Gowler and Legge 1982). It is often argued that an individual's position in the organization's hierarchy is manifested and maintained by the amount and nature of his rewards, for example pay and fringe benefits. Even if one is not prepared to accept these interpretations, individuals certainly make frequent reference to them. It is often claimed in the rhetoric of bureaucratic control that status should be related to reward, and that both status and reward should be related to achievement. But these relationships are notoriously difficult to establish in terms of definition, measurement and consensus. We believe that many would protest that such positive relationships between achievement, status, effort and reward represent an ideal state of affairs unlikely to be found in the rapidly changing world of practical affairs. But such views return us directly to an issue raised above – the idealization of achievement.

To adopt or, more precisely, adapt a view from social anthropology, it is possible to treat the principle of achievement in quite another way. First, it may be that the semantic links between achievement, motivation, reward, and so on are restricted to certain cultures (Hofstede 1980: 35). Second, it is often asserted that all societies have some form of social differentiation, which is conventionally discussed in structural terms, with reference to age, sex, class, caste, race, and so on. Moreover, there are those who convert forms of social differentiation into forms of social stratification, where such factors influence or even determine individuals' life-chances. The suggestion that in Western capitalist societies it is the principle of achievement that actually defines and legitimates inequalities in social status and opportunity structures is of considerable interest. In the words of Offe:

> the achievement principle does not operate merely as a norm which ensures equality, but just as much also as a legitimating principle to justify social inequality – it restricts social inequality in the very moment that it propagates a claim for it. The achievement principle sanctions those forms of inequality which have resulted from individual achievement and in this way it is also a norm of inequality. (Offe 1976: 41)

Further, discussing the social functions of this normative flexibility, he writes:

> Our basic assumption is that *the achievement principle is a prescriptive model of status distribution*, providing for formal organizations in industrial societies the sole principle by which social status is legitimated, where status includes both differences in existing status and changes of status by means of occupational mobility. (Offe 1976: 55, emphasis added)

From a social anthropological point of view, two distinct interrelated interpretations of the principle of achievement emerge. First, Offe seems to be saying that the principle of achievement not only provides a charter myth for the hierarchical structuring of formal work organizations, but also that it 'accounts' for any individual's position or mobility within or between them. Second, there seems a remarkable correspondence between what Offe claims as the social functions of the achievement principle and what some social anthropologists claim as the social functions of totemism. Totemism, like ritual, myth and magic, has been the subject of a considerable amount of speculation and controversy. Lienhardt (1964) neatly sums up the classical view, pointing out that among traditional societies the recognition of common life is often expressed in 'religious' acts, for example sacrifice and totemism.

> Among many peoples, the relationship existing between whole groups of people – notably those claiming common descent and belonging to the same clan is symbolized by a totem. Totems are of many kinds, but are often one or another species of animal, sometimes regarded as an ancestor of the clan. A common totem therefore stands for a community of interests of one sort or another. (Lienhardt 1964: 181)

Under the influence of Lévi-Strauss (1964), this view of totemism has been challenged. It is now also seen as a universal cognitive device that enables people, particularly non-literate people, to organize their experience of the world into a framework of values and meaning, where the differences in culture and nature are brought into relationship.

> Totemism is not a separable 'ethnographic' specimen peculiar to the Australians and some other peoples but a particular instance of a much more general phenomenon, one indeed that all societies have to face in one way or another: the problem of how men perceive, select, intellectually order and socially structure the

similarities and differences in both the natural and cultural realms respectively, and how connections are established between these two orders. (Worsley 1967: 142)

Given this view of totemism, it is instructive to consider what Swingle (1976) has to say when writing on the dysfunctions of what he terms the 'mythology of management'.

We believe, in our society, that rewarding people simply and non-discriminately on the basis of merit or achievement reflects true fairness and democracy. . . . I am always stunned by the naiveté of people caught in such organizations who accept the myth of meritocracy as a basic tenet of their modern religion. In all meritocracies someone or some . . . group (even if it is the entire organization) must evaluate achievement and decide on appropriate rewards. (Swingle 1976: 14)

He argues that the myth of meritocracy is an outgrowth of social Darwinism, this being a cluster of ideas (for example, the 'struggle for existence' and the 'survival of the fittest') which expresses the popular normative adaptation of the concept of evolution. We suggest that the symbols and meanings of meritocracy, achievement, and so on categorize, justify and – at times – celebrate social, economic, political and physical differences between people. When these differences are expressed and validated in a 'survival of the fittest' form, they mirror the principles and processes that are claimed to 'select' and differentiate all forms of life. Put briefly, social Darwinism relates the order of culture to the order of nature and, as such, meets Lévi-Strauss' main criterion for totemism.

In support of this assertion that certain meanings, symbols, and forms of achievement provide the 'abstract' totemism of contemporary Western societies, it should be noted that ethnographic research frequently associates totems with a variety of patterned avoidances. For instance, Beattie reports:

a custom of ritual avoidance of the totem is widespread. In Africa members of totemic groups are generally prohibited from killing and eating their totem (if it is edible), though others may do so. A Nyoro believes that if he eats his totemic species he may become ill and perhaps die. He respects rather than fears it; certainly he does not worship it. He uses the same term, meaning 'respectful avoidance', for his relationship to his wife's mother as he does for his relationship to his totem. (Beattie 1974: 220)

In contemporary British society it is not only the symbols of group unity – for example flags, badges, uniforms, and ceremonies – that are the objects of subcultural ritual respect, but also the symbols of, and reference to, achievement are often accompanied by linguistic and other forms of patterned avoidance. For instance, this may take the form of an ostentatious display of the trophies and tokens of achievement accompanied by an exaggerated expression of diffidence about the acquisition of these prizes. In Britain, successful people sometimes attribute their achievements to 'luck' or 'good fortune'. This 'luck-labelling' (Fairhurst 1975: 181) is often said to be a means of coping with the anxieties generated by participation in highly-competitive organizational hierarchies, while at the same time espousing commitment to cooperative values and behaviours. Obviously, the whole issue of the taboos that appear to surround the question of achievement is worthy of more attention.

From a social anthropological point of view the attribution of luck may be a taboo that draws attention to the ends of achievement while, at the same time, backgrounding and blurring the means of achievement. In other words, such taboos protect the 'sacred' principles of achievement by deflecting questions about agency, merit, and so on in those circumstances where the 'facts' are especially difficult to determine. This does mean, of course, that 'luck-labelling' may only be used sparingly, since too often a recourse to this form of explanation may raise serious questions, among even the most gullible of people, about the 'facts' of achievement.

To summarize, we have drawn attention to the idealization of achievement and have argued that the ensuing rhetoric may be analysed in terms of totemism and taboo. Certainly, management is not only said to be about 'getting things done' but also about 'getting things done well', which inevitably introduces a whole complex of meanings, including 'success', 'competition' and 'performance', that characterize the semantic order of what Offe (1976: 40) terms the 'achieving society'.

This approach to the theme of achievement suggests how it is bound up with the theme of hierarchy. For example, people frequently justify their position or status within the managerial hierarchy on the grounds of their achievements. What is more, the rhetoric of bureaucratic control is often used in support of the idea that a hierarchy of roles and controls is absolutely necessary for the achievement of organizational goals.

Similarly, the theme of achievement is frequently conflated with the theme of accountability. During appraisals, assessments, interviews and so on, managers are required to account for their achievements. Such occasions are likely to be conducted in the language of accounting, and with liberal use of vocabularies of economic exchange and industrial relations, making reference to 'effort', 'standards', 'rewards', 'performance', and 'output'. Given this, it is not surprising that in the managerial subculture, ideas, values, and beliefs about achievement have become reified into a totem. And, like all totems, it comes to be treated with exaggerated respect, even to the extent that a critical discussion of the issue may become difficult.

There is also the possibility that all this talk about achievement is yet another facet of the 'right to manage' issue. Put bluntly, in the so-called achieving societies the managerial prerogative is likely to be legitimized by the assertion that the right to control power and exchange relationships should be in the hands of those who have demonstrated 'a good track record of achievement'.

Conclusion

What immediate propositions emerge from our analysis of management as an oral tradition? First, through embodying and expressing such ideas, management means hierarchy, accountability and achievement. Second, with regard to the management of meaning, we contend that:

1 management eulogizes 'plain speaking' but, on examination, examples of apparently 'plain speaking' are revealed as rhetorics disguising and legitimizing values about order and control in industrialized society;
2 rhetoric about hierarchy, by surfacing a techno-social justification for delegation and downward-looking relationships, submerges the reality of management dependency on superordinates;
3 rhetoric of accounting in an industrialized society, through its myth-making functions, serves to simplify and clarify the ambiguities inherent in an uncertain world;
4 rhetoric, by presenting achievement in totemic forms, safeguards and perpetuates its idealization

Generally speaking, we consider the fact that managers spend a great deal of time talking is more than a matter for passing comment, and not necessarily something to be deplored. This endless talk, especially the rhetoric, may be the way in which social control is maintained while, in situations of great uncertainty and complexity, managerial prerogatives are simultaneously accomplished and legitimated. This is not an inconsiderable achievement. Indeed, this may be what 'achievement' is really all about. Heller (1972) and Offe (1976) would appear to lend support to this view. However, in the course of this analysis, the management-as-achievement theme grew in significance for us.

Our generalizations about the three themes selected here are as follows. The management-as-hierarchy theme expresses meanings about social order, while the management-as-accountability theme expresses meanings about the moral order. It is the management-as-achievement theme that cements the social and moral orders into a rational, 'natural' order, where any other state of affairs would be seen to result in anarchy and despair.

The preferred image of the natural order is produced by the rhetoric of bureaucratic control, which presents the proper access to, and allocation of scarce resources as a 'neutral' technical business. But in order to accomplish this, it simultaneously incorporates, though backgrounds, ambiguous and controversial moral-aesthetic meanings. Turner (1971) has gone so far as to suggest that the manager has to acquire the political ability so to manipulate his verbal and written outputs. Thus, he comments:

> The overt meaning content of a message cannot normally be ignored and the most skilful practitioners of this sort of manoeuvring are those who are able to link both the hidden and apparent meanings. A successful manager can be expected to present cases that are both accurate *and* calculated to advance his own cause. (Turner 1971: 110)

Our analysis has concentrated upon Parkin's (1975) crucial distinction between plain speaking and rhetoric-as-ritual. We have emphasized the relationships between language and social control, that is how language might be used to exercise power over people. But there is a body of management research, opinion and practice that on the surface appears to be concerned with power over things. This includes the world of 'management science', which its practitioners might reasonably claim lies squarely in the domain of techno-social meanings, and happily free of the pernicious use of moral-aesthetic meanings. But, as social anthropologists, we would be surprised if this were the case, since the 'technical order' of any society requires some form of symbolic representation. Furthermore, such representations are un-likely to be cast within an inviolate system of unequivocal meanings. Even if this were the case (and some might point to mathematics here), technical designs and choices always require presentation and justification, at which point the moral-aesthetic domain would be likely to make its shadowy ap-pearance. While this topic awaits further research, we leave the stage to a member of a 'young managers' programme' who, when describing his job in production to other course members, confidently observed: "You often have to make decisions on sparse information. Then you stick to it. You don't change it . . . afterwards you just have to justify it.'

References

Barthes, R. (1972) *Mythologies*. London: Jonathan Cape.

Beattie, J. (1974) *Other Cultures*. London: Cohen and West.

Binnie, J.H. (1981) letter to *Personnel Management*, 13(4).

Burchell, S., Clubb, C., Hopwood, A., Hughes, J. and Nahapiet, J. (1980) 'The Roles of Ac-counting in Organizations and Society', *Accounting, Organizations and Society*, 5(1).

Chambers, R.J. (1980) 'The Myths and the Science of Accounting', *Accounting, Organizations and Society*, 5(1).

Clark, C.R. (1979) letter to *Management Accounting*, July/August.

Cohen, A.P. and Comaroff, J.L. (1976) 'The Management of Meaning: On the Phenomen-ology of Political Transactions', in B. Kapferer (ed.), *Transactions and Meaning: Directions in the Anthropology of Exchange and Symbolic Behavior*. Philadelphia: Institute for the Study of Human Issues.

Colville, I. (1981) 'Reconstructing "Behavioural Accounting"', *Accounting, Organizations and Society*, 6(2).

Crick, M. (1976) *Explorations in Language and Meaning*. London: Malaby Press.

Davis, T.R.V. and Luthans, F. (1980) 'Managers in Action: A New Look at Their Behavior and Operating Modes', *Organizational Dynamics*, Summer.

Douglas, M. (1970) *Natural Symbols: Explorations in Cosmology*. London: The Cresset Press.

Douglas, M. (1973) 'Tacit Conventions', in M. Douglas (ed.), *Rules and Meanings*. Harmonds-worth: Penguin.

Douglas, M. (1980) *Evans-Pritchard*. London and Glasgow: Fontana.

Drucker, P.F. (1974) *Management: Tasks, Responsibilities, Practices*. London: Heinemann.

Fairhurst, E. (1975) 'Expectations, Chance and Identity-Stress', in D. Gowler and K. Legge (eds), *Managerial Stress*. Epping: Gower Press.

Fleet, A.H. (1979) Letter to *Management Accounting*, July/August.

Fowler, R., Hodge, B., Kress, G. and Trew T. (1979) *Language and Control*. London: Rout-ledge & Kegan Paul.

Golding, D. (1979) 'Symbolism, Sovereignty and Domination in an Industrial Hierarchical Organisation', *The Sociological Review*, 27(1): 169–97.

Golding, D. (1980a) 'Authority, Legitimacy and the "Right to Manage" at Wenslow Manufac-turing Co.', *Personnel Review*, 9(1): 43–8.

Golding, D. (1980b) 'Establishing Blissful Clarity in Organizational Life: Managers', *The Sociological Review*, 28(4) pp. 763–82.

Gowler, D. and Legge, K. (1981) 'Negation, Abomination and Synthesis in Rhetoric', in C. Antaki (ed.), *The Psychology of Ordinary Explanations of Social Behaviour*. London: Academic Press. pp. 243–69.

Gowler, D. and Legge, K. (1982) 'Status, Effort and Reward', in A.M. Bowey (ed.), *Handbook of Salary and Wage Systems* (2nd edn.). Aldershot: Gower Press.

Hanson, F.A. (1975) *Meaning In Culture*. London: Routledge & Kegan Paul.

Harré, R. (1980) 'Man as Rhetorician', in A.J. Chapman and D.M. Jones (eds), *Models of Man*. Leicester: The British Psychological Society.

Heller, R. (1972) *The Naked Manager*. London: Barrie and Jenkins.

Hofstede, G. (1980) *Culture's Consequences: International Differences in Work-Related Values*. Beverly Hills: Sage Publications.

Lévi-Strauss, C. (1964) *Totemism* (translated by R. Needham). London: Merlin Press.

Lewis, I.M. (1977) 'Introduction', in I.M. Lewis (ed.), *Symbols and Sentiment: Cross-Cultural Studies in Symbolism*. London: Academic Press.

Lienhardt, G. (1964) *Social Anthropology*. London: Oxford University Press.

Mintzberg, H. (1973) *The Nature of Managerial Work*. New York: Harper and Row.

Offe, C. (1976) *Industry and Inequality: The Achievement Principle in Work and Social Status*. London: Edward Arnold.

Paige, M. (1981) letter to *Accountancy*, September.

Parkin, D. (1975) 'The Rhetoric of Responsibility: Bureaucratic Communications in a Kenya Farming Area', in M. Bloch (ed.), *Political Language and Oratory in Traditional Society*. London: Academic Press.

Peacock, J.L. (1975) *Consciousness and Change*. Oxford: Basil Blackwell.

Pym, D. (1975a) 'The Demise of Management and the Ritual of Employment', *Human Relations*, 28(8).

Pym, D. (1975b) 'The Crisis in Authority', *Management Education and Development*, 6(3).

Stewart, R. (1976) *Contrasts in Management: A Study of Different Types of Managers' Jobs. Their Demands and Choices*. London: McGraw-Hill.

Swingle, P.G. (1976) *The Management of Power*. Hillsdale, New Jersey: Lawrence Erlbaum Associates.

Tannenbaum, A.S. and Cooke, R.A. (1979) 'Organizational Control: A Review of Studies Employing The Control Graph Method', in C.J. Lammers and D.J. Hickson (eds), *Organizations Alike and Unlike: International Inter-Institutional Studies in the Sociology of Organizations*. London: Routledge & Kegan Paul.

Turner, B.A. (1971) *Exploring the Industrial Subculture*. London: Macmillan.

White, M. (1981) *The Hidden Meaning of Pay Conflict*. London: Macmillan.

Willis, P. (1979) 'Shop-Floor Culture, Masculinity and the Wage Form', in J. Clarke, C. Critcher and R. Johnson (eds), *Working-Class Culture. Studies in History and Theory*.

Worsley, P. (1967) 'Groote Eylande Totemism and Le Totemisme Aujourd'hui', in E. Leach (ed.), *The Structural Study of Myth and Totemism*. London: Tavistock Publications.

Zijderveld, A.C. (1982) *Reality in a Looking-Glass: Rationality through an Analysis of Traditional Folly*. London: Routledge & Kegan Paul.

3

Producing Clarity – Depoliticizing Control

David Golding

When Vladimir says to Estragon, 'But at this place, at this moment of time, all mankind is us, whether we like it or not' (Beckett 1956), he encapsulates the problem of the non-omniscient being. We do not have the facility for being everywhere and knowing everything, and therefore, it is not possible for us to encompass the complexities with which we are faced at any moment in our lives – accepting the assumption that there exists, in some form, a world *out there* (whether practical or idealized) which we experience as being separate from ourselves. One consequence of this predicament is that (in order to deal with these complexities) we find ourselves generating, and being subjected to, extensive processes of abstraction and simplification. These processes appear to be ontological, not merely psychological, and they form part of the means by which we try to ensure that we have at least a reasonable chance of maintaining our day-to-day survival. They are one of the foundations upon which we establish, and make provision for the continuation of, apparently mundane communications.

One consequence of the necessity to abstract and simplify is that, by their very nature, interactions produce views and perspectives which are partial. Unfortunately, because of insufficient time and/or inclination to check any particular contribution against other available views and perspectives, this sometimes has the effect of investing partial contributions with unjustified universality. This presents a considerable problem to the conduct of cooperative ventures.

To the extent that views and perspectives take on an existence which transcends and neglects alternatives, they are susceptible to processes which grant them authority as the only possible versions. This occurs precisely because the ontological status of human existence precludes the facility of omnipresence. We generate accounts of events in accordance with our partial perspectives, and we are doomed to pay less attention to the potential for alternative perspectives because we are mortal, anxious, time-bounded, and cannot be everywhere at once.

The processes of abstraction and simplification enable a complex world to be given meaning through particular social constructions, but in a way which tends to result in each construction being seen as the best, the privileged, or the only *possible* way of viewing the world. The whole process, in other words, has a tendency to become self-fulfilling. The views of the world produced by our abstraction and simplification processes in fact achieve the continuing confirmation required to perpetuate their existence by the transformation of possibles into apparent absolutes. This redefining in turn serves to divert us from (although it never entirely denies) access to alternative views. Through these processes, *particular* contributions are transformed into *general* ones, and become accepted, in direct relation to the extent that access to alternatives is effectively blocked.

A troublesome though fundamental side-effect of this is the vulnerability of such processes to manipulation and exploitation. This leaves them at the mercy of any particular individual and/or group who may be in a position to ensure that certain preferred definitions of situations prevail, and in turn to make certain that those preferences are reinforced and maintained. This chapter examines examples of such inherent dangers, involving the way in which a principle of control – deriving from one possible way of organizing – is transformed and given life such that it appears in effect to be the only way to organize.

What follows draws upon concerns raised by managers in a study of two particular organizations. Sometimes these concerns would be expressed as vague dissatisfactions, such as, 'you know, I really used to enjoy coming to work . . . look[ed] forward to it . . . but now . . . I could cheerfully drive straight past the entrance in a morning . . . and spend the day in the hills'. On other occasions they would be expressed rather more directly: 'I no longer feel that I can manage in this situation . . . no . . . more than that . . . I don't *want* to. . . . It's as though . . . it just doesn't seem *right* anymore'. In each case the perceptions of the managers in question seemed to indicate something which went to the heart of what might be called the nature of management.

I also want to consider the extent to which ossification of ideas about the nature of management may be said to have occurred. Ideas concerning the nature of management have been taken for granted even by those involved in the construction and development of management theories, due to the prevalence of so many ahistorical approaches to investigation. Indeed it has been recognized for some time (see, for example, Clegg and Dunkerley 1977; Salaman 1978; Whitley 1977) that the preponderance of work which fails to locate organizations in the societies in which they exist has led to the development of oversimplistic theoretical frameworks, and resulted in an impoverishment of organization theories in general. The neglect of history, and 'embeddedness' in particular organizational and societal contexts, has undoubtedly compounded this.

Nevertheless, any consideration of historical factors must necessarily take a more sophisticated approach than studies which treat the everyday world as given, relying upon members' unexamined assumptions and understanding as though they were shared, unequivocally, by everyone. The proper consideration of historical factors presents a fundamental requirement to examine the origins and development of common-sense assumptions and factors which give rise to the *appearance of being shared by everyone*. As the process of transforming possibles into apparent absolutes suggests, important underlying factors can only be uncovered by an examination of implicit understanding and 'taken-for-granteds'.

The Ticking Seconds of History

The means by which everyday life is made possible are an elusive but central problem for social analysis. The way in which each ticking second recedes into history leaving behind it an element – a part of its one-time existence, a part of its life-that-was – is at the heart of this problem. The existence of elements which come to be taken for granted in everyday life is largely determined by the (manipulated and exploited) abstraction and simplification processes acting as a series of selection filters in the development of assumptions and understandings. The extent to which everyday transactions provide means for continual reinforcement of selections, gives rise to the possibility of perpetuation of those elements which do survive such filtering.

As an example, consider a transaction in which A gives B one penny in payment for something received in the form of goods or services. At time t minus one second, A prepares to give B one penny, because that is the done thing in this situation. B has provided goods or services for A, and A knows that those goods or services have to be paid for; A knows that money is legal tender, and that one penny is the going rate. At time t, A gives B one penny. At time t plus one second, A has given B one penny, payment has occurred for goods or services provided, one penny has been established as the going rate, and money has been confirmed as legal tender. The assumptions concerning going rates, legal tender, and so on, and the way in which the whole process comes to be seen as 'the done thing', are necessary to the extent that they simplify the task of exchange. The legitimization of the transaction is used and confirmed by A and B as a language of exchange which enables concentration to be diverted to other more important things, such as the state of the weather.

The elevation of some things to a position of more importance in itself underlines the necessity of simplification processes in which shared assumptions and understandings can be developed to facilitate everyday transactions. The development of shared assumptions and understandings is always subject to continual reformulation in members' interactions, but the reformulation itself becomes second nature (thus transforming a possible way of exchange into an apparently absolute one), in that members are not (normally) aware of the essence of what they are reformulating. They do not consciously reformulate alternatives. A does not (usually) consider whether to give B a turnip rather than a penny – at least not in those societies which have developed economies based upon specialization, division of labour and monetary exchange. Thus, one thing this simplification may be seen to have produced is a more convenient means of exchange (that is, one which is more convenient in terms of time and expenditure of energy). The derivation of this, however (located in history as such transactions take place and become more convenient following increasing specializations and divisions of labour) has tended to become lost, as one *possible* means of executing exchanges has become *the* way. This loss of historical derivation may not be too serious in the case of monetary exchange (in fact, because the increase in convenience is so obvious, perhaps it is never entirely lost); however, in more complex considerations, the loss can have severe consequences.

What are the more serious consequences of such a loss of historical derivation? Although this 'forgetting' of historical derivation is based in individual consciousness, the loss becomes shared, and the shared existence – divorced from a historical *raison d'être* – is experienced as a rule. This experience rests upon a shared belief *in* such a rule, such that the sharedness represents an incorrigible manifestation of the *done thing* – reproduced as apparently *the only rule possible*. It thus represents a myth – in the sense of being a message – as a system of communication (the extent to which it tells a story) and as a kind of speech – a message purveyor.

Barthes, in fact, has argued that myth has the task of giving a historical intention a natural justification and making contingency appear eternal:

> In passing from history to nature, myth acts economically: it abolishes the complexity of human acts, it gives them the simplicity of essences, it does away with all dialectics, with any going back beyond what is immediately visible, it organises a world which is without contradictions because it is without depth, a world wide open and wallowing in the evident. It establishes a blissful clarity: things appear to mean something by themselves. (Barthes 1973: 143)

Abstraction and simplification, contingent, purposeful and necessary to facilitate the complexities involved in accomplishing everyday life, achieve self-fulfilling properties in creating myth. The isolation of nature (the present – the apparent absolute) from history (the ticking seconds containing the possibles – the alternatives) is made innocent by the *depoliticized speech* of myth. As Barthes has suggested: 'myth is constituted by the loss of the historical quality of things: in it, things lose the memory that they once were made' (Barthes 1973: 142).

Thus any underlying political relations are divested in producing 'blissful clarity' and the essence of the depoliticizing lies in the message purveyed. Such resulting myth, therefore, operates in the realms of the submerged and tacit elements of everyday life (as distinct from an overt storytelling kind of myth). Message becomes myth to the extent that its origins have been lost and its intentions have been depoliticized. The paradox is that the *necessary* processes have resulted in alternative origins and intentions being suppressed, precisely because they have become *unnecessary*.

The Principle of Control at Wellblown Manufacturing Co.

The following illustrations underline this depoliticizing (as a loss of memory) by demonstrating the way in which the depoliticized speech of myth is ·

subsumed into the normal speech of everyday life. The material (with names and positions changed to protect identities) is taken from field notes I prepared during an extensive period of participant observation spent as a manager (the authorial imputation of meaning therefore stemming partly from the perspective of acquiring membership, see Golding 1986) in Wellblown Manufacturing Co., a medium-sized engineering manufacturing company in the north of England. The company is the UK subsidiary of a USA-owned multinational company with household name products.

The following scenario is reconstructed from a lunchtime conversation between John Manners, the machine shop manager, and Roger Metcalfe, the training manager. I was seated at the next table.

Scenario
'You know Roger, I think the biggest problem facing us at the moment, is the question of morale.' John Manners, the machine shop manager, clattered some more potatoes on to his plate.

'Why do you say that?' Roger Metcalfe asked somewhat curtly, being so concerned in his job as training manager with the unfortunate preoccupation of his colleagues with a searching for solutions, rather than with a defining of problems.

'Well you know, I can go round the shop and . . . well . . . just . . . it's almost as though people's faces told me.'

'Told you what?'

'Told me that people are not . . . well, I don't know . . . I know it's not fashionable to talk about being happy – about being happy . . . contented . . . satisfied at work. But there's certainly something wrong . . . somewhere . . .' Manners' voice trailed away.

'Why don't you ask them then?' Roger Metcalfe suggested.

'Ask them what?' Manners laughed.

'Ask them what is wrong.'

'Well I can hardly do that can I? They wouldn't be likely to tell me would they?

'It depends what you want them to tell you.' Metcalfe warmed to his argument. 'In my experience people are only too pleased to talk about themselves. They're so unused to anyone taking an interest in them.'

Manners became more agitated.'But it's not a matter of being interested in them . . . of course I am . . . that goes without saying . . . that's why I want to know what to do about morale . . . it's my job to manage, and I must do something. How can I motivate them . . . ?'

A Reading of John Manners' Account

In the foregoing scenario, John Manners' account of his problem as being one of morale suggests that his concern is grounded in the view that the workers in the machine shop are in some way dissatisfied with things, and that this is an undesirable situation. When asked to explain why he feels this is a problem of morale, he has some difficulty, but opts to talk in terms of happiness, contentment and satisfaction at work. His normal speech is thus concerned with identifying a cause (low morale) for some perceived symptoms (unhappiness).

The search for a cause seems to be underlain by two key assumptions. First, the observation that people's faces indicate that they are not happy/contented/satisfied suggests that Manners feels that they ought to feel happy/contented/satisfied. The appearance that they do not is taken as evidence that something is wrong. On the face of it, Manners' view might be taken as being indicative of an implicit, benevolent, altruistic social theory in which work is good and to be enjoyed, irrespective of the manner in which it is organized. Whether this is the case, however, is less important and it is not necessary to have such benevolent foundations for the articulating idea that unpleasant tasks can be accommodated, since at Wellblown Manufacturing Co. the overriding nature of work is held to be towards the basic 'good' of increasing production, which is largely unquestionable. The possibility of non-commitment to this idea of the basic 'good' of increasing production (benevolent or not) is depoliticized by implicitly defining as deviant anyone not subscribing to the (abstracted) idea of increasing production.

The second key assumption underlying Manners' 'normal speech' concerns the fundamental structures of relationships at work. The inherent premise here stems from the dominant ideology that, in order to achieve the processes of production, a separation is required between those who 'manage' and those who 'work' (for a comprehensive pre-Braverman treatment of such conceptual separation, see Sohn-Rethel, 1978). This separation is located in the acceptance of specialization, following from perceived economic advantages in the division of labour (the particular historical circumstances in the society in which Wellblown Manufacturing Co. exists) and the gradual distinction (albeit partial) developed between management and ownership stemming from perceived economies of scale. The particular historical circumstances are depoliticized by transforming the resultant separation between those who manage, and those who do not, into an apparent absolute. That is the way things are – that is the only way things could be – everyone knows; and access to the derivation is blocked by defining any attempts to *gain* access as subversive.

Two examples will illustrate this blocking, and thereby the perpetuation of this particular apparent absolute. The attempt to question the supposed advantages of the economies of scale – symbolized by the slogan, 'small is beautiful' – had, in managers' lunchtime conversations at Wellblown, previously resulted in proponents of decentralization and reduction of operating size being defined as idealistic (a nice idea, but really!). Defining it as idealistic implies impracticality and therefore deviance, in a situation where increasing size is the very foundation of the structure of the separation of work relationships into 'managing' and 'working'.

A further demonstration of the blocking can be seen in the implicit exclusion (and on occasions at Wellblown, the explicit defining as subversive) of those arguments which may seek to conceptualize the development of specialization and division of labour as resulting in exploitation of the surplus value of the labour of some by others (as an inevitable consequence of advancing from a commodity exchange into a monetary exchange economy).

Manners thus – whether oblivious of, or deliberately excluding, such potential transforming forces – chooses to see the problem facing him as one of morale, existing and requiring a resolution within the inherent (depoliticized as apparently absolute) structure. The myth (of apparently absolute structure) pushes Manners into manipulating the pieces on the board, because the rules of the game are given.

Metcalfe's suggestion, that Manners should talk to the people and ask them what is wrong, is viewed as not taking the matter really seriously, since 'if the manager does not know, how can they know?' (that is, given the definition of the problem as a technical one of morale). This portrays the hierarchical structure in which Manners sees himself engaged as a hierarchy of knowledge and expertise, and suggests that since morale is such a complex problem, it needs a manager (as expert) to understand it. This compounds the problem because, while it might be reasonable to assume that someone specializing in such things will develop some relevant expertise, the process of depoliticization clouds the reality that becoming a specialist does not equate with becoming an absolute specialist. Nor does it exclude others from becoming knowledgeable as non-specialists. In this way, however, Manners' depoliticized speech implicitly forecloses alternative views of the situation, of which the rejection of the suggestion made by Metcalfe is but one example.

The location of the problem in this way leads to the acceptance of an apparently total responsibility for the situation by Manners. As far as John Manners is concerned, he is a manager and, as a manager, such matters are his problem. According to his scheme, *he* has to solve it. He needs to know how to motivate his people. That is the answer. Motivation will cure morale.

Of course, an account such as this is severely limited in that the account itself is an abstraction and simplification of, for instance, Manners' speech, a speech which contains many other elements and implicit assumptions such as a recognition that his position is by no means as simple as a division into 'managing' and 'working' might first imply (for example, 'they wouldn't be likely to tell me would they?'). Such limitations, however, do not render impotent counterposed accounts such as this but merely define their status (for example, simply alternative, counterposed, inevitably partial, persuasive accounts).

One of the basic underlying assumptions operating in the speech of John Manners is concerned with the control of workers by management, but the emotive, negative connotations associated with controlling someone are avoided by the *less emotive* term of motivating (to motivate someone is a 'good' thing to do). The transformation of control into motivation makes the depoliticization of control (based on the historical separation of managing and working) more acceptable. The belief in a rule of the *right* to control (for a more detailed treatment of the notion of a right-to-manage in this context, see Golding 1980) becomes a *need* to motivate, through the production of a 'blissful clarity', and is thus firmly entrenched in the bedrock of Wellblown Manufacturing Co. As depoliticized speech, it tells a story. It is a myth, but a part of the very necessary abstraction and simplification processes which enable the complex to be made simple.

Theorists who have examined the consequences of such processes have tended to base their arguments upon reinterpretations of Marx (see for example, Hyman 1975) and Weber (see for example, McNeil 1978; Clegg 1990) and clearly such critical/interpretative schemas are relevant here. Whether following the Marxist idea that capitalist production (as an exploitation of the surplus labour of some by others) represents the domination of one class by another, or the Weberian idea that in bureaucratic organization there is a 'need' to control (in order to calculate and measure success – that is, assess profitability) which leads to the domination of others by those in control, the results are similar. They are similar in that those in control (whether conceptualized as a class, as a particular group of managerial élites, or as a dominant coalition – see for example, Child 1972) have the means of influencing the abstraction and simplification processes (for example, Manners' implicit foreclosing of alternative views of the situation), thereby perpetuating the domination. (For an interesting account of the way in which this may be seen to acquire a kind of symbolic permanence, see Bourdieu 1977.) Therefore, the depoliticization process is, as might be expected, not exclusively a feature of the organizational context in which it occurs. Indeed, it is possible to conceive of organizations as being one means of perpetuating societal structures of domination (through the influence of 'those in control', see Whitley 1977; Clegg 1989).

Thus what was originally perceived as an economically advantageous division of labour has been transformed into an apparent absolute, and is maintained as such by the very structure of domination it has produced. This is not to suggest that those in control have a monopoly in myth creation. In fact, as long ago as 1978, Brown argued that the modern worker must make myths in an *ad hoc* manner, 'to reconcile the work processes with official rhetoric of "the organization"' (Brown 1978). Ignoring the reification, this suggests the idea that all members are potentially amenable to the development of shared myths in order to simplify everyday transactions; and clearly any such myths are liable further to cloud the access to derivation of what might be termed 'core myths' or 'charter myths' (see Gowler and Legge, Chapter 2 in this volume), since members will probably experience this sharing in a multitude of incrementally different ways.

The idea of some having control over others suggests an acceptance of the principle of control as a fundamental component of organizational life, and such acceptance is clearly grounded in a belief that this is the way things are done. Through this simplification, it has therefore come to be taken for granted that some will have authority over others. In fact, Weber's now classic categorization of authority into different types (legal-rational, traditional, and charismatic) in addressing the question of authority, conceptualizes that meaning in terms of a belief. In Weber's scheme, legitimacy may be bestowed in different ways associated with different types of authority, but legitimacy in each case is said to be founded on some kind of belief. Thus, legal-rational authority 'rests on a belief in the "legality" of patterns' and traditional authority is seen as 'resting on an established belief in the sanctity of . . .' (Weber 1947). The kind of belief which sustains such an acceptance is not, however, of the elaborate messianic kind involving fulfilled expectations. Rather, it is a belief which is continually and simply satisfied in the way things are. Such a belief is confirmed and reconstituted in everyday transactions, precisely because it is self-fulfilling – it simply does not occur to people that things could be otherwise. This is indeed suggestive of a kind of belief which might draw credence from a rule system. Garfinkel has expressed the idea of a rule-governed aspect to everyday life succinctly:

> the moral order consists of the rule-governed activities of everyday life. A society's members encounter and know the moral order as perceivedly normal courses of action – familiar scenes of everyday affairs, the world of daily life known in common with others and with others taken for granted. (1967: 21)

The acceptance of the principle of control thus confirms the apparently absolute nature of one particular alternative conception of organization. It is not of course absolute in a finite sense, since a chapter such as this would not be possible if such were the case. Rather, it represents a myth to the extent that it is merely a particular historical development in the structure of organizations, but is reproduced and sustained by a belief in the familiar as the only thing possible. Bourdieu has captured something of the self-fulfilling nature of this, arguing that the 'realized myth' ('realized', that is, in the sense of being achieved rather than being aware of) reproduces the reconciliation of subjective demand and objective necessity which appears as the grounding of the belief of a whole group in what that group believes:

> Every established order tends to produce (to very different degrees and with very different means) the naturalization of its arbitrariness. Of all the mechanisms tending to produce this effect, the most important and the best concealed is undoubtedly the dialectic of the objective chances and the agent's aspirations, out of which arises the sense of limits, commonly called the sense of reality, i.e. the correspondence between the objective classes and the internalized classes, social structures and mental structures, which is the basis of the most ineradicable adherence to the established order. (Bourdieu 1977: 164)

This 'sense of limits' experienced as a 'sense of reality' thus appears as a rule or rule system, and is founded in the myth or myths which are made possible by the undiscriminating belief in rules. Thus a structure of domination is created and maintained by the abstraction/simplification process – transforming a particular historical development into an apparent absolute (the very necessary simplifying of complexity), and is perpetuated by the myth so formed (some manage; some work). The access to derivation is blocked by the 'sense of limits' of the (apparently absolute) social order manifested as a rule, enabled by the depoliticizing (isolating) of the past, and influenced by those with most interest in maintaining the myth. In these circumstances it is not too difficult to see why the argument, that those being controlled have themselves an interest in perpetuating the structure of domination (for example, reciprocity arguments wherein the structure of domination is seen as providing safety, in the form of satisfaction of security needs), comes to be seen as a justification/rationalization – effectively confirming the original myth (some manage; some work) through the development of a further myth (the myth of reciprocity). This is a direct consequence of the neglect of submerged dimensions in organizational relations. It is akin to similar arguments which conceptualize organizational relations as representing in some way a kind of 'corporate society', involving, for instance, collaboration of trades unions with management (whether seen as maximizing members' welfare within the system, or as temporarily accepting the existing order until ready to institute revolutionary change). In neglecting submerged dimensions, such arguments inevitably result in theorizing which overemphasizes the degree of conscious awareness in organizational transactions.

The Fragility of Myth

The second piece of illustrative material demonstrates the somewhat pervious foundations upon which such myths are built. Although the myth outlined above (some manage; some work) gives life to the idea that management have the right to control, it was also suggested that the negative connotations of control are often modified into less emotive terms such as to motivate. This aids the clouding process that enables those in control to perpetuate the blocking of access to alternative views and the particular derivations of the rules of control, by making control appear more amenable. In the following example, however, management (perhaps innocently) come extremely close to exposing such a myth by overemphasizing the more overtly controlling aspects of the structure of domination, thereby risking the encouragement of possible alternative views of the situation. The day is only saved by humour defusing the feelings of those being subjected to overt control. In saving the day, the humour can be seen further to underline the pervasiveness of this particular myth. The central problem for those being controlled reverts to a question of how to survive *within* the structure interpreted as given (no doubt reinforced by the myth of reciprocity), even when the overemphasis of certain managers creates an opportunity for apparent exposure of the myth.

The following, collected by previous participant observation, concerns the reorganization of the North Midlands Board – an area board of a then nationalized utility company. The reorganization, planned and executed by a small team of top management of the area board, was a major upheaval which was aimed mainly at mechanistic structural change. It was decided to change the existing three-tier structure (consisting of one HQ, five areas and twenty districts) into a two-tier structure (with an HQ and just ten districts). This particular example concerns an unofficial debriefing given to Sheila, a shorthand typist who had just returned from an interview with the management team. The interview had been held as part of the changeover process; it had been decided to reduce the staff in the district office where Sheila worked, leaving approximately one-quarter of the existing staff. The work being carried out by the other three-quarters of the existing staff was to be transferred to another district office (Central District), some 40 miles away in Central Town.

Scenario
Several engineers (including the author, himself working as an engineer at the time) are standing around a coffee machine as Sheila enters.

First voice	How did it go then Sheila?
Sheila	I . . . don't know really . . .
Second voice	Have you got a job?
Third Voice	What have they offered you?
Sheila	A job in Central District.
Second voice	In Central . . .?
Third Voice	How can you . . .?
Sheila	They said there would be a job for me in Central District.
Second voice	But . . .?
Sheila	And when I said, 'I can't move, my husband works here', . . . they said . . . I still haven't really got this . . . they said, 'Can't your husband get a job in Central Town?'
Second voice	They said what?
Third voice	Oh come on!
Fourth voice	Bloody hell!
Second voice	Hey Ted, have you heard this? . . .

Exeunt in uproar.

The management team, so obviously involved in their task of achieving reorganization as quickly as possible, appear to have abstracted/simplified beyond sustainable limits. Their suggestion that Sheila's husband should consider obtaining a job in Central Town, simply to accommodate their own plans for reorganizing North Midlands Board, is received with incredulity. It matters not whether the management team really believed that this was a possibility, the crucial factor being that they relegated any problems of that nature to second place, below the importance of their own job in hand.

In communicating this simplification, the myth of apparently absolute management control was, for a moment, threatened with exposure, because it contradicted an even more pervasive domination myth in the context in which it occurred – the masculinist myth of male domination (which can be seen as a myth, in the same sense, with the husband being seen as primordial breadwinner in the structure of the family). Yet, that the management reorganization team *was* seriously suggesting that Sheila's husband should contemplate a job in Central Town and give up his present job to enable Sheila to move to Central District, is confirmed by the engineers themselves taking it seriously.

The myth of apparently absolute management control was subsequently rescued from complete exposure by the introduction of humour – 'Hey Ted, have you heard this?' – and later the engineers enacted an action replay in which the roles played were exaggerated, enabling the issue to be diffused in hilarity. Despite the diffusion, the episode did become part of folklore and remained for some time a potential exposure threat, perhaps underlining the necessity for the continual reinforcement of myth.

One way in which the rules underlying myth are reinforced, thus underlining the belief in those rules, is by the development of rituals. The relationship between myth and ritual is obviously reflexive, and therefore rituals develop from the formation of myth and, concurrently, support myth maintenance. The manipulation of rituals in order to maintain the principle of control, and with it the existing structure of domination, is a further feature of the relationship between myth and ritual. Cohen has suggested that continual attention is required in order to perpetuate such myths:

> All the intellect, skill and cunning of the ideologist, the politician, the theologian, and the artist and all the techniques of colour, music, poetry and drama are needed to create, accomplish and perpetuate the myth of authority in the face of continually subversive processes of different sorts. (Cohen 1974)

The development of secrecy rituals (for example, at Wellblown Manufacturing Co., only certain things are allowed to be discussed and decided upon by particular levels of the hierarchy) is a potent source of defences against forces which might threaten exposure of the myth of absolute authority. Those in control legitimate the right to act (that is, to control) in secrecy and the ritual feeds the myth. Thus the subversive processes are stemmed by the very defining of them as subversive; they are defined in this scheme as threatening the secrecy which is so necessary to manage (control) in such a complex competitive world. The threat of competition becomes a justification in the development of secrecy, but in effect legitimates the whole myth/ritual structure. Hierarchy is, thereby, mystified in secrecy rituals. The impact of rituals in this structure of control is examined in more detail in Chapter 5.

A Paradox in the Management of Supremacy and Control

The myth of apparent absolute management control is at the heart of the structure of organizations such as Wellblown Manufacturing Co. and North Midlands Board, and the apparent superiority of those in control is manifested as representing a hierarchy of knowledge and expertise. The manifestations of that supremacy have to be tempered, however, in relation to the strength of the myth in the society in which it has developed, an indication of its strength being given by the preponderance of reinforcing myths such as myths of reciprocity.

Unfortunately, many organization theorists have implicitly overemphasized the forces which suggest a tempering of this supremacy and, in so doing, have opted for some kind of pluralistic stance. This has subsequently led to the neglect of considerations of the derivation of that manifested supremacy, presumably under the assumption that- if it is not total supremacy then it is not supremacy at all. Like an observer discovering that the branch of a tree has leaves which largely determine the directions in which the branch will be blown by the wind, the failure to realize that the branch (and the tree) are *relatively* unmoved by this process – due to the underlying structure – is a fundamental oversimplification. In this chapter, I argue for the reinstatement of hierarchical factors to prime importance in studies of power in organizations – which is not to say they should be all-important, since those being controlled can organize their worlds to some extent to oppose/modify the manifestations of control.

Not *all* managers at Wellblown Manufacturing Co. are as conceptually simplistic as John Manners, the machine shop manager highlighted in the first example, or as the reorganization management team at North Midlands Board in the second example. The extent of conceptual sophistication is a constant source of trouble due to the continual reformulations made necessary by the need to reconcile the apparent contradictions inherent in trying to manage complexity through processes of abstraction and simplification. On the other hand, perhaps there is a sense of complementarity, as Schroyer (1973) has suggested, following the manner of Chinese symbols denoting crisis – one meaning danger, the other opportunity. Far from being mutually exclusive, these processes may *be* the addressing of complexity.

Such a paradox, however, constructs an extremely pernicious arena within which to perform the awesome task of management. The problems of this arena are illustrated in our final example from Wellblown Manufacturing Co. This demonstrates some of the difficulties by indicating the way in which any attempt to address the complexities of organizational life is (as part of the blocking process) defined as subversive – 'not being a responsible manager'.

The following is an account given to a small group of staff (of which I happened to be one) by a manager who had recently attended a company-wide managers' meeting (these being formally held at two-monthly intervals). FHJ is the industrial relations director and DJS is the managing director.

You might not believe this, but you'll find it interesting – for Christ's sake never tell anyone who told you – but, during the meeting we'd had FHJ . . . a right performance that was . . . reporting on the strike results. . . . Really bloody childish it was . . . holier than thou – how we won the war because we were the goodies – pathetic. Anyway, at the end of the meeting DJS gets up and asks all non-managers to leave . . . there were one or two deputies there – asks them to leave. What now, we thought as we started exchanging looks. Then DJS launches into a . . . well I don't know whether you'd call it a plea or a lecture – he was

certainly very angry underneath. His hands were shaking, although he didn't shout
– he spoke very quietly – about how he's heard so much back-biting and criticism of
late that he's sick to death of it. Management is difficult enough without all this
criticism. In future managers will behave like responsible men . . . there will be no
more criticism – yes he actually said that – there will be no more criticism . . . by
managers about managers, and by managers about him! If it hadn't been so deadly
serious I'd have pissed myself. . . .

In issuing this directive of 'no more criticism', the managing director seems
to assume that he only has to issue a command and it will be obeyed – a kind
of Dalek management, as it was described by one of the listeners. His
authoritarian invective perhaps suggests that he himself has difficulty in
addressing the complexities of managing, and his consequent emphasis upon
simplification (by defining criticism as unnecessary) reinforces the principle
of control by implicitly suggesting that there are no alternatives. Furthermore, the underlining of the hierarchy of command in confirming the
apparent absolute, implicitly denies the existence of any paradox, and
thereby makes the addressing of complexity even more difficult for other
managers who *are* trying to cope with the paradox.

The difficulties inherent in obeying the chief, in the light of his strangely
simplistic invective, is illustrated by the way in which the manager giving the
account again uses humour to diffuse the seriousness of the managing
director's pronouncement. Yet the managing director has to be obeyed and,
therefore, managers who do not comply (irrespective of the fact that they
may regard themselves as being more realistic) find themselves at odds with
the enactment of the principle of control. This invariably leads to some form
of castigation, if not on occasion to 'departure'. Departure in such
circumstances is addressed in more detail, as a feature of certain rituals of
control at Wenslow Manufacturing Co., in Chapter 5.

The blocking of access to alternative views is reinforced by defining
anything which does not subscribe, in effect, to the myth of absolute
management control as not being *responsible management*. Those who persist
in trying to be more realistic can then be defined as subversive, and a part of all
the similar problems (indiscipline, apathy, low morale, and so on) which
serve, in the eyes of the directors, to make the job of management more
difficult. The existence of such tensions (symptoms perhaps of a legitimation
crisis, see Habermas 1976) is seen (by DJS et al. at Wellblown) as indicative of
the impossibility of being a manager unless you are tough and determined to
stamp out potential opposition (that is, alternative perspectives). The
paradox is animated. Attempts by managers to address complexity are
frequently resisted by directors imposing their own preferred definitions
which suggest that the problems are insoluble, and therefore unapproach-
able. It is then a short step towards the defining of any manager who attempts
to address complexity (in the interests of being more realistic) as a subversive;
following which, should they persist, they can always be 'persuaded' to leave.

'I understand' he said. 'You speak of the city whose foundation we have been
describing, which has its being in words; for there is no spot on earth, I imagine,
where it exists.'

'No,' I said, 'but perhaps it is laid up in heaven as a pattern for him who wills to see, and seeing, to found a city in himself. Whether it exists anywhere or ever will exist, is no matter. His conduct will be an expression of the laws of that city alone, and of no other.'

'That is likely enough,' he said. (Plato, *The Republic*: Book IX)

References

Barthes, R. (1973) *Mythologies*. London: Paladin.

Beckett, S. (1956) *Waiting for Godot*. London: Faber and Faber.

Bourdieu, P. (1977) *Outline of a Theory of Practice*. Cambridge: Cambridge University Press.

Brown, R.H. (1978) 'Bureaucracy as Praxis: Towards a Political Phenomenology of Formal Organizations', *Administrative Science Quarterly*, 23(3): 365–82.

Child, J. (1972) 'Organizational Structure, Environment and Performance: the Role of Strategic Choice', *Sociology*, 6(1): 1–22.

Clegg, S. (1989) *Frameworks of Power*. London: Sage.

Clegg, S. (1990) *Modern Organizations*. London: Sage.

Clegg, S. and Dunkerley, D. (eds) (1977) *Critical Issues in Organizations*. London: Routledge & Kegan Paul.

Cohen, A. (1974) *Two Dimensional Man*. London: Routledge & Kegan Paul.

Garfinkel, H. (1967) *Studies in Ethnomethodology*. Englewood Cliffs: Prentice Hall.

Golding, D. (1980) 'Authority, Legitimacy and the Right to Manage at Wellblown Manufacturing Co', *Personnel Review*, 9(1): 43–8.

Golding, D. (1986) 'On Becoming a Manager', *Organization Studies*, 7(2): 193–8.

Habermas, J. (1976) *Legitimation Crisis*. London: Heinemann.

Hyman, R. (1975) *Industrial Relations: A Marxist Introduction*. London: Macmillan.

McNeil, K. (1978) 'Understanding Organizational Power: Building on the Weberian Legacy', *Administrative Science Quarterly*, 23(1): 65–90.

Salaman, G. (1978) 'Towards a Sociology of Organizational Structure', *The Sociological Review*, 26(3): 519–54.

Schroyer, T. (1973) *The Critique of Domination*. New York: George Braziller.

Sohn-Rethel, A. (1978) *Intellectual and Manual Labour*. London: Macmillan.

Weber, M. (1947) *The Theory of Social and Economic Organizations*. London: Hodge.

Whitley, R.D. (1977) 'Concepts of Organization and Power in the Study of Organizations', *Personnel Review*, 6(1): 54–9.

PART 2

DEFAMILIARIZING MANAGEMENT PRACTICE

4

Competence, Symbolic Activity and Promotability

Omar Aktouf

Competence is generally agreed to be both a necessary and a sufficient condition for promotion within an organization. In order to be regarded as 'promotion material', individuals should need only to demonstrate initiative and technical knowledge along with a reasonable degree of success in their undertakings. In this view, however, the term 'competence' refers essentially to the mastery of a set of technical skills and abilities.

While there are indeed a number of competences to be developed by the individual who intends to be noticed and to go up the promotion ladder, I would argue that it is primarily social rather than technical competence which is the determining factor. In this chapter, I shall draw upon my own 10-year experience as a mid- and upper-level manager and as a researcher to highlight and analyse the symbolic interactions involved in this process. In particular, I shall refer to a comparative study of two breweries in Canada and Algeria which I conducted as a 'participant-observer' (using the ethnographic model) to study these phenomena in the middle and lower echelons of the organization.

The question which must be asked at this point concerns the *nature* of the competences which are deemed to be essential and sufficient for promotion. Does everyday reality reflect – as commonly held 'theories' and beliefs would have it – an amalgamation of know-how, efficiency, resilience, and leadership potential? Let us ask the question in another way: what, *precisely* and *concretely*, must the ordinary worker demonstrate in order to advance to the first rung of the management ladder? Is this some sort of individual 'gift' which is objectively observable and for which managers have a valid evaluation instrument? After all, promotions are supposed to happen this way and this is also the way industrial tradition likes to portray the situation.

This may, in fact, be the case but 'competence' is hardly ever measured or sanctioned in a value-neutral manner. On the contrary, it is more frequently totally subject to the arbitrary 'discretion' of the hierarchy. The obvious question, therefore, is to determine *how* one goes about demonstrating the necessary competence. Hence, it is necessary to identify the signs and indicators involved in order better to understand the symbolic process at work. This is all the more important in that this symbolism does not manifest the same meanings or the same foundations for different actors. We know, for instance, that the 'misunderstanding' surrounding promotion systems (especially at the lower levels) is one of the factors most often noted[1] as a cause of 'distance' between the firm and its employees: 'those who "climb" earn their promotions by means which have nothing to do with their knowledge of the work' was the usual comment made by workers in the two breweries. 'They' (the management) choose them 'from among those whom they believe able to oppose the workers' . . . while at the same time the 'policy line' of management affirms choices 'based on competence', 'the capacity to lead', to be 'listened to and respected' and 'to instill collaboration' (Aktouf 1986a).

As a participant observer in both breweries, I was able to note and analyse a large number of daily interactions. These point to a much more complex problem than had hitherto been anticipated. There are, in fact, three types of behaviour that workers can use to 'send signs' to management concerning their career orientations: to express a desire (and the aptitude) to be promoted; to express indifference; or, at the other extreme, to express antipathy toward promotion. I am primarily interested in the first type of behaviour. In this chapter I will show the manner in which promotion-related mechanisms are 'signalled' implies highly symbolic activities, including verbal and non-verbal modes of communication. I will examine the promotion process for foremen and team leaders at the two breweries to illustrate the power-play, double-talk and collusion[2] involved in these activities.

A Typology of Competence

On the basis of the data collected at both breweries, it becomes evident that line workers who are interested in the position of team leader or foreman[3] must learn to demonstrate that they are worthy of belonging to the hierarchy; that they possess something 'extra' or 'different' in comparison to 'ordinary' workers. One of the first things necessary is to show these 'qualities' very early on; the quicker one appears 'promotable' the better, because the eventual effort required will be much greater if one wastes time establishing an 'ordinary' employee identity. Hence, promotion candidates will generally adopt the necessary 'attributes' on entering the plant, even as temporary workers (or 'temps').[4]

First of all, the would-be foreman must *interiorize the productivity culture unconditionally* and without any reservations. First and foremost, candidates must be zealous; they must also *do more*. They must become production machines who are ever and always what the workers call 'shit eaters',[5] never satisfied unless they are 'at the maximum'. In sum, they must be 'obsessed' – as if their entire life were at stake (the machinist who used his breaks to clean up his machine and 'prepare' his workplace, or the quality-control operator who telephoned the plant on his days off to make sure that 'everything was running smoothly', are good examples). Next, an equally unconditional degree of *submission and obedience* is required: no matter what happens, the hierarchy is always right, and anything it requires is always justified. The ideal here, for the administrative director in Algiers, is the worker 'who doesn't raise his head, who has respect for authority and says nothing'. Paradoxically, this same worker must show a *strong capacity to direct other men* and 'keep them in line'. How is this to be reconciled with a state of total submission?

Another quality which our management candidate must show, is '*ruthlessness*': the end (productivity) justifies the means. From the moment rates and quotas are at stake, nothing else matters. Modern-day Stakhanovism is the rule. Nothing should temper the candidate's commitment to productivity – not friendship, compassion, or (even less) solidarity. The conduct to be encouraged could be expressed as: 'In case of accident, look after the machines first'.[6] All of this is summed up well by the workers' formula: 'The company doesn't like "nice guys" as foremen'.

Next is the requirement to '*keep one's distance*' from the other line workers.[7] Moreover, the candidate must also take care to *master the discourse* and speech patterns of managers (Aktouf 1986b) in order to be seen as 'promotion material'. This type of linguistic imitation is apparent in all aspects of language. Pronunciation is important: the man must 'sound' like a foreman. So is vocabulary: slang and 'unsuitable' popular expressions are to be shunned in favour of the buzz-words and bureaucratic expressions of the hierarchy. On a discursive level, the candidate must simultaneously show his respect for authority and his distance from his peers. The candidate must demonstrate both the willingness and the ability to wield authority, and discourse becomes a powerful way to do so. For instance, language serves to show unconditional support for the official positions of management. This need not be done publicly, as long as it is heard in the right quarters.

The last competence vehicle we shall discuss here is *appearance*. Briefly, the candidate must imitate the appearance of his immediate superiors and of management in general. I will present a profile of a typical candidate and look at the symbolic mechanisms involved later in this chapter. For the time being, suffice it to say that the candidate must show proximity to the world of management in a number of verbal and behavioral ways.[8]

In order better to understand the nature of these competences, let us compare the descriptions of the 'good foreman' (and more briefly of the 'good employee') given by management on one side, and workers on the other. Interestingly, the picture is virtually the same at both locations

(Montréal and Algiers). As far as management is concerned, the 'good employee' (who has the potential to become a foreman) is the one who is:

- submissive: ever consenting, obedient and disciplined;
- punctual: does not lose a half-minute[9] of production time;
- serious: 'does not talk', totally absorbed in his task;
- malleable: lets himself be 'formed', acquires the 'right' bent;
- ambitious: 'wants it', 'works his guts out' to succeed, gives 'his maximum'.[10]

On the subject of foremen, they should (as presented, in order of importance by different managers):

- achieve their assigned objectives: quotas are first and foremost, everything else comes 'after';
- set the example: particularly concerning the points listed above;
- be 'firm': never yield on any issue, do not be 'soft', put output before all else;
- be a policeman with 'velvet gloves': supervise and obtain productivity without problems;
- 'have a grip': be able to boss the men, be inflexible and uncompromising;
- not 'try to please': 'to please' the employees is 'playing their game';
- know how to be tough: 'deal severely with', 'sanction' and 'make an example of offenders to avoid shirking' on the part of the employees;
- be 'able to solve their own problems', 'to show initiative';
- at the same time, know how to 'communicate' while 'maintaining discipline' and 'not going further than they are asked'.[11]

The following are criteria for the evaluation of foremen in Montréal (as given by the technical director of that brewery):

- production per line
- production per machine
- production per job
- number of breakdowns
- number of conflicts

The spirit and orientation of this type of 'criteria' are unworthy of comment, but it is very interesting to note that technical competence is never even mentioned! It would appear, in effect, that a knowledge of the work to be done is only a minor consideration with respect to what is required of a foreman.

We do, however, often find the term technical competence in the comments of the employees (who see only *in*competence in the overwhelming majority of their immediate superiors): 'they (foremen) don't know anything about the job and they just come around to be embarrassing'. Following is the workers' idea of what makes a good foreman:

- competent, first;
- has confidence in us, doesn't feel obliged to be incessantly on the workers' backs;
- we can have confidence in him; he isn't 'two-faced';
- a man of his word, dignified, a 'true example';
- talks to the employees, listens, 'has a heart';
- 'respects' the employees, treats them like 'people';
- is fair;
- is not 'uptight' (obsessed with outputs and who transfers this obsession to everybody)'.

While this portrait from the workers themselves is a sort of 'ideal', reality abounds with foremen who are exactly the opposite. This is hardly surprising in view of management's preoccupations in this regard. The profile of the typical foreman can be summed up in the following comments which are highly representative of the employees' point of view:

- 'Most of the guys are chosen (to become foremen) not because they're competent hard workers, but because they're "two-faced" or "hard-headed";[12] these are guys who climb over the backs of their colleagues, I don't like that.'
- 'They don't know anything, don't do anything except to catch you out[13] just to embarrass you! Those are the types that are encouraged.'
- 'Good or bad, they're all the same . . . a dog doesn't eat dog, so they close ranks against us . . .'
- 'There are some here who only want to crush you, crush you with work and filth'.
- 'They never stop pushing . . . one might think they're only here to make trouble.'
- 'One time I injured my hand, blood was pissing out of me, and all the boss was interested in was that I fill out a report before going to the hospital! And they come around every year to shake your hand!'.[14]

The list could be lengthened considerably but it would become repetitive. Let us move on to a discussion of the symbolic activities involved.

Symbolic Activities

By 'symbolic activities' I mean the ways and means, implicit and explicit, by which the employee will 'signify' (establish through a series of 'signs') a desire to be promoted and his or her mastery of those competences which make the employee a good candidate for promotion. From the results of field-observation, there are two major categories of 'sign games': verbal and non-verbal.

The Verbal Signs

One of the first verbal symbols identifies the career-minded employee in what I have called elsewhere the adoption of the 'language of officialdom'.[15] This can go from simple daily use of accounting, technical and administrative terms, right up to the repetition at every opportunity of well-known slogans which serve to identify one's 'side' unequivocally. This last type of sign was more evident in Algiers, but in both cases it is a question of demonstrating that one interiorizes the language of the power-holders and adheres to their values. For instance, employees will talk about costs, productivity, rates, and so on when dealing with superiors (notably when senior managers are around).

It is also apparent that this type of imitation goes beyond vocabulary and takes place at all discursive levels. The ambitious employee will make an effort to detach himself from 'common' parlance and to speak in a 'correct', authorized, competent manner (in the 'official' and 'dominant' sense that Bourdieu (1982) gives to the term). For example, Algerian promotion candidates make an effort to speak 'classical' Arabic which is markedly different from the vernacular variety used in everyday life.

Verbal signs also include the imitation of management's discourse. This takes two distinct forms: amplification and praise. From what I was able to observe in the field, those who involve themselves in this activity act as a kind of 'multiplier' of management information. Promotion candidates will make sure to issue such statements in front of senior executives. This type of linguistic behaviour also serves to mark the distance from their 'less well informed colleagues'. They will usually 'add something' to show that they have clearly understood or that they are 'in the know'. At the same time, they are likely to heap praise on new developments in working methods, regardless of their nature. They justify them meticulously and endorse all official policies without any reservations.

This explains the difference between those workers in Montreal who find the 'new production line' totally inhuman, and those (rare ones) who excuse all its problems straightaway in the name of 'the competition', 'progress', 'productivity', and a 'bigger cake to share'. The phenomenon is much more obvious in Algiers, where it essentially becomes a matter of repeating hollow abstractions officialized as 'projects' or 'transformations'. As one of the workers explained, 'everything is always in the future . . . so it's a question of boasting in advance of the benefits of something which is still an abstraction in the minds of top managers'.

There is another element which is specific to the Algerian brewery. Promotion candidates are usually well-known, so their use of discourse comes as a surprise to no one. These are the people who 'know someone', who are well connected with someone in management, in the party or even in the union. In their discourse, everything that the management does is good and legitimate, regardless of circumstances or consequences. These people will go up, no matter what.

Next comes the ability to modulate one's own discourse to conform to that of management. This is the mirror image of the mechanism described above which can be described as 'discursive adaptation'. This is more readily apparent in the plant in Algiers (though present on a smaller scale in Montréal, especially among the older employees and union representatives). Briefly, any changes in direction, justification of delays, cancellation of measures and promises by the authority in place finds unconditional support among promotion candidates. This can reach the point of defending a position which is in complete opposition to yesterday's official line, simply because the authorities have changed their discourse. In Algiers, this is called 'talking like the newspapers'.

Another form of behaviour which is similar to those described above is that of the 'echo-discourse'. In short, promotion candidates are expected to send back to management an echo-image of the organization's official discourse. This type of discourse inevitably reflects management's reinforcement of productivity theories, banners and slogans. Career-minded employees usually have a very clear understanding of the echo-discourse requirement. This role could be fulfilled by repeating the company's advertizing theme (as in Montréal), or by repeating entire sections of official propaganda (as in Algiers).

The foregoing has two serious consequences for the linguistic behaviour of promotion candidates. First, they must integrate the clearly anal (i.e. affirmative, calculating, authoritarian, time-conscious) characteristics of the organization. Then, they must develop an equally clear capacity for double-talk. Briefly, career-minded employees tend to ape the anality of management discourse to differentiate themselves from the primarily oral nature of workers' behaviour (Abraham 1966).

The second consequence, double discourse, is the direct corollary of all the support and modulation activity which is centred on management's position: double discourse across time, as well as in the perception of the situation. In effect, this represents the pure and simple sharing of the systematic obfuscation of reality: situation and events are one thing, what one says about them is quite different. In this way, some employees maintain the language of the 'united family', the 'benevolent father-figure' of management, and the 'worker-king', all the while extolling the virtues of ultra-Taylorist and fundamentally demagogic practices.

The Non-Verbal 'Signs'

The non-verbal symbolic activity demonstrative of the desire for promotion is much more varied. I will briefly review what I consider to be its main manifestations. These are divided into three major groups: those involving behaviour, those involving attitudes, and those involving a relational mode with one's colleagues. First, concerning 'behavioural' symbolism, we should note in ascending order of importance:

- Adopt behaviour which is in absolute conformity to management's prescriptions (zeal in observing rules and quotas) and as visible as possible.
- Do all possible to 'help' management by different actions, from 'seeing with the master's eye' to outright spying. All sorts of actions, incidents, facts and even quotes can, and should be, reported to the hierarchy.
- Avoid becoming unionized, and, if it is inevitable, show clearly that is against one's will. Boycott and systematically counteract all union activity.
- Use one's breaks to improve one's output at work; systematically use a part of this time to clean up and check workspace/machines, observe and 'learn', and so on.
- Be constantly 'on the bosses' coat-tails': use every occasion to speak to them, show them, warn them, attract their attention . . . but these exchanges must invariably concern production!

Secondly, we should observe the following manifestations of attitude-related symbolism:

- 'Keep your distance' and 'know your place'; do not 'mix' with other workers and do not exaggerate the intensity of one's contacts with the bosses. This can even go as far as exaggerated obsequiousness toward bosses, and disdain for all others.
- 'Appear to suffer', look worried and unsettled. 'Bosses' like to see intense concentration and a 'serious' mien in 'good' workers.
- Care for one's appearance: this can range from the 'always freshly shaven' to a style of clothing which reflects management's 'fetishes' (shirt and tie, avoiding jeans, and so on).
- Appear ambitious – 'want it' – notably by mimesis, which can consist simply of being seen to always have a shirt pocket full of pens, or a pencil behind one's ear. In addition, one can carry a briefcase, and loudly proclaim that one is 'taking some courses'. Essentially, it is important to manifest one's 'white collar' fantasy.
- Evidence a sort of 'output obsession', even outside of working hours, and outside of one's proper area of responsibility. In this, breaks, and starting and quitting times are the ideal moments for playing one's role of 'informer' to the bosses: reminders and notices of a thousand little things that slow up production, or cause additional waste, or increased costs.
- Appear ideologically impeccable; never miss an opportunity to underline one's total adherence to 'the system' (especially by the positions one takes – verbal or not – during confrontations, strikes, general assemblies, and so on).

Thirdly, concerning the symbolic implications of one's relations with other workers, I have observed the following phenomena:

- Be the one who is not liked. This is very important because it shows immediately that one is 'trustworthy' and not interested in 'fooling around'. By definition, only agitators are liked by workers.

- Be obviously 'out of', and if possible opposed to, all 'activist', 'unionist', or other 'worker-oriented' groups. The more one provokes their rejection and aggression the better it is for one's career.
- Use all possible means to keep one's distance from peers, including mealtimes, leisure and social activities.
- Put the 'interest of the firm' before all else, particularly solidarity and community. Avoid like the plague anything that looks like a petition or group action which questions the established order, even outside the workplace.
- Lastly, and above all, demonstrate unconditional adhesion to the 'sink or swim' mentality, show clearly that one is able to become the foreman who 'at work, doesn't even know his own mother!'

It would be fastidious to give examples illustrating each of the points reviewed here. Suffice it to say that daily plant life supplies a thousand illustrations. The machinist in Montreal who talks to no one, eats his meals alone, looks like he's dying as he works at his bottling machine, rushes breathlessly to 'un-jam'[16] the line all around him in order to ensure that the flow of bottles never slows down, and who is clearly identified by his fellow employees as 'the one who wants to climb the ladder' is an excellent example. There are also the cases of a few well-connected workers in Algiers who are immediately better off than their peers, who have direct access to the best jobs, and who are instantly identifiable as potential bosses or union delegates. They also maintain a climate of ostracism towards their peers; their situation as 'string-pullers' virtually forces them to do so. They have little choice but to adopt the behaviour of a career-minded employee.

It is even more enlightening to note the groups of expressions used by employees to describe promotion candidates: 'block-heads', 'shit-eaters', 'brown noses' and 'limp wrists' in Montreal; and 'traitors', 'lickers', 'porters', and 'yes-men' in Algiers. It is important to indicate that these terms in their respective environments have connotations of treachery, obsequious submission, weak dependence, misplaced zeal, the absence of self-respect and dignity, and even – in some more masculinist quarters – a lack of virility! This is what the overwhelming majority of workers think of those who will eventually become their bosses.

Naturally, those who wish to signal their absence of promotion ambitions use what could be described as 'reverse symbolism' and are immediately classified (by the chiefs) as undisciplined, not serious or ambitious, and unworthy of confidence. In this sense, the reasons invoked by workers who do not intend to be promoted (the large majority of workers at both plants) are extremely interesting:

- 'I want to stay right where I am until retirement, I'm not interested in stepping up. If somebody goes up, he becomes awful . . . if he does what the bosses want, he becomes a dog; . . . you mustn't be friends with the workers if you want to go up'.

- 'I'd rather stay clean. I refuse any promotion. . . . I don't want any trouble . . . I don't want to whip the guys.'
- 'I don't want to become a pig.'
- 'I'm staying the way I am – at peace."
- 'I'm not a boot licker. . . . What counts is who you know . . . to help you climb . . .'
- 'A serious attitude, education and work don't help . . . that's not what's important, it's being able to be a dog.'

These workers are described by the foremen as 'useless foot-draggers' who 'refuse all challenges', a view which is generally shared by management.

From any viewpoint one must be careful not to see in these attitudes only spite, rationalization or fecklessness. I have personally witnessed at least two cases of voluntary demotion on the part of team leaders who preferred returning to their jobs as line workers, after a few weeks of promotion, because the required competences were simply too onerous.

Conclusion

The main focus of this study is undoubtedly that the observations and facts 'in the field' indicate a fundamental rift in the perception and interpretation of identical symbolism. From the organization's point of view, it is a matter of seriousness, desire, challenge, ambition, leadership and great potential; whereas for the workmen it is question of pettiness, shabbiness, mendacity, lowness, treachery – and something approaching prostitution!

We are uncontestably in the presence of opposed systems of representation (Aktouf 1986a) which necessarily implies a type of 'collusional' relationship (Laing 1969), wherein double discourses and occultations dominate the scene almost totally. The central question is how these competences are being transmitted (with their attendant symbolisms) and held by promotion candidates. While official management discourse (in several circumstances, the *only* discourse) centres on such concepts as 'family atmosphere', 'helping and understanding the worker' and 'benevolent authority', it is the daily behaviour and discourse of managers in their official activities which highlight the differences between the projected and actual conditions in the plant.

To me, the dichotomy is glaring: the organization does the utmost to maintain an official discourse, and then acts in direct opposition to that discourse. Foremen act in accordance with their own perceptions of those areas in which they feel supported and encouraged. When asked about the reasons for the systematic promotion of foremen whose behaviour and attitude are a blatant contradiction to the organization's official position, managers inevitably answer that it was 'because the workers did not want to be promoted!' Apparently, very few of them were interested in the reasons for this state of affairs.

There is an abundance of contradictions: between reality and discourse, between discourses themselves, between symbolic activities and practices, between required and expected abilities, between being promoted and degrading oneself. This means that as soon as one enters into the 'career' game, there follows a whole self-maintained process of collusional relationships, and the induction of experiences and interactions based on a systematic false-self.[17] The least that one might say is that the systems of symbolic manifestations of 'the love of management' and 'the love of employees' appear to be mutually exclusive and irreconcilable.

Even at the heart of political-economic and cultural differences as vast as those between Canada and Algeria, all the mechanisms in play are, surprisingly, identical. Can the factory system, even in its totally automatic variety, induce behaviour, relationships and representations that are truly harmonic? An even more serious question is how to ensure the social and psychic integrity of a hierarchy whose basic structure is made up of people who must successfully traverse a schismogenic process in order to 'prove their mettle'?[18] What sort of working atmosphere 'or organizational culture' can one reasonably expect in such conditions?

References

Abraham, K. (1966) *Oeuvres complètes*. Paris: Payot, Tome II.
Aktouf, Omar (1986a) *Le travail industriel contre l'homme?* Alger: ENAL-OPU.
Aktouf, Omar (1986b) 'La parole dans la vie de l'entreprise: faits et méfaits', *Gestion*, 11(4): 31–7.
Bourdieu, P. (1982) *Ce que parler veut dire*. Paris: Fayard.
Laing, R. (1969) *Self and Others*. London: Penguin Books.
Terkel, S. (1975) *Working*. London: Wildwood House.
Winkin, Y. (1981) *La Nouvelle Communication*. Paris: Seuil.

Notes

1   This is also clearly confirmed by our research. In both factories, promotion is always 'suspect' for the employees: there 'must' be some under-the-table activity, in terms of favouritism or co-opting . . . never 'competence' or 'value at work'.
2   Collusion: a term borrowed from R.D. Laing (*Self and Others*, 1969), designating a mechanism of mutual self-dupery in which each partner confirms self and partner in a reciprocal game of false identities and consciences.
3   The 'team leader' stage represents a sort of trial period in the hierarchy. If the newly-promoted person confirms the potential he is trying to show as a 'boss', over several months, the way is then open for him to become a foreman.
4   The period wherein a workman has 'temporary' status (at the complete mercy of arbitrary cuts or affectations), which can last from three to eight years, is a sort of 'purgatory' where the person is 'used' in a manner which will render him a future 'good worker'.
5   'Shit eater': the workman who 'the more you pile it on (work), the more he asks for'. A kind of unconditional 'hyper-zeal' (workaholic).
6   S. Terkel, in his *Working*, reports the example of the foreman who rushed to restart the line (which a workman had stopped as a result of a serious accident which happened to one of his

colleagues), before giving any attention whatsoever to the injured person. In our breweries too, we have had witnesses describing foremen who 'looked after the machines first, and the man afterwards' in the case of accident and even very serious injury.

7 It was possible for us to observe a typical case in Montreal. Someone who had been identified as an 'up-and-coming kind of guy', constantly exhibited a closed appearance, didn't talk to or smile at anyone, ate alone, and so on: as his colleagues said 'you mustn't be pals with the workers if you want to go up'.

8 Such as, for example, the table at which one sits during breaks and at mealtimes, the type of food one eats, the places (clubs, restaurants) one frequents, and the sports and leisure activities one practises (golf, ski, squash, and so on).

9 'Half-minute', because production lack of earnings are based on 30 second slices of time. Every 30 seconds of down time must be justified and ascribed to a particular position – and, therefore, to a particular person.

10 We note that for the workmen, this represents a 'pathological' case: a 'shit-eater', or a 'blockhead', or a 'boot licker'.

11 Here, management made allusion to a foreman (whom we called 'S'), particularly 'perverse' and 'detested', who 'went too far' in 'severity'. But all of that is merely words and rituals because, in fact, 'S' and his ilk are largely encouraged. As long as they deliver, nobody will be asked any questions – and especially not foremen who are reputed to 'push them till they drop'.

12 'Two-faced' and 'hard-headed' describe members of the lower levels of the hierarchy and those who are preparing to join it. These are 'hypocrites' who 'don't keep their word', who pass their time 'sucking up' to the bosses (hanging on their coat-tails).

13 'Watcher' (French slang): obvious surveillance, examining someone minutely while he is working. This is generally the equivalent (or the prelude) to 'being timed' (MTM analysis).

14 Alludes to the 'hand shake' which management offers the workmen each year at New Year.

15 A type of language stereotype destined to operationalize a sort of permanent occultation of reality (demagogy, paternalism, cynicism, propaganda, etc.).

16 'Un-jam': one of the factors slowing the production of beer occurs when containers 'jam up' the mechanisms, one must unjam them to re-establish regular flows.

17 False-self: it is from within the false-self that collusion is set up. The term is borrowed from R.D. Laing (1969), designating the false identity which people having identity problems develop. In daily life, the games of 'being' and 'appearing to be' derive from the same mechanism.

18 Schismogenesis: a term borrowed from G. Bateson, designating a process of progressive 'rupture' characterized by a permanent exposure to a 'double-constraint' mechanism (contradictory demands which are very costly psychically and affectively). Cf. Y. Winkin (1981) (ed.) *La nouvelle communication* (New Communication). Paris: Seuil (Points). Chapter 2.

5

Management Rituals: Maintaining Simplicity in the Chain of Command

David Golding

This chapter focuses upon some of the everyday rituals encountered in a single and particular organization, and seeks to illuminate something of the way in which such rituals appeared to contribute to the accomplishment of the practice of management. The material discussed is drawn from a longer study of managers, and focuses upon various activities encountered among individuals and groups who were considered to be part of management by definition of their own accepted job titles. The study spanned different hierarchical levels of management, covering job titles including assistant manager, manager, senior manager and director. The overrriding consideration in this defining process was a community inclusion feature (and by implication excluding feature) encompassed in the notion, 'we who manage'.

The analysis of everyday rituals is thus approached through an examination of activities among a particular community who saw themselves as being part of what *they* called management. The focus in this chapter is, therefore, upon the social articulation of control *among* different levels of management rather than upon control as a feature which managers exert *over* others, as might be the focus in certain resistance-and-control approaches and in much of the labour process literature. Storey has argued (1983: 189) that control is always 'precarious and conditional', and indeed a central focus of this analysis will be the way in which control is socially constructed and maintained.

The study in question was carried out as part of the work previously introduced in Chapter 3, and concerned, in particular, the industrial manufacturing company in the north of England referred to as Wellblown Manufacturing Co. The company is the UK entity of a USA-owned multinational company, with a range of household name products. The material for this analysis was obtained over a period of 15 months, during which I was employed as a manager in the organization. The material discussed, being anthropological in origin, necessarily implies no geographical, cultural, or professional generalizations.

The Idea of a Chain of Command

In Chapter 3, an analysis was made of processes perceived as contributing to the depoliticization of a principle of control, which I suggested were central to the way in which management was accomplished at Wellblown Manufacturing Co. In this chapter, the argument will be extended by an examination of the way in which certain activities appeared to contribute to the continual reinforcement of such a principle of control.

Given the variety of perspectives involving the differing values, aspirations and expectations that exist between managers in a complex organization, it is not surprising to find that a great deal of time is spent in simplifying situations and interpretations. One way in which this is achieved is through the idea that management essentially involves the maintenance of a chain of command, which is seldom overtly articulated but which everyone appears to understand.

Although it may be common in complex organizations for the process of establishing shared meanings and understandings to be a regular feature of interaction, the idea that such processes are seldom made more explicit than absolutely necessary is a little more curious. It is clear that alternative meanings and understandings abound. Less clear is that pervading those, there are certain preferred definitions of situations which are reinforced periodically. Some individuals, because of hierarchical position, have a greater ability to ensure that their definitions are enforced in preference to other possible alternatives. This is one of the dynamic features of what we call management, although we do not find it written in job specifications, nor do we find it the focus of attention in many management textbooks. Perhaps this is to be expected, given that the very nature of such activities entails an avoidance of explicitness.

The idea of a chain of command is one example of the way in which such dynamic features may be articulated. Such an image has a certain appealing simplicity, yet it is also far too simple – far too crude. An image which *is* so simple cannot be made too much of a focal point or it would not survive; therefore, it has to be continually blurred in order to be protected and sustained. At Wellblown Manufacturing Co. the image of a chain of command is alternately expressed and obfuscated in a variety of ways, and through these processes achieves its more or less subtle perpetuation of (ultimately) manifest control. The image of a chain of command is invoked in order to simplify when complexity is felt by some to be getting out of hand. It is used to clarify and 'bring things down to earth', but it cannot be invoked to do this very often; the 'chain' is fragile.

Images such as this exist in a complex arena of socially-constructed and alternatively-available meanings. It is only through the maintenance of an aura of apparent ambiguity, that they become capable of immense accomplishment. This is achieved and becomes sustainable largely because such expressions appear as *innocent* options in a rich network of symbolic communication. Members are entirely familiar with the need socially to construct the boundaries of their own understandings from the variety of often implicit and potentially ambiguous communications with which they are bombarded. Indeed, a great deal of the very information that a manager needs in order to become a competent member is conveyed in a covert, referential manner (Golding, 1986).

Managers therefore expect that a great deal will be transmitted symbolically through what might be termed unarticulated communication – that is, that which provides a richer network of potential meanings than may initially be apparent. An image such as a chain of command is protected by this richness (control could not possibly be so crude) while simultaneously being expressed (there has to be a *shared* way of demonstrating control). In this latter respect, Firth has argued that, in fact, one of the functions of symbols is to provide convenience and simplification in order to facilitate social organization.

> Or we can hold that for much of our life we deal with reality, in our relations with people and things, both mental and physical, and that symbolisation is a mode of operation which is basic and ubiquitous, but not the sole mode of dealing with reality. Its functions are those of convenience and simplification, of giving scope for imaginative development, of providing disguise for painful impact, of facilitating social interaction and co-operation. (Firth 1973: 90)

The idea of 'providing disguise for painful impact' underlines the fragility of an image such as a chain of command. There are some occasions when the chain of command *is* made explicit – an incident deemed to require the invoking of disciplinary procedures being one example of this – but the majority of action is conducted without such explicitness. Indeed, because such explicit expression normally *does* involve individuals being disciplined, reprimanded, dismissed, and so on, the chain of command is regarded as in some way an expression of 'unpleasantness'. Yet at such times, organizational interactions clearly *do* follow a hierarchical responsibility and accountability structure, and there is thus a sense in which the chain of command has to be protected from becoming untenably 'unpleasant'. It is, therefore, both crude in its essential simplicity, and immensely subtle in its variety of expression, in 'providing [that] disguise for painful impact'. Furthermore, the penalties for attempting to expose the crudeness of the chain of command can be severe.

> An Industrial Relations Manager at Wellblown Manufacturing Co. lost his job after he circulated photocopies of a warning letter he had received from his superior. The copies with Mr Clark's own comments endorsed were circulated to managers, foremen and chargehands, and some ended up on the factory notice boards, an Industrial Tribunal heard yesterday.
> Counsel for Wellblown Manufacturing Co. said: 'This was an act tantamount to sabotage by a man minding his machine.' (*Northern Morning News*)

The sabotage metaphor used by counsel for the company provides a vivid underlining of the perceived fragility of the chain of command, even in the legal representatives of those most concerned to ensure its continuity. The attempt by the particular manager to invoke support for his position leads not only to his dismissal, but also results in the formal arena in which he was legally able to appeal against the decision to dismiss him being used as an opportunity to express the necessity of maintaining confidentiality and secrecy in hierarchical transactions. The manager's action as a response to *particular circumstances* is thereby elevated, through interpretation, to a perceived attack upon the *entire fabric of command*.

Management as Artful Practice

The intricacies of the above example underline the difficulties of any symbolic interpretation. Different perspectives are often in competition and tension. Douglas has argued that symbols cannot be understood in isolation, and that meaning essentially involves patterns: 'A symbol only has meaning from its relation to other symbols in a pattern. The pattern gives the meaning' (Douglas, 1973: 11). An image such as a chain of command involves a multitude of symbols, expressed in a variety of alternately crude and sophisticated patterns. Thus, one way in which patterns of control are expressed is through the skilful, seldom explicit, but always bounded performances of managers.

Grafton-Small and Linstead (1985) have, for example, argued that these skills can be seen as a constant process of professional symbolic legitimation associated with kinship relations, where a community of managers can be considered to have *quasi*-kinship relations.

> We consider that, as participants in and consumers of a fluctuating but particular stock of knowledge, professionals are an occupational kinship group. Indeed, organizations may be fruitfully considered to be shaped, at least in part, by the negotiations of such kinship groups, and kinship relations may be seen to be at the symbolic heart of both the rational/technical and the commercial/economic systems of organizational activity. (Grafton-Small and Linstead 1985: 55)

The emphasis placed upon skill is not to suggest some kind of technique in the sense of a learned series of responses or reactions. Rather the focus is upon the way in which everyday activities, which come to represent competent membership of a quasi-kinship group (in this case managers), constitute a series of what ethnomethodologists might call 'artful practices'. The practices are artful in the sense that the potential ambiguity in many alternative perspectives is managed so as to maintain control without making it too explicit (except on certain well-defined occasions where control *is* more openly expressed). The maintenance of control is, therefore, not an exclusively top-down activity. It is, rather, a sense-making activity, in which all managers are involved.

In focusing upon sense making, the analysis in this chapter will attempt to highlight a process of evocation (following, for example, Sperber 1974). In this respect, the aim will be to examine the significance of certain (artful) symbolic practices, although not through the explication of a system of signification, as might be the case in approaches attempting to identify supposedly encoded systems of signifiers. Rather, the approach will be to suggest an interpretation of meaning through a process in which members improvise *ad hoc* responses according to interpreted experience, as a means of confirming some kind of order and of resolving potential contradictions. In this schema, rather than learning a code of signified meanings, organizational members are viewed as being involved in a constantly changing process of 'learning to make things fit'. This is never a finite or totally-bounded process, but is always in transition, with certain parameters coming to be evoked more consistently than others. The conceptualization of 'making things fit' draws upon the idea of 'bricolage' in the work of Lévi-Strauss (for example, 1966, 1977). The idea has been developed illuminatingly by Linstead (1984) and by Grafton-Small (1985), its application being further extended by the same authors jointly in Linstead and Grafton-Small (1990).

The Significance of Rituals

One way in which managers' artful practices are manifested is through the construction, adoption, and maintenance of elaborate networks of rituals, which articulate patterns of control. The concept of ritual is, however, fraught with difficulty, with little agreement even among analysts working in similar traditions – whether they be social anthropologists or social interactionists, or whatever. In this chapter, an initial perspective is one in which ritual action represents mundane action which does not involve explicit awareness. Mangham and Overington (1987) have identified a similar starting point in their illuminating study of organizations as theatre. They suggest that:

> Participation in social rituals is largely nonreflective. People do what they do, they get on with it; they do not think about what they are doing, how to do it, or what it means. Rituals are the performance of stable, successful solutions to the problems which repetitive social occasions present. (Mangham and Overington 1987: 46)

They further suggest that, because few occasions are simple enough to present only one solution, rituals might best be considered as involving actions which draw upon 'a repertoire of optimal solutions'. In this analysis then, the focus will be upon the way in which such repertoires come to be manipulated for the expression and maintenance of certain preferred themes, and the extent to which these themes reproduce images of control.

However, there is yet another way in which the concept of ritual is enmeshed in conceptual difficulty. Organizational members themselves occasionally use the term ritual in everyday language. This obviously *does* involve some degree of explicit awareness. Such awareness, however, may not extend to identifying that some individuals and groups deliberately use such explicit rituals as a further means of alternately blurring and bringing into sharp focus the chain of command. Furthermore, where actions are seen and identified by members as rituals, there is a tendency to define these rituals as almost exclusively negative ones. The idea of ritual often has, in this context, a connotation of representing in some way 'mindless behaviour' (for example, 'it's just a ritual'; 'I don't know why we bother'). This deprecating of ritual obscures the potential achievements of ritual, one example being the way in which apparently empty activities may be used in a far from negative way by members (for example, as defences against anxiety). This raises the question as to whether a distinction might be made between positive and negative aspects of ritual, and indeed Douglas has argued for a differentiation between positive ritual and 'ritualized' ritual, with regard in this instance to religious practice.

> It is fair enough that 'ritualised' ritual should fall into contempt. But it is illogical to despise all ritual, all symbolic action as such. To use the word ritual to mean empty symbols of conformity, leaving us with no word to stand for symbols of genuine conformity, is seriously disabling to the sociology of religion. For the problem of empty symbols is still a problem about the relation of symbols to social life, and one which needs an unprejudiced vocabulary. (Douglas 1973: 21)

The problem with such a distinction in work organizations is that the positive aspects are perhaps even less evident. The idea of members regarding rituals as being functional is in fact anathema to the dominant administrative logic (see McNeil 1978). The connotations *of* emptiness prevent the acceptance of positive views of ritual. The fact that there is a great deal of activity which could be said to *be* empty (for example, pretending to be working even though the day's work is done, simply because it is not yet five o'clock) contributes to the more or less exclusive view of rituals as negative activities in the view of members of Wellblown Manufacturing Co. Nevertheless, members do use these apparently empty ritualistic activities on occasions as protections against anxiety, and as means of manipulating apparent constraints so as to express individuality.

It is evident that the same activity may be defined as ritual by some and not so by others. Equally the same activity, when defined as ritual, may be seen as negative by some and as positive by others. These apparent contradictions are, of course, important aspects of the means by which perpetuation of preferred definitions of situations are achieved. It will be an aim of this chapter, therefore, to attempt to embrace some of these differences.

There is one further level of complication in the treatment of the concept of ritual. This chapter is my account as an ex-member of the organization. This presents a problem in the sense that my reading of any situation is likely to be different to that of at least some other members of the organization. Again this underlines the idea that such factors can only be treated as a function of the persuasiveness (or otherwise) of the account.

Secrecy Rituals

One of the ways in which control is achieved is by the construction of a mesh of secrecy rituals. The way in which the discussion of certain items is only

permissible on sections of agendas ('starred' business) which concern higher
levels of hierarchy is one example. Moreover, this is achieved not simply
through restricting the discussion of certain matters to particular levels of
hierarchy, but also in actually ritualizing the production of secrecy. The very
mechanisms which are used to close off access to certain items are
themselves legitimized in the process. The legitimation, of course, is not
absolute and secrecy is a favourite target of humorous stories. Humour,
however, is generally more indicative of coping devices than any expression
of the prospect of achieving real change. In fact, as highlighted in Chapter 3,
there often seems to be an acceptance that because real change is impossible
'you have to laugh'.

A particular example of this kind of secrecy is found in the way in which
certain financial information is restricted to higher levels of the hierarchy at
Wellblown Manufacturing Co. Considering that organizational transactions
contain numerous references to the idea that the organization is supposedly
in existence to make profits, it is paradoxical that secrecy even extends to the
concealment of actual operating figures. The following piece of illustrative
material demonstrates the contradictions inherent in the way financial
matters are treated. The material comes from an impromptu, and certainly
unofficial, debriefing given by a financial manager, shortly after leaving a
meeting which had been held to discuss the annual forecast of expenditure
(the budget) for a particular production department.

> Well, at the end of the meeting . . . I just gave up. It really is a waste of time you
> know, we have these meetings and fix – well supposedly fix – figures . . . but really,
> as we all know, the figures are already fixed. How could we fix the figures anyway?
> As you know managers are not given access to profit figures . . . and I'm not
> allowed to tell them – which is bit of a laugh, since I don't really know either.
> Budgetary control, eh? Oh sure, you could say it was control, and not just
> forecasting – in that targets have to be met, or else! But since those actually
> controlling the resources – people, raw materials – don't know . . . can't relate to
> actual profits, it's control from above – so what are we doing? It's not involvement,
> it's appeasement. Why don't they just hand down the targets? That is what they're
> doing anyway in effect.

The suggestion here seems to be that the meetings between managers to
decide annual forecasts of expenditure are a waste of time, since the actual
amounts they will be allowed to spend will be decided elsewhere (by the
board of directors). This suggests that such managers' meetings are in some
way empty rituals, and that the real decisions are taken in secrecy in a higher
level ritual. Such an account, however, fails to acknowledge that other
people at lower levels of the hierarchy equally regard such managers'
meetings as secrecy rituals, and their own activities (in providing information for use in managers' meetings) as empty rituals, since anything they
do will be overriden by the managers acting in secret.

Thus the definitions of 'empty' and 'secret' are dependent upon who is
defining the situation, the same ritual being defined as both in different
circumstances, depending upon hierarchical position and the part that is
expected of the definer in maintaining the chain of command.

Another example of secrecy is found in company appraisal-of-performance practices, which constitute a whole structure of rituals involving periodic assessment, carried out and recorded in secrecy. This kind of secrecy is often justified on the grounds of protecting an individual's personal details, but this masks the question: protection from whom? In fact, assessment schemes in many organizations have been known to develop identities quite independent of the supposed reasons for their existence (as contributions to improving performance) and have taken on lives of their own.

At Wellblown Manufacturing Co., this kind of secrecy is raised to an even higher plane, since there is no openly-used appraisal scheme. There is, however, a covert scheme, which most managers (but not all other staff) know about. Those (secretly) identified as potentially promotable are sent (secretly) to London to spend a day with a 'trained psychologist' who produces a (secret) assessment on the suitability of the testee for a higher position. The ensuing report is kept – for all time – in the (secret) personal file of the person concerned. In fact, a recent innovation has been introduced: the individual is also given a copy of the report – minus conclusions and recommendations! This is regarded as a demonstration of openness, and serves to highlight the way in which even declarations of openness can in effect legitimate secrecy, by imposing preferred boundaries to such openness. The emptiness of the contents of that part of the report which is made available to testees vividly illustrates the vacuity of this demonstration of openness. 'Well actually, it didn't tell me anything I didn't already know about myself. In fact, it was basically . . . what I had myself told him.'

A further example of the imposition of preferred boundaries occurs in what managers at Wellblown refer to as 'communications'. As in many organizations, managers at Wellblown spend a good deal of time talking about improving communications. This invariably takes the form of a 'broadcasting to the people' framework, in which *some* are defined as having a responsibility to inform *others*. This is applied by managers not only to the problems of communicating with subordinates (for example, 'we must keep them in the picture'), but extends also to their own criticisms of directors. Here too, however, managers' attention is almost exclusively focused upon the lack of information which directors provide for managers (for example, 'they always keep us in the dark'). By implication there is almost a suggestion that such communications *could only be one-way*, so seldom do managers' criticisms focus upon the extent to which directors do not *listen* to managers.

Preferred boundaries are ingrained in this and, in fact, the whole idea of improving communications at Wellblown Manufacturing Co. is entrenched in a chain-of-command view of organization. The resultant widespread use of training courses in communication skills has thus transformed a structural problem (that is, the tendency for communications to be one-way) into an interpersonal solution. Not surprisingly, communications courses at Wellblown have come to be rather paralysed by over-expectation, and are frequently regarded as an expression of empty ritual, as indicated by one manager on his return from such a course. 'What a waste of time. Oh sure I enjoyed it . . . but look at this lot . . . nothing changes. I now have to shift this, before I get jumped on. Huh . . . he doesn't even know I've been on a course, let alone care.'

Rituals of Distinctiveness

Underlying rituals of secrecy, there are whole series of rituals which emphasize the distinctiveness of certain groups of people. The dominant coalition is a good example, and even quite senior managers at Wellblown are made very much aware of their position in relation to the directors to whom they are subordinate.

This enlightenment is not achieved through expressions of command directly (although commands are sometimes used) but is built up and sustained in an elaborate structure of rituals which subtly demonstrates the distinctiveness and, thereby, the superiority of directors. This is nicely demonstrated in a comment from one manager: 'He may be an acting-director, but he doesn't eat in the board room . . . no . . . well he hasn't been awarded his knife and fork yet.' The bitter sweet reward of a knife and fork, which is given to a manager only when finally confirmed as a permanent and accepted member of the board of functional directors, is one of the ritualistic expressions of control associated with distinctiveness. The reward of eating in the board room represents a badge of promotion and celebrates a rite of passage, but it is not given lightly. It is not, for instance, given to those who may very well be doing the job but are regarded as in some way being on trial, as are acting-directors.

The demonstration of distinctiveness is illustrated by the way that directors of Wellblown (the board in question consists of the managing director and five functional directors) go to lunch fairly consistently 15 minutes after everyone else on second sitting (directors are all on second sitting, of course). This provides considerable scope for alternative perceptions of such consistent action, but the origin of most alternatives is located in accounting for distinctiveness. Thus an explicit account which emphasizes the functional responsibilities of a director ('one cannot just leave everything like lesser mortals – one needs the additional 15 minutes in this job') is accounting for distinctiveness, just as is an implicit account which evokes the ceremonial expression of status difference (for example, some are 'chosen' to eat at a different time). That directors invariably return from lunch 30 minutes later than the majority of managers, further reinforces such distinctiveness. Again this reinforcement may also be achieved in the form of an explicit functional account ('lunch in the board room is a working lunch, one cannot just switch off when one has such responsibilities') or in the evocation of ceremonial (being a director involves certain privileges).

Thus the subtle hand of control is articulated against an immense web of complexity, in which alternative interpretations abound. Members are continually generating *ad hoc* responses, but they generally have to be made to fit. Patterns develop in ways of accounting for things, and perhaps this can be seen as the production of a kind of storyline. Cohen (1974) has in fact identified a series of markers upon which such a storyline may rest. The creation of mythologies of descent is one such marker, which is used freely by members of the board of directors at Wellblown Manufacturing Co. Evocation may take place through elaborate association of common public school (for example, name dropping in routine conversation) or university (for example, pointing out that candidates for appointment have attended a less prestigious university – even though several directors did not attend university at all). Another marker involves association with religious symbolism (such as dissemination of information about common church attendance) or quasi-religious masonic involvement (for example, common lodge membership). Yet another marker may emphasize moral exclusiveness (for example, fraternizing, eating together, parading a common moral conscience). Style of life is another significant marker symbolized, for instance, by dress code (for example, sober/expensive suit-wearing, involving consistency: a director never removes his tie – even in stiflingly hot weather, when all about him are losing theirs!).

Inherent in this kind of distinctiveness is the idea of belonging to a group, and anthropologists have developed the notion of totemism in connection with the idea of belonging (see Gowler and Legge, Chapter 2). Lewis (1976: 51), in interpreting Durkheim, has provided one definition of totems as 'mystically charged symbols of group cohesion and identity – badges of belonging'. The way in which status symbols are collected and emphasized at Wellblown certainly has something of this flavour. The existence of the 'Wellblown Manufacturing Co. Men's Club' is a good example. Membership is restricted to managers and supervisors, and, although there are no women managers at Wellblown, there are a good number of women supervisors who are thus excluded (employment discrimination legislation does not apply to registered clubs), with any attempt to consider the offensiveness of this being defined as deviant. In addition to such overt gender exclusion, there are other explicit dimensions to the social construction of exclusiveness in this club, as the following extract from the bye-laws of the club illustrates.

Article 2 – Membership
Membership shall be open to the following persons subject to the approval of the Wellblown Manufacturing Co. Men's Club Executive Committee.

(a) Executive, Foremen and Heads of Department
(b) Employees holding a responsible position subject to the approval of the Executive Committee.

An interesting link between secrecy and distinctiveness is highlighted by an engineer's story about a hierarchy of dining rooms. Such a hierarchy is central to the eating habits of different levels of management at Wellblown, and this particular illustration emphasizes the importance attached to such a hierarchy. The engineer who related the story, on this occasion with the explicit purpose of underlining the importance of secrecy, had himself been involved in the action as a services engineer for an extension to the amenities block of a previous employer – a competitor of Wellblown. He had been given the task in question by a director, which in itself was unusual, since – as he was quick to point out – that had been the first time he had had the privilege of actually speaking to a director.

The task involved the engineer in providing a service layout for an extension to the part of the building which housed the managers' dining room, and comprised an extension to the original dining room. It appeared that the managers' dining room was to have a section partitioned off from the main part of the room, which would then be for the sole use of 'senior managers' (a new rank to be introduced between that of director and manager). The actual extension was to comprise a toilet block, 'so that senior managers [would] not have to pass through the managers' dining room to get to the toilet'. The engineer who related the story was instructed, by the director who gave him the task, to 'keep it under his hat'. The managers were not to learn of this new level of hierarchy until it had actually happened. The engineer complied with the instruction and got a good deal of amusement out of the situation, particularly the secrecy aspect, although the real hilarity came much later when it was discovered that the operation had been conducted in such secrecy that planning permission for the building had not been obtained!

Dining rooms are generally closely guarded. At Wellblown, the managers have a meals committee which is entrusted with watching over the sanctity of the place. For example, it is traditional – despite hierarchical supremacy – for a director not to enter the managers' dining room unless invited to do so by a meals committee representative. A story related by a manager at Wellblown will illustrate the importance attached to the sanctity of the space.

The manager concerned had scheduled a meeting with employees in one of the sections under his control, and he described it as a crucial meeting involving a matter of redundancies. He was finding it difficult to locate a room in which to hold the meeting because all the rooms normally available for meetings were occupied, due to the visit of external auditors. Eventually another manager (on reflection perhaps mischievously) suggested the managers' dining room. The meeting was duly arranged for 4 p.m. on a particular Friday afternoon (always a good time to announce redundancies). On arriving some minutes before the time scheduled for the meeting, the manager found the door to the managers' dining room barred by the chairman and deputy chairman of the meals committee, who categorically refused him entry. He was informed that he could not use the room, because he had not sought the prior permission of the committee. Biting his tongue, he proceeded to ask permission but, on stating the purpose for which he required the room, permission was refused on the grounds that people who belonged to a trades union could not possibly be allowed access into the room in which managers actually ate! An angry exchange followed but, short of physically forcing his way into the room, it was clear that the manager would be unable to gain access. He then had to quickly contact all the employees who were due to attend and inform them that the meeting had been postponed, to avoid the embarrassment of having them turned away at the door.

The structure of status symbols in general is naturally integrated with the expression of distinctiveness, and with means of reward – and indeed punishment – administered through status degradation and intimidation rituals (see Garfinkel 1956; Gephart 1978). The importance of such dimensions at Wellblown has been underlined in Golding (1986) but, for the purposes of this chapter, suffice it to say that hierarchies of status are common bases for the development of rituals, many of which evoke the image of a chain of command. To mention just a few at Wellblown, in addition to hierarchies of dining rooms, there are hierarchies of car parks (with distinctiveness periodically reinforced through illustrations of dire consequences for anyone caught parking in the 'wrong' car park), hierarchies of office size (and all the trappings associated therewith), and – of course – hierarchies of toilets. As an example of the latter, there are separate exclusive toilet facilities for directors, directors' secretaries (not for the use of managers' secretaries), managers, other male office staff, other female office staff (including managers' secretaries), male works people, and female works people. To be seen in the wrong toilet is to invite, at the very least, raised eyebrows or even disciplinary procedures.

Rituals of Oppression

Status degradation and intimidation rituals referred to above are essentially rituals of oppression, but activities of that nature are usually more intentional and directed at specific individuals. The concentration in this chapter is upon more general features of patterns of control which, although not as overt as such specifically-directed intimidatory schemes, may be seen nevertheless to constitute ritualistic oppression. Again, however, the articulation of such felt oppression is achieved through sense making, by all kinds of managers at different levels, rather than being a simple top-down expression of explicit structure. The chain of command, although on occasions being experienced as oppressive, is therefore not generally brought into question; rather, it seems to be treated as inevitable.

Terkel (1975) has suggested that work, by its very nature, is about 'violence to the spirit' as well as to the body.

> To survive the day is triumph enough for the walking wounded among the great many of us. The scars, psychic as well as physical, brought home to the supper table and TV set may have touched, malignantly, the soul of our society. More or less ('more or less', that most ambiguous of phrases, pervades many of the conversations that comprise this book, reflecting, perhaps an ambiguity of attitude

towards the job. Something more than Orwellian acceptance, something less than Luddite sabotage. Often the two impulses are fused in the same person). (Terkel 1975: 1)

The 'fusion of two impulses in the same person' was certainly in evidence in the following events, related by a manager at Wellblown who had had to convince his wife that she had not been to a race meeting to which he had taken her on the previous Saturday. The circumstances surrounding this strange sequence of events concerned a race meeting at which Wellblown were sponsoring a race – the Wellblown Stakes. This was a new advertising area for the company and managers had been invited to take their wives to a special launch party immediately preceding the race. The following week, however, on the day that some of the same managers and their wives were to attend a function at which the 'boss-man-international' from the USA parent company was to be present, all managers concerned were gathered together and instructed to erase the race and the excursion from their memories – and were told they must also instruct their wives to do the same. It transpired that the managing director had discovered that the 'boss-man-international' had religious objections to horse racing and, consequently, it had been decided to issue an order to re-write the history books. All future sponsorship was cancelled, and all reference to that which had already taken place was forbidden (even the drafts of the next issue of the company house-journal were searched to remove any reference to the said sponsor-ship). The exercise was later estimated to have cost the company a substantial five-figure sum (of measurable costs) and one manager was heard to remark, 'have you read 1984? . . . Well that's what it's like – all bloody doublethink'.

There are occasions when the 'fusion of two impulses', identified by Terkel, is tested almost to destruction, with considerable 'violence to the spirit' being inflicted. An example of this occurred at Wellblown during the coincidence of a 25-year award presentation ceremony with a death in the same department. The award in question was scheduled to be presented to a chargehand, a few days after the foreman to whom she was responsible had suffered a heart attack. On the morning of the presentation, the chargehand was collected from her home, as was the custom, in a hired Rolls-Royce motor car, and so would have no contact with other staff until she arrived 'on stage' at the presentation. Tragically, early that morning, the news was received at the company that the foreman to whom she had been responsible, having worked in that capacity for many years, had died during the night. It was realized by the directors of the company that the chargehand would, at the very least, be extremely upset by the news, but rather than postpone the presentation ceremony, they decided that it should go ahead ('you can't put off a 25-year award – that would be unfair on the recipient – after all, it is her day'). Accordingly, instructions were sent round the company that under no circumstances was the chargehand to be informed of the death of the foreman until after the ceremony. The ensuing stress placed upon her close colleagues (and the deceased foreman's), having to display pleasure and congratulations while feeling inner grief, made for a most bizarre ceremony. More fundamentally, however, the decision to proceed also took no account of the chargehand's eventual reaction when, having coming to terms with the shock, she realized the extent of the concealment. (I am grateful to Dan Gowler for illuminating the resemblance which this episode has to the marriage ceremony, at least in traditions prevalent in the society in which Wellblown Manufacturing Co. exists in the north of England. The emphasis placed upon the bride – dress, attendants, and so on – serves to mask the underlying structure of male domination, in that the woman is the one who is changing and losing most – that is, her name. The elaborate structure of rituals, however, serves to conceal this and reproduce the event as a glorification.)

At Wellblown, the domination of the award ritual (the show must go on) legitimated a considerable degree of oppression, which at the time was masked by the overwhelming feelings of grief felt by most of the chargehand's colleagues. Afterwards, however, came the realization of the manipulation of events, and the circumstances were used many times subsequently to illustrate more explicitly the 'unpleasantness' associated with the chain of command.

> But a glazier in the factory believes that the position has now reached a stalemate, and she believes the management will never give in. But equally significantly she refused to have her name published, an indication of the feelings of worry and fear which are not so very far from the surface. (*Northern Evening News*)

Even managers sometimes refer to Wellblown Manufacturing Co., as 'Colditz Castle' – an artful dissipation in humour. The chain of command cannot express absolute domination of course. That is not a practical possibility in most circumstances – not even as Sykes has demonstrated, in a maximum security prison: 'The custodians of the New Jersey state prison, far from being converted into tyrants, are under strong pressure to compromise their captives, for it is a paradox that they can ensure their dominance only by allowing it to be corrupted' (Sykes, 1958: 58). In a curious way, that Wellblown Manufacturing Co. is not a maximum security prison may, in fact, be seen to licence more, rather than less oppression, since inmates are free to leave at any time – and they frequently do, although not always voluntarily! 'In the end I felt that I had to leave, because I couldn't face having to put up with what the man above me was doing – and of course, I knew that I couldn't change that . . .'

Managers make sense of their experience, with respect to the more 'unpleasant' aspects associated with the chain of command, in various ways. Some occasionally find it all too much and, like the industrial relations manager in the earlier example, engage in action to generate more alternative perspectives than can be tolerated (resulting in speedy departure). More typically, however, managers conceal their discontent, dissipating bad feelings in humour ('this place really is a case of, never mind the ball, get on with the fucking game') and in outside activities ('right, I'm really going to knock the cover off this ball').

The compromising of the reactions and feelings of individuals, in fact, extends even to oppressive ritual elements in the selection of new managers. Cleverley (1971) has highlighted the way in which recruiting a new member into an organization is effectively acting out a rite of passage, and Silverman and Jones (1976) have captured some of the ritualistic nature of carrying out recruitment. The compromising is demonstrated in the degree to which candidates are able to anticipate, and subscribe to, what will be expected of them. Typical ritual questions are ingrained in recruitment interview practices, such as, 'which daily newspaper do you read?' The 'correct' answer at Wellblown is, the *Daily Telegraph*; *Financial Times* readers are regarded as being 'far too dangerous'; those who say that they read *The Times* are seen as being 'too clever by half'; and, of course, the *Guardian* does not exist (the *Independent* was not established at the time of carrying out the original fieldwork from which this analysis has been drawn). This, again, is part of a storyline and only has significance *in* that story, not least underlined by the fact that interviewers at Wellblown feel that the 'correct' answer has significance, and act upon such information – or as one manager, in reaction to the perceived absurdity in this, put it: 'Come and be headhunted for real!'

Conclusions

This chapter has focused upon one aspect of control, and the way in which an image of a chain of command is articulated in one particular organization. The emphasis has been placed upon the part played by such an image in the sense-making activities of managers in the organization. It has been suggested that these sense-making activities involve continual generation of *ad hoc* responses and initiatives. Such *ad hoc* responses, however, in order to make sense, have to be 'made to fit'. Thus patterns tend to develop, but this is by no means a unitary top-down view of control.

To suggest, as Meyerson and Martin (1987) appear to do, that such features represent a monolithic view, emphasizing 'integration' (as distinct from 'differentiation' and 'ambiguity'), is to attempt to create an unsustainably static view of organizational life. It is also to suggest a curiously constrained conceptualization of ambiguity. Action moves frequently from integrated to differentiated control, sometimes without immediate directional intentionality, and sometimes with it. That is how organizations become avenues for the articulation of membership, which can express inclusion and expulsion at the same time. Patterns are shaped (for example, through the establishment of particular competence criteria such as the ability to identify the 'correct' daily newspaper) and change is a way of life (as members are geared towards making their responses 'fit'). Tensions are thus sustained in interminable ambiguity.

This chapter has highlighted some of the areas of ritual which articulate control. In imposing a particular-observer-derived framework for shaping this analysis, a considerable richness has inevitably been destroyed. Perhaps there is a sense in which any analysis that involves standing back from the action and expressing ideas in a supposedly analytical way, must destroy something of that richness. This is one dilemma of the so-called social sciences. It is not an argument for avoiding analysis, but is a call for the development of more alternative analyses (accounts) to be treated as metaphorical expressions which enliven organizational analysis – rather than attempting only general and literal descriptions and analyses, which tend (and may even *in*tend) to produce ossification. It is also a potent reminder of the temporal nature of any analysis. We may attempt to stop the clock, but fortunately (in the short term) we are doomed to failure. The idea of stopping the clock is simply a metaphor of social analysis. The clock, on the other hand, is real enough.

References

Cleverley, G. (1971) *Managers and Magic*. London: Longman

Cohen, A. (1974) *Two Dimensional Man*. London: Routledge & Kegan Paul.

Douglas, M. (1973) *Natural Symbols*. London: Barrie & Jenkins.

Firth, R. (1973) *Symbols Public and Private*. London: Allen & Unwin.

Garfinkel, H. (1956) 'Conditions of Successful Degradation Ceremonies', *American Journal of Sociology*, 61(3): 420–4.

Gephart Jr, R.P. (1978) 'Status degradation and organizational succession: an ethnomethodological approach', *Administrative Science Quarterly*, 23(4): 553–81.

Golding, D. (1986) 'Inside story – on becoming a manager', *Organization Studies*, 7(2): 193–8.

Grafton-Small, R. (1985) 'Marketing Managers: the evocation and structure of socially negotiated meaning', PhD thesis, Sheffield City Polytechnic (now Sheffield Hallam University).

Grafton-Small, R. and Linstead, S.A. (1985) 'The everyday professional: skills in the symbolic management of occupational kinship', in A. Strati (ed.) *The Symbolics of Skill*. Trento: Universita di Trento.

Lévi-Strauss, C. (1966) *The Savage Mind*. London: Wiedenfeld & Nicholson.

Lévi-Strauss, C. (1977) *Structural Anthropology*. London: Peregrine.

Lewis, I.M. (1976) *Social Anthropology in Perspective*. Harmondsworth: Penguin.

Linstead, S.A. (1984) 'Ambiguity in the workplace: some aspects of the negotiation and structuration of asymmetrical relations', PhD thesis, Sheffield City Polytechnic (now Sheffield Hallam University).

Linstead, S.A. and Grafton-Small, R. (1990) 'Organizational Bricolage', in B.A. Turner (ed.), *Organizational Symbolism*. Berlin: De Gruyter, p. 291–309.

McNeil, K. (1978) 'Understanding Organizational Power: Building on the Weberian Legacy', *Administrative Science Quarterly*, 23(1): 65–90.

Mangham, I. and Overington, M.A. (1987) *Organizations as Theatre*. Chichester: Wiley.

Meyerson, D. and Martin, J. (1987) 'Cultural change – an integration of three different views', *Journal of Management Studies*, 24(6): 623–47.

Silverman, D. and Jones, J. (1976) *Organizational Work*. London: Collier-Macmillan.

Sperber, D. (1974) *Rethinking Symbolism*. Cambridge: Cambridge University Press.

Storey, J. (1983) *Managerial Prerogative and the Question of Control*. London: Routledge & Kegan Paul.

Sykes, G.M. (1958) *The Society of Captives*. Princeton: Princeton University Press.

Terkel, S. (1975) *Working*. London: Wildwood House.

6

There to Here and No Way Back: the Late Life of a Cocaine Dealer

Michael L. Rosen and Thomas P. Mullen

A Lifetime in the Death of a Dealer

The Devil left Akhsa a message, either before or after she died – I'm not certain. Buried inside the feathers of her pillow. Isaac Bashevis Singer understood. 'The truth is that there is no truth' (Singer 1953: 371), he made the words read. She clutched them in her dead hand. The Devil's words. About truth.

Ponder that.

Attaining truth. Mastering and owning it. Dispensing it to the misinformed. Defending and purifying it against the assaults and profanations of others. Twisting it slowly in the sunlight for others to catch its sparkle and recognize there the power of your insight and the value of your authority. These are (only in large part?) the obsessions of the academic.

> 'I your Wizard, *par adua al alta*, am about to embark
> upon a hazardous and technically unexplainable journey
> into the outer stratosphere, to confer, converse and
> otherwise hobnob with my brother wizards, and I hereby
> decry that until what time, if any, I return . . .' said
> the Wizard of Oz.

Truth, well, truth. Mastering and owning it.

'It was a farce, in a way, our breakfast,' he said about our meeting with Roy two years earlier. 'Or at least a sort of delusion.'

We were sitting in Pat's West Village office. It was near five o'clock on a business day as the streets through his professor's window were filling with the City's density of rush hour traffic – motors revving cars trucks buses bicycles motorcycles pedestrians food carts brakes screeching three card monty games horns blowing street hawkers selling everything fake Rolexes Gucci labels broken blenders clothes stripped and neatly folded from the back of a bum who'd died last night up on 42nd Street the still living homeless and a drug dealer or three hustling from here to there just a day in the City – and the surrounding pre-cast concrete deco buildings were cloaked in the late afternoon warm orangish glow of the summer's sun. It was 5 June 1990. A Tuesday.

We had gotten together again to talk about Roy. We hadn't done that for a couple of years. 'Crack is really like a vortex,' Pat began, leaning back in his chair, eyes off on the wall.

'The circle was so far out in '87 that you didn't feel the velocity. You have to understand that in the early phases of the vortex the circle is so large you just don't feel the velocity. That was in '86 and '87. But by '88 and '89 it was right here,' Pat's hand waving, shaping a cyclone, with his finger narrowing and picking up speed dropping to the bottom – withdrawing and pointing fast, pointing right there. To the bottom, spinning in place. That was Roy, I guessed. Ending 'right here'.

'Now, part of what he was saying is true. But a lot of it was just dreams and rationalizations of what he wanted to be.'

For a little over a year we had studied a man named Roy, largely in his role as a petty merchant in the cocaine trade. We had identified him as 'Jim', that he lived in the Mission Hill area of Boston. 'A neighborhood to be young in', we wrote. Crowded, frenetic, filled with the excitement of shops and restaurants, boutiques and small apartments. But Roy lived in New York's Greenwich Village. We said that Jim was an electrician. But Roy was a plumber. What matter a person's name, location or occupation?

'The last I knew,' Pat continued as the sun finally set outside his window, 'someone said that Roy was totally addicted. That he was living with a cocaine whore. He hadn't paid his rent in months, was on the verge of being evicted, and had his electricity turned off. His phone was disconnected. The last time I was there, Con Ed [the municipal electric company] had already turned off the power, but he'd bypassed the electric meter by going down to the basement and rewiring his electricity around the box.'

We observed and interviewed Roy/Jim and those associated with him in many settings; while sitting in restaurants, shopping for food, standing on street corners, hanging out in his apartment playing cards and backgammon, helping to set irrigation and plumbing systems in new homes, partying and so on.

Roy/Jim knew that we were conducting a study. The others we observed came to know us only as relatively new members of their group. As people Roy trusted.

Précis

We first began to observe Roy in 1984, interviewing and otherwise collecting data over the period of roughly one year. Two years later, in late 1986 and early 1987, we met again with Roy for a series of short conversations, culminating in a lengthy meeting on 8 January 1987. And nearly three and a half years after the completion of our original research, 5 June 1990, we met with another in Roy's circle – this long conversation forming the third and final aspect of our research.

We therefore 'went to the field' three times. On each of the last two 'field trips' we encountered a reality contradicting what we had originally assumed and written.

'The Great Oz has spoken,'
his voice boomed electric.
'Pay no attention to that man behind the curtain.'
But Toto had already drawn back the curtain. Time might
not be progressive. But it certainly appears to be
linear. The curtain had been opened. It was too late.

In a shamanistic turn of phrase, Tyler plumbs the place of ethnography in a transcendental return to an arena which never was. His is an intriguing signpost before deciding to hit the throttle, jam the brakes, spin the wheel off into the desert. Before beginning to write.

The ethnographic text is not only not an object, it is not the object; it is instead a means, the meditative vehicle for a transcendence of time and place that is not just transcendental but a transcendental return to time and place. (Tyler 1986: 129)

Hit the gas pedal. Spin the wheel. Take a ride with us. You drive; I'll navigate.

I am Oz
the Great and Powerful
the voice boomed electric.

But the Navigator has a few words of warning: 'Don't *believe* me.' And a map:

first tranche of research

....

second tranche of research

....

third tranche of research

....

you don't need a compass.

Roy looked better than he had in years. He said that he hadn't lost any weight, but he looked trimmer, faster. His face looked tighter. Some of the distended look of the addict, Sartre's nausea of bloat, had dissipated. His eyes were darker, more focused, lucid, mean. Roy said that he hasn't been doing as much dope for the last three months or so. That his new girlfriend wouldn't let him.

'That's the good thing about crack,' Pat commented on my assessment of Roy's new look of health. 'Crack makes you feel like a million bucks, at first,' he continued. 'But Roy wasn't any better. You just saw him as better.'

So much for precision.

We met on the corner of 4th Street. Roy recommended a nearby Greek diner. We spoke for half an hour or more about a thousand different things, catching up on the years. No one mentioned our earlier study of him – several written versions of which he had read. Then he brought it up. He told us that he more or less liked what he'd seen. 'But I want co-authorship of these things,' he said, referring to the papers.

'Sure,' you can be a co-author', I smiled, answering a question or demand I took as nothing more than a piece of the conversation.

'There are only two things I didn't like about those papers,' he continued. 'You said I was a "pusher". But "pusher" conjures up a bad public image,' Jim started. 'I don't "push" at all. People come to me. "Pusher" gives you images of someone hanging around school yards selling to little kids.'

> Jim is now in his late forties, and he says that it is harder to be a dealer the older one gets. It is not so much the selling that is tiring, but the buying. Having to travel around the state, keeping up your old contacts, making new ones as the old go on to different things or get busted. He has been buying bootleg quaaludes from the same person for the last five years, acid from the same source for the last eight years, marijuana from maybe five or six people, and the same for cocaine.
>
> One the other hand, Jim has gotten into a stride, a gliding rhythm of conducting his affairs that he says is comfortable. He says there is nothing to stop him, nothing at sixty that will be different than at fifty. 'It is only getting better from here,' he shines. A proudness of endurance, that he has lived on his terms. He is ageing but in a sense easily, strongly. He exercises now and then, but says that he should do so more frequently.
>
> He says he would like to 'get out of the business someday.' Maybe move down to 'the Islands. Maybe to Jamaica and hang out on the beach', but there are no immediate plans.

'We don't know if he's alive', Pat continued. 'We don't know if he has AIDS. We don't know if he's homeless or dead.'

> Jim is far from wealthy. He dresses and lives simply, and he says that he does not know *anyone* at his end of the business who has made real money. Jim is a big man, around six feet tall, with extra weight on him – not so much a belly *per se*, but all around. He has big hands that you expect to envelop yours in a crush. But they are too soft for that. So is his face. Lots of fleshy lines. He looks wide awake, young, but a bit abused by the years. Phenomenal amounts

of dope have passed through him. But he does not look 'wired', that notion of the coke fiend, darting eyes and tenseness. He looks more mellow than that, almost tired.

He pays attention to news selectively, so selectively it tends towards little attention. Music is closer. And he is a connoisseur of dope. He will look at something, smell, touch and taste it and tell you its quality and street value – in a way tending towards sensuality.

'It's a youth culture,' Jim says, referring to the drug scene. People who ten years ago used to buy an ounce of marijuana a week from him now smoke an ounce every two or three weeks. People get older and they slow down, becoming more a part of the surrounding society.

On the other hand, 'you only go around once,' he says. That being the case, you might as well do what you enjoy. As a friend of his put it: 'You want to get high, he wants to get high. So let's get high together.'

In Jim's world, he is providing a service. Participating in a victimless crime. He maintains standards to keep it this way. He does not sell heroin, for example, nor does he sell to people 'who are too fucked up'. If a client is using 'too much', Jim will ease off, telling the person that there is not enough to go around. In his scale of harm, 'using dope' is no more harmful than drinking alcohol. That his drugs of preference are illegal while the preferred drugs of those in the business and power communities are legal – scotch, bourbon, wine, beer, and so on – is socially myopic.

To carry on the type of trade that Jim does, it would be impossible not to use the goods he sells. In his life, as will be seen more closely below, drugs are part of a world different from the means–ends orientation of the technocratically rationalized one spinning around him.

In Jim's world, the sale and use of dope is not an end in itself. It is, instead, part of a life where 'partying' is primary. For example, a number of evenings during the week – he has slowed down to four or five – Jim will party with friends. He will eat dinner and then go to his or another person's place – preferably his own as the paranoia of being a dealer sets in – and party. And partying is always, or almost always, linked to both drugs and sex.

At its basic level, partying is a social event, one withdrawn from the normal strictures of social structure. It is a liminal space, an escape, a unit in social process which is the opposite of the system of roles, statuses, and positions which might be understood as constituting social structure (Myerhoff 1975: 33). Partying is in this sense an anti-structural, anti-organizational process.

Accepting partying as an emerging, increasingly key construct in

Jim's life 17 years ago lends a continuity to his transition from one-time suburbanite to city dope dealer. He was not always a pusher. He was once living in a house with a yard and a garage, and wrapped in boredom. He was married with children, and stifled.

He had been a manager in a branch office of a national corporation. He had been moving up in the ranks. There were promises of a promotion to regional manager. He knew the ways of Weberian bureaucracy; separating the public from the private domains, acting according to the career concept, following the formal rules, playing coalition politics.

There was a shake-up at the top of his division, and he was in the losing camp. He found himself without a job, and with an acute distaste for Weber and his bureaucracy. He took a position in a smaller, competing firm, but felt tired with 'the whole suburb bureaucracy thing'. He 'felt bored.'

Boston provided a break from the monotony, and he spent more and more time there until the suburbs were no longer home. After 15 years of marriage, he filed for divorce, sold his house and quit his job.

Jim increased the time he spent with a small group of friends who partied a lot. To save money – a scarce commodity for all of them and not something worth spending too much of the week trying to get – he and his friends started to buy dope in bulk – maybe a pound to divide among four people. Of his quarter, Jim might sell off a couple of individual ounces to other friends, increasingly realizing that by buying in bulk and individually ouncing some of it off he was left with free dope. The division between what is normally considered play and what is considered work – buying marijuana for his own use while helping his friends by getting good stuff at a low price, versus dealing – became increasingly clouded. He was, or was becoming, a dope dealer who played at his work.

The world of the Protestant work ethic – of hard work, saving money, delaying gratification for a future date, of strongly separating work from play and repressing the latter while deriving prestige from the material accumulation enabled by the former – the very world enabling bureaucracy to rise, is not Jim's world. It is not until one refocuses on the specific question of work, asking what work is in juxtaposition to other human activities, that Jim's work of being a dealer begins to make sense to those inhabiting a more segmented world. Thus, for example, while the literature recognizes that within occupational communities the distinction between work and leisure becomes blurred (Van Maanen and Barley 1984: 29), even the understanding here of what is work and what is leisure is too culture bound to adequately capture the essence of Jim's world.

The Nature of Work and Play

The English term 'work' ultimately derives from the Indo-European base werg-o, which is 'to do, act' (Turner 1977: 39). This definition of work as goal-oriented action, regardless of the goal, is reflected in traditional societies which equally define as work the activities of the hunter, the farmer, and all participants in rituals. In this world, work also includes what we would call play, as opposed to the post-Industrial Revolution notion of work as something solemn, something devoid of play. In traditional cultures work is an activity which inherently includes 'a good deal of what we and they would think of as amusement, recreation, fun and joking' (Turner 1977: 40), of spontaneity and creativity. It has a ludic quality.

As the segmentation of human activity into discrete, distinct realms advanced with the urbanization and subsequent industrialization of society, work increasingly became an activity separated from, and devoid of, play. Here play, in the ideal sense, is understood as a multidimensional activity, a generally non-restrictive form of behaviour necessitating creative conduct. Play is a rich, flexible activity, allowing freedom to the player. On the other hand, work (productive work in particular) increasingly became a rationalized mode of organization ideally empty of the freedom to be creative, the freedom to be a multidimensional human in the workplace.

It is in contradistinction to this technocratically rationalized definition of work that leisure exists. It is an alternative mode. Leisure is a 'non-work, even an anti-work phase in the life of a person who also works' (Turner 1977: 41; 1982: 36). Two basic conditions are thus requisite for the development of leisure. First, social relations come to be individualized to the extent that, at least in theory, some activities become subject to personal choice rather than governed by the obligation of common ritual; and second, the means by which an individual earns her or his living is 'set apart from his other activities; its limits are no longer natural but arbitrary.' Free time thus stands in contrast to work time. Further, in addition to including play time *per se*, one's free time also includes 'attendance to such personal needs as eating, sleeping, and caring for one's health and appearance, as well as familial, social, civic, political, and religious obligations. In tribal society all of these would have been parts of the work-play sacred-profane continuum' (Turner 1977: 45). In our society, on the other hand, work stands alone, in disjunctive relationship to all these other activities.

In our segmented world, therefore, leisure is a social construct incorporating the experience of what Fromm (1941, 1942) terms 'negative' freedom, which is the absence of constraint, and 'positive' freedom, which is the experience of human autonomy and integrity (see Willmott and Knights 1982: 208). Similarly, Turner writes that leisure is freedom from a whole array of institutional obligations prescribed by the basic forms of technological and bureaucratic organization of the work domain. It is also freedom from the forced, chronologically regulated rhythms of factory and office, and a chance to recuperate and enjoy natural, biological rhythms again, on the beaches and mountains, and in the parks and game reserves provided as liminoid retreats. More positively, it is freedom to enter, even for some to help generate, the symbolic worlds of entertainment, sports, games, diversions of all kinds. It is freedom to transcend social structural normative limitations, freedom, indeed, to play . . . (1977: 42)

Given our culture's stratification of work and freedom into discontinuous realms with freedom characterizing leisure, Jim's work of being a dealer is not captured within the Protestant ethic, technocratically-rationalized notion of work. His is specifically a world of play, of consciously transcending 'social structural normative limitations', of avoiding the routinized strictures of bureaucratized and technocratized life. His is a world of experimentation – sexually, chemically, socially. His is a world of not working hard, of not saving money, of not delaying gratification, of not deriving prestige from financial and material accumulation, of not separating 'work' from 'play'. The texture of his life, his *Weltanschauung*, is not thus readily captured using our typology for understanding occupational activity. We are instead thrown back to his notion of play as the starting point for the development of an alternative typology.

To begin, Jim is an adventurer, a seeker of thrill. Within the past year alone, and only for fun, he has travelled to California, Europe, and Central and South America. He used to parachute for sport. He has rafted down the white water of the Colorado River. He has owned some, and ridden on many more, motorcycles. He 'chopperized' one of them to look like a bike from *Easy Rider*. And on his thin earnings he also used to have a motorboat. But after five or six summers it sank, never to be raised or replaced. He likes to ski, and tries to get to Colorado once every couple of winters to catch some good Western snow.

There is not much differentiation between one day in Jim's week and the next, except for Friday, which is market day. His time flow seems merely a series of fluid days punctuated solely by Fridays. More than performing a particular job – leave the house, drive or catch the train to work, clock in, clock out, go home – his activities seem a string of liquid episodes strung together around partying with friends and marketing on Fridays.

On a day that he is not earning a legal income, Jim gets out of bed between 11 and 12 in the late morning. He usually answers some of the messages on his phone machine, gets a cup of coffee, walks down to the street to check on his car, does some errands, and maybe does a dope deal in the late afternoon. He might buy some dope on a Wednesday, but this could just as likely be on a Saturday or Monday, depending on demand and availability.

If he gets an electrician's job he will not work on it more than three or four days a week, four or five hours a day. If it is in a private house, for example, or some other place to which he has access, he might arrive on the site at midnight, after dinner and a little partying, and work till sunrise.

If he is installing an alarm on the Cape he might leave his apartment around 11 a.m. and work until early evening, then come home and plan to party up. He installs alarms maybe 12 weeks out of the year, and spends an average of one or two days a week doing electrician's work the rest of the weeks of the year. On one level this work is only to show the authorities a legitimate income; on the other hand, he seems to enjoy its craft.

Jim is involved in a wide range of activities with, essentially, the same small group of people. And he is in this way, among his many others, similar to one within a traditional society. Jim often has friends and/or family members help him with his electrician's jobs. He eats with these people and others within the circle, parties with the same, travels, fights, loves, and relaxes within the closeness, trust and fun of those he knows well.

Jim's 'inner circle', this 'total institution'-like mode of behaviour (Goffman 1961), is reasonably seen as the outcome of the illegality of his activities and the nature of his non-stratified style, of partying as a locus of social process. If partying is an idiomatic expression of institutionalizing play as a primary goal, breaking down the work versus play distinction, it is consistent that Jim's activities are carried out among a relatively small set of people. His 'inner circle' of trusting relationships.

Where there is an 'inner circle', we create an Other. This, Jim's 'outer circle' of substantially more instrumental relations – nevertheless coded in the rubric of friendship and loyalty, of caring and closeness – is noteworthy for a manipulation of symbols wherein, through sleight of mind, the instrumental is transformed into the moral. Or at least it appears to be; where appearance is everything.

A situation is created in which people instrumentally interact but also enjoy each other in their own right. This is so much more so when those engaged in a transaction are exchanging something that is illegal and taboo. It is more comfortable to sell dope to someone with whom you eat, drink, laugh, and get high; someone with whom you play.

Friday Nights

The majority of Jim's income comes from direct sales to end users: friends and acquaintances, the inner and outer circles. About a third of these sales occur on days other than Fridays, sales placed randomly throughout the week. But Jim also has a wholesale drug business, selling in bulk to other dealers. Approximately two-thirds of this business is also randomly placed about the week, on days other than Fridays.

Friday is market day, a partying day. The rough structure of the day is this: from 2 p.m. until 4.30 p.m. Jim sells mostly wholesale, a great deal of the sales being telephone orders with home deliveries. Jim has a one-man delivery force. From 4.30 p.m. until about 10.00 p.m. Jim's trade goes retail. From 10.00 p.m. until late he parties with friends, and from late until he falls asleep and subsequently wakes up, he makes love with someone there from the evening. Either male or female. Boundaries are not formal.

Jim lives in a five or six storey 'walkup'. There are over 20 apartments in the building; his is near the top and in the back. A twisting, somewhat narrow and old wooden stairway is the only way up.

From the front stoop a visitor buzzes the intercom, Jim asks who is ringing, and if he knows and/or is expecting the person, he or she is buzzed in. Jim stands by his door, gazing through his peephole once the approaching steps of the visitor on the creaking stairs become audible.

His apartment is roughly 500 sq feet, a small place, approximately 45 feet by 12 feet. The floors are wood; not the fancy hardwood teak floors of those in the upper tax brackets, but the oddly-put-together, four inch, ill-fitting wooden slat floors of those not (yet?) achieving the American dream. A bathroom is at the end of the apartment nearest the street. Out of the bathroom and into a small room separated from the dining room/entrance/kitchen area by a vertical half wall, you find dope scales, kilos of marijuana in bags on the floor, cocaine and its specialized accoutrements, bottles of booze in all shapes, colours and degrees of fullness, cans of food, a calendar of women in bathing suits hanging on the bathroom door.

Things are piled everywhere. The rough oak dining room table, the first thing you hit when you enter the apartment, is piled with papers, soda cans, beer cans, magazines, junk mail – the stuff of urban life. No signs of anyone eating a home-cooked meal there in the remembered past. The refrigerator is almost completely filled with cans of Budweiser and Pepsi. Cans upon cans upon cans.

The back room is the largest. Jim's mattress lies on a sort-of-platform an inch or so off the floor. It is neatly covered with a blue quilt and matching plaid pillows. A poster of a woman hangs on the wall above his bed. You see her from the waist up, dressed in a wet, almost invisible white T-shirt with 'Jamaica' written in dark block letters across her large round breasts. Other posters and paintings hang from the walls. Sensuous things. A framed cover from *Time*

Magazine pictures a champagne glass filled with white powder. The screaming red headline shouts, 'High on Cocaine'.

One half of the wall across the room from his bed is lined with shelves. Some books have been placed there, together with a full series of *National Geographic* and *Skiing* dating back more than a decade and a half. Piles of cassette tapes. Boxes of photography slides. A large round ashtray filled with more dope roaches than any human being has ever seen, a lifetime of roaches piled in one huge place. Odds and ends. An old stereo system, never particularly expensive, worth nothing now. His is the rag-tag apartment of male adolescence.

By the early afternoon on Friday, Jim's phone begins to ring with serious intent. He does not answer. He never does. A machine picks up, and his outgoing message is played. Regulars know that he is probably in, and they expect him to pick up after recognizing their voice. Depending upon who is calling, he does. Small talk for a short while, and then a discussion about what time he wants the person to come by that evening. For the transaction. For friendship.

One Friday afternoon we arrived around 1.30 p.m. A friend of Jim's was already there, the assistant. He was helping to measure marijuana out into one-pound bags. He would go out to run a delivery, return to package some more dope and so on. He has been helping Jim for a couple of years now, paid in cash or kind. He is gay, and there are understandings of romance between them.

We were watching the wholesale trade in operation. Local deliveries. In between transactions we sit and talk, drink beer and Pepsi, and watch cocaine packets being prepared. Large sheets of white freezer paper were cut up into hand-width strips, and then into squares. Child-like origami was then performed for illegal intentions, multiple little folds precisely transforming the paper finally into little packets – marvels of engineering to hold a half or a gram of cocaine. Easy to fit into your wallet or shirt pocket; easy to open up anywhere out of the wind and to take a snort or two. That is one of the things about coke. A gram sells for $100 and packs down to no size. You buy the stuff in bulk from a connection, cut it by up to 50 per cent with maltose or something else white and powdery, and your income starts to outpace your expenses – unless you snort a lot yourself and are too generous with friends. But selling coke looks like good business on the back of an envelope. Jim says that he never intended to get into selling it, but it was too hard to ignore. Except for the danger. You see folks who carry guns, who are mean.

So he sells coke for the money, for the dope he gets, for the friendship. And he is paranoid. Paranoia becomes a palpable dimension in the life of a dealer.

The first retail business buzzed the intercom at 4.30 p.m. She identified herself from the street as 'the Ghost of Christmas Past'. They hugged and kissed when she walked into the apartment.

It was winter, and she was tanned. She was on her way to Jamaica. Permanently. To sell real estate in the sun. To wear white T-shirts. She said that if she could find a way of packing Jim in her suitcase she would.

Other people started to arrive. One couple in their mid-twenties brought their one-and-a-half-year-old boy, a baby wearing maroon OshKosh coveralls. The kid was a terror, putting his hands into everything. Jim has an old bubble gum machine in his living room/bedroom, the type they used to have in department stores. You put in a penny, push a lever, and two squares of gum slide down and out. Only Jim's machine does not require money, and you get M&M candies instead of bubble gum. The kid caught on to the free food, dropping candy all around. The parents, clean-cut middle class types, white, played with their child, tidied up after him, and talked with others in the living room. By 6 p.m. there were about 10 people at Jim's and countless M&M candies scattered everywhere. Rounds of backgammon were being played by people sitting on Jim's bed.

Jim's assistant had been reading people's futures from a deck of cards. Cans of beer and soda were making their way from the refrigerator. Joints were circulating. They just appeared, to take a hit and pass on.

Jim, in the meantime, never entered the bedroom after about 5 p.m. Instead, he stood near the door, in the dining room/kitchen area, making occasional forays back into the dope room for a sale. The metamorphosis from partier to purchaser is a transformation from seemingly moral to instrumental relations. A guest turns into a buyer after playing backgammon, getting her or his future predicted, smoking dope, and/or just sitting and talking in the bedroom/living room. The soon-to-be purchaser would say good-bye to those in the front room, and move back towards Jim. If he was there but with someone, they would dance the dance of catching his attention to secure their place in line, of fluttering and gesturing to be seen while being seen as calm and disinterested. They would wait if he was not there. But if he was there and free, a deal is to be done in the pantry. So there they go, back, behind the privacy of a drawn black curtain. Jim measures dope in full view of his customer. Notions of honesty. He has two scales; both are Ohaus – state of the art for a dope dealer. The marijuana scale has browned with thick resin of 15 years' passage. It is reliable down to one tenth of a gram. The cocaine scale is newer, smaller, more fragile. More expensive. Accurate to one hundredth of a gram. At the price of coke, a customer likes the security of precision. Jim likes to reassure his friends.

Dope is weighed and packaged, and exchanged for cash or an entry in Jim's accounts. As noted, most people leave soon thereafter. But sometimes people buy when they sense a lull in Jim's activities. They buy, chat with him a bit, and then find their way up to the front room party.

Just about every person there on a Friday night, at one time or another, is on a rotating credit system. Jim has up to three or four thousand dollars outstanding in credit at any one time. His debt ledger is a wad of papers. Someone is noted by their first name and last initial. He ruffles back through the papers to find the last amount owed to him by the customer, calculates the current total debt, and makes a new entry on the top sheet. Jim also occasionally buys on credit, but only infrequently, and then only with an old time supplier.

The dope world at Jim's level, like much of the petty underground economy, settles out only by cash or barter. People do not pay by cheque. There are no credit cards. But given that one trusts one's friends, Jim's credit system becomes not only common, but the norm.

Similarly, Jim does not like to haggle over prices. Nor does he like people to insist on sampling the quality of his dope. It is good. His prices are more than fair. Because he wants to keep his people happy. Which keeps him happy. That is why he has a multi-tiered pricing system, where the charge depends on the closeness of the person buying.

Leaving Jim's apartment involves not only saying goodbye to friends and acquaintances, but also a handshake and/or a hug and/or a kiss with Jim. He might ask a guest to wait a moment before leaving, however, until someone else is on their way up the old wood stairs. To minimize the creak from one particularly loud spot, he times a guest's exit so that the two people going in opposite directions hit the same spot at the same time. Only one audible event occurs. He says that it is important to time comings and goings to camouflage the number of people visiting on a Friday night – so as not to attract attention.

He used to have an apartment across the street from his current home. But the owner discovered that he was dealing, and encouraged him to leave. He moved across to his current place and, for a short time, tried to deal out of his old apartment. A separation of work from play, of one realm from the other. In the tradition of Weber and the bureaucratization of the labour process. After that arrangement fell through, he convinced friends living lower in his new building to lend their apartment. Less stairs for a customer to climb. Less noise to attract attention. Living above and dealing below – a metaphor for the social construction of a dealer. Concerns by the tenants of that apartment, however, eventually led Jim to abandon the use of the lower apartment. In retrospect, those who participated in the Friday night activities at that time recall an uncomfortable 'coldness' partying outside Jim's home, in his official workplace. Jim recounts the same uncomfortableness. He gave up his attempt at separation, and started selling in his home again.

We talked with Roy about his new girlfriend. She doesn't like the lack of privacy in his lifestyle, he said. So on a Friday night, after three or four people arrive, she gets up and leaves. She comes back after the partying, but the resulting definition of partying has been affected. Roy said that most of his business is now transacted between 6 and 7 p.m.

This means that the Friday night market party, as we originally understood it, no longer exists. Partying is lying back and letting the week roll off. Relaxing after dinner, getting high and staying up late because you don't have to go to work tomorrow. Partying is not buying dope for an hour between 6 and 7 o'clock, and then leaving to go elsewhere.

'He was into drugs then', Pat was saying of Roy, referring to crack. 'And all the rationalizations about the Friday night party were just that. Rationalizations. He was too paranoid to have all those people around, and he didn't have the inventory any more. He couldn't afford it. At one point he had $10,000 of inventory. He needed that to do business. He needed the diversity and quality of goods. But it was all gone and he couldn't save the money anymore to keep the inventory or build it up again. He was spiralling down. The vortex.' Pat's finger twirled again.

Concentric Circles Don't Touch

The notions of 'inner circle' and 'outer circle' are used to distinguish between those 'friends' closer to and those further from Jim. Closeness to the presumed 'real Jim', the man remaining when stripped of his structural accoutrements; this is the Jim that emerges in the anti-structural conditions of partying, under the nominal conditions of play and creativity. And here Jim has manufactured an inner world defined by degrees of friendship.

Those on the immediate outside are largely clients clothed as friends. They come to purchase drugs for their own use in other places. Jim sells to them to earn a living. But behaviours are enacted within the idiom of friendship.

Various aspects of the Friday night party help to cloud underlying dichotomies. As stage director, Jim stakes a position on the cusp between the moral and the instrumental realms, slipping from one to the other as the drama of the evening is played out. He parties with those from the inside, who come early and stay throughout the evening. They provide a backdrop of play against which Jim can conduct the instrumental as if it were the moral, interacting with those from the outer circle as if they too were members of the inner circle, or could be if they only had time to stay. As if they too were 'real friends'.

In the early part of a Friday evening, before things get too busy and while only four or five people are around, Jim will sit, talk, and do dope with his friends, much as he will again late in the evening with some of the same. A joint will make the rounds. If someone has brought nitrous oxide Jim has the balloons and handles. Every 15 or so minutes Jim dips into his cocaine reserve and passes some around. He makes neat lines on a small round brown polished piece of stone. People snort the stuff through a cut straw, the white and red candy-cane striped kind kids use for soft drinks. Jim does not bother with the niceties, snorting his off the corner of the piece of cardboard he used to make the lines. Then he stopped bothering to make lines for anyone. He dumped coke onto the stone in rude two-nostril sized piles, one per person. Even later he just offered coke off the edge of the cardboard.

As noted, partying is a social event, creating and reinforcing a certain solidarity. One is handed a joint, smokes it and passes it on – hand to hand, mouth to mouth – necessitating interaction beyond speech, a spatial-temporal exchange. People give and accept, by the nature of the activity, physically interacting in a cooperative manner. Each takes into her or his mouth – through inhalation into his or her body – the same essence, a communion, understood to transport everyone together to a different consciousness, an altered state where all will dwell to the exclusion of others not present.

The same holds true for cocaine, passed from person to person, each giving and receiving – replenished again and again by the master of the ceremony. There are social differences between the worlds of marijuana and cocaine, however, one of division and hierarchy. Marijuana can be picked right off the plant and smoked. But cocaine requires specialization and hierarchy. Silver, gold and crystal accoutrements are used to snort this fine white powder through crisp, tightly rolled hundred dollar bills. Important people snort cocaine. Wall Street types and and corporate executives. Entertainers. Thin straight lines cut with gold handled razor blades on the smooth perfect surface of a Tiffany travel mirror.

The people at Jim's snort piles of cocaine through bits of candy cane plastic straw. Jim uses only the edge of the cardboard. The drugs they share, the inebriation from beer, nitrous oxide, marijuana, cocaine and more, experienced by each, is an obvious link among them. When enough chemicals bounce around in your brain, when your heart races and your muscles do not move, when you see sound and touch infinity, when you completely understand the meaning of the universe, social structure takes a temporary back seat to circumstance and you are undifferentially and existentially bound with those sharing the experience. An acute com-munality is engendered as a result of the psychoactive agents ingested under the particularly anti-structural circumstances of Friday night partying at Jim's – a strong cessation of the normal relations of social structure, a strong sense of freedom from the strictures of society, and freedom to experience and act in non-standard fashions. This is a communality of ecstasy and its anticipation, an intense and temporary liberation from structure. From conformity. At best, beyond our orbit, an escape into another closed world.

Jim's is, relatively, also a world of sensuality and sexuality, with ecstasy in both. Touching, hugging, kissing, making love, having sex (with either sex), all reduce distance. Sensuality affirms belonging. Sexuality does. While bureaucratic organization desensualizes and desexualizes the lives of its members in the quest for control (Burrell 1984), Jim's world refuses to do so, resists doing so, recognizing these aspects as integral to communality. The paintings and posters on Jim's walls attest to this non-parcelling out of the human, this anti-bureaucratization. A member of the inner circle had been the subject of a graphic pictorial in a pornography magazine. A copy of the issue made its rounds as we sat together, clothed. Admirers paid their compliments to the man as the pages were turned and his abilities viewed. 'Whatever makes you feel good', Jim had offered in another circumstance.

Drugs are a part of this capacity to play, to flow, to enjoy the moment of the now as its edge travels inexorably forward. Chapple notes that

> you can read a thousand law enforcement manuals or sociological puff-papers without understanding why 30 million American citizens smoke marijuana. Here's why: Marijuana makes fucking even more fun. It relaxes the frenetic and makes the shy giddy. It relieves boredom and it turns sunsets a deeper orange. (1984: 238)

A while later, after more people had arrived, the cocaine disappeared and Jim assumed his stance at the door, managing the backstage of the event. Various circles of closeness and types of trade etch a pattern in the flow of a Friday night. From closeness to more instrumental relations and back to closeness. Partying, managing sales, back to partying, and so on. Dave is an example of a particularly instrumental relationship in this world. He is in his late twenties, and has been buying from Jim for several years. Unlike most of the people there, who wear informal clothing – jeans, T-shirts, pullover knit cottons, peasant dresses – Dave was wearing a light grey business suit, a white shirt unbuttoned at the collar, and a loosened tie.

Also, unlike most of the people there, Dave was noticeably nervous, almost jittery. He was not socializing with the people in the front room, just staying back in Jim's area, hugging that part of the apartment, waiting for his turn to buy. Also unlike the other people there for the partying and the buying. Dave talked about his work – exclusively about this work, about being an insurance salesman. In a couple of years he is going to get into real estate. When he gets the money.

When Jim and he got together they were back in the dope room within moments. A couple of minutes later the nervous salesman was gone. That is the way it is with him, Jim says. In and out.

Standing Still

Jim purports to have had a 'no new customer' policy in place for approximately the past five years. If someone asks to bring along a friend, Jim says that he says no. He says that he gets angry if someone brings along a friend for a Friday night without asking. But he also says that he might sell the new person some dope, depending upon his mood – his mood being one crack in the system.

Like any supposedly static social system, Jim's structure allows for change. Many in the inner circle have been with Jim for only two or three years. They are largely single and without children. Good clients for the dope trade.

Jim says that he uses the same criteria in evaluating potential clients as does a landlord: a steady job, a good demeanour. He wants adults who can handle the complexities of the dope world. People who will not betray him. People he can build a trust in. Security is his only reason for limiting the acquisition of new customers, he says, for limiting the adding of new friends. The paranoia of drug dealing. He could 'easily double' his sales, 'because everyone has a friend who would like to meet me.' The perception that he 'has dealt with the same people for so long' leads Jim to say that he 'mostly feels secure' with dealing. In addition, he says that the first time he gets arrested he 'will get off with a warning, probably with probation', regardless of the stiff legal penalties concerning dealing cocaine; because, Jim says with a twinkle, 'I'm a moral, upstanding person.' There are lawyers who specialize in defending dope dealers. He knows one, a friend of a friend – his security blanket tucked away for a special night.

The denial and the paranoia of dealing. One of Jim's worst nightmares: going to a party where he does not know many of the people. But everyone there knows him. Knows what he does for a living.

Dragged Down by Gravity

It is perhaps relevant in the non-bureaucratized world Jim seeks to inhabit that the substantive core of dealing dope is not technically complex. While the transition into this activity is likely to be disjunctive (unless one is raised by dope dealers), given its marginality, dealing is technically simple. One can easily and excitedly converse with non-expert friends about it. One can readily involve them in play: in communality, in ecstasy.

Jim's effort to leave the differentiated, formally rational, bureaucratized world, his effort to achieve an integrative life of play within work, has led to the construction of a life chasing the bonds of *communitas*. Social process, however, is dialectical, with pressure for change arising from the activities being performed. One structure tending to anti-structure tending to another structure. In Jim's quest to achieve freedom from the surrounding society, to strive after ecstasy, to live in the anti-structural domain of *communitas*, an alternative social structure has largely been formed – a contradiction in his terms. It is precisely within the process of differentiating his life from the surrounding social structure that Jim participates in and directs the construction of an alternative structure; one more readily fused with this world of play than was the structure he escaped, but a structure nonetheless.

This apparently contradictory concept of creating structure within *communitas* has been discussed by Myerhoff, who writes that *communitas* itself

> may become bounded and rigid, a kind of totalitarianism of the sacred. . . . Thus communitas 'becomes what it beholds' and is engulfed by internally originating structure. The 'group mind' absorbs the individual, and once more duty replaces freedom. Communitas has now come full circle and is its own opposite, social structure. (Myerhoff 1975: 65)

For Jim this process of structuring has come to include many elements. Most basically, he segments people and time in a manner enabling him to enact an occupation beyond the margin of legitimate social intercourse. With Friday nights, we see the creation of a taxonomy of clients, one hierarchically differentiated by levels of closeness. We see Jim partying with those in the inner circle, people who arrive early and stay late, or all night. He shares drugs with these people. He shares love and sex with them. But not with everyone there on a Friday night. Some people are only clients.

> 'That's too wonderful to be true.'
> Dorothy said somewhere in Oz

There is an instrumentality here. A non-*communitas*. The management of a backstage, with Jim as director. When the time comes, Jim stays near the front door, to manage comings and goings. He moves into the dope room to sell and then moves out again to be available for the next buyer; back and forth between rooms, realms and dimensions, weaving an intricacy between flow and structure whose swirl in the vortex accelerates with such momentum that, in the end, in the very end, the challenge is merely to survive.

But the eddies did not always seem so perilous. The backstage to a Friday night was once neatly layered and categorized. Boundaries of inclusion and exclusion were neatly structured. Jim escaped the suburbs, the divisionalized world of the Protestant ethic, of bureaucracy. En-route he created an alternative structure, one more closely fusing 'work' with 'play'. Being was stressed over having. Sort of.

We think, now, that Roy is dead. The Great Wizard, *par adua al alta*, slipped away in the carnival air into the outer stratosphere. 'I hereby decry that until that time, if any, I return . . .' But the truth does not float back. Akhsa died, clinging to it. Pat's finger twirled.

References

Burrell, Gibson (1984) 'Sex and Organizational Analysis', *Organization Studies*, 5(2): 97–118.
Chapple, Steve (1984) *Outlaws in Babylon: Shocking True Adventures on the Marijuana Frontier*. New York: Pocket Books.

Fromm, Eric (1941) *Escape from Freedom*. New York: Farrar and Rinehard.

Fromm, Eric (1942) *The Fear of Freedom*. London: Routledge and Kegan Paul.

Goffman, Erving (1961) *Asylums*. New York: Anchor.

Myerhoff, Barbara G. (1975) 'Organization and Ecstasy: Deliberate and Accidental Communitas among Huichol Indians and American Youth', in Sally Falk Moore and Barbara G. Myerhoff (eds), *Symbol and Politics in Communal Ideology*. Ithaca, New York: Cornell University Press. pp. 33–67.

Singer, Isaac Bashevis (1953) 'A Crown of Feathers', in *The Collected Stories*. New York: Farrar Strauss Giroux. pp. 352–71.

Turner, Victor (1977) 'Variations on a Theme of Liminality', in Sally Falk Moore and Barbara G. Myerhoff (eds), *Secular Ritual*. Atlantic Highlands, New Jersey: Humanities Press. pp. 36–52.

Turner, Victor (1982) *From Ritual to Theater: The Human Seriousness of Play*. New York: Performing Arts Journal Publications.

Tyler, S. (1986) 'Post-modern Ethnography: from Document of the Occult to Occult Document', in J. Clifford and G.E. Marcus (eds), *Writing Culture*. Berkeley: University of California Press. pp. 122–40.

Van Maanen, John and Barley, Stephen R. (1984) 'Occupational Communities: Culture and Control in Organizations', in Barry M. Staw and L.L. Cummings (eds), *Research in Organizational Behavior*. Vol. 6: Greenwich, Connecticut: JAI Press. (Used here in manuscript form, November 1982.)

Willmott, Hugh and Knights, David (1982) 'The Problem of Freedom: Fromm's Contribution to a Critical Theory of Work Organisation', *Praxis*, 2(2): 204–25.

PART 3

RETHINKING SYMBOLIC MANAGEMENT

7

Management in Context: Culture and Organizational Change

Steven P. Feldman

The recent interest in cultural analysis of organizations is based on the belief that organizations have symbolic aspects that affect organizational behaviour. Underlying this research, however, are different assumptions about the nature of symbols and the role they play in organizations. The majority of writers have assumed that symbols perform an expressive function and are used in a type of action they call 'symbolic action' which they contrast with 'substantive action'. This dichotomy between symbolic and substantive action has resulted in the development of models that assume culture is a causal factor in organizational change, and should be controlled by the management of symbols. In this chapter, this approach – the management-as-symbolic-action approach – is examined and found to be inadequate. An alternative approach is developed – the culture-as-context approach – that assumes all actions have a symbolic aspect, all actions are value-laden, symbols are meaningful only in terms of their relations with other symbols, and symbols are dispositions to action – not causes of it. The study of culture is seen, then, as the explication of action in terms of the system of symbolic forms – goals, plans, ideas, roles, and traditions – that people use to give meaning and order to their experience. This approach is applied to the interactions of the members of the 'transition team' in a Bell Telephone operating company preparing for the deregulation of the American Telephone and Telegraph Company (AT&T), its parent corporation, in 1981. It is demonstrated empirically, and explained conceptually, that culture leads to a certain class of possible actions which makes certain attempts at change, or reactions to change, probable in a given situation.

A Bell Telephone company manager once described a rather difficult-to-work-with superior as a small terrier that attacked little stuffed animals and ripped them to shreds. This symbol from the Bell cultural context – manager as vicious small dog – points to two aspects of organizational culture. First, the symbol led to a *motivation* to avoid this overly competitive and petty superior. Second, it created a *mood* of caution and frustration. Thus, the cultural symbol has a dual nature: it establishes an inclination in the individual that directs him or her to accomplish an end, and it represents the conditions or circumstances in terms of which this end makes sense. This latter aspect – creating reality as opposed to pre-adapting to it – has been given little attention in the literature on organizational culture. This has impeded our understanding of organizational culture and its relation to other aspects of organizational behaviour. In this chapter, my objective is to develop a concept of culture that takes into account the dual nature of the cultural symbol, and to demonstrate the significance of this concept in our efforts to understand organizational change.

To base this analysis in an actual change process, I will analyse the interactions of the members of the 'transition team' in a Bell Telephone operating company preparing for the deregulation of AT&T in 1981. This transition team was composed of a dozen line and staff assistant vice presidents (AVPs), but all management levels were involved in its work. In this chapter, the empirical data are taken from my observation of three transition team meetings, and interviews with the participants. These meetings, and the Bell System divestiture that prompted the transition planning, were causes of considerable anxiety and fear in these managers. What the transition team members, especially the line managers, feared most was their loss of control over the means of production of the telephone service. They had spent their whole occupational lives controlling the operational variables that made up this production system. As they started to lose control over these variables their managerial instincts, which had become an almost automatic part of their behaviour over their 30-year careers, revolted against this loss. The telephone company managers, as always, gave the appearance of compliance – in this case with the deregulation order – but then tried their utmost to limit their loss of control. To understand these reactions, we must investigate the telephone company cultural system, because it established the moods and motivations in terms of which these managers approached the deregulation process.

I will begin with a review of the literature on the concept of culture and its role in organizational change. From this discussion I will develop an interpretive concept of culture (Geertz 1973b) to investigate the dual nature of organizational symbolism. The following section summarizes the cultural context of the telephone company as it is described in my previous work (Feldman 1985, 1986a, 1986b). In the penultimate section, I present and interpret data from the three transition team meetings in light of the telephone company culture. Finally, I draw general conclusions about the nature of organizational culture and the role it plays in organizational change.

Organizational Symbolism and Organization Action

The concept of culture has recently attracted much interest in the field of organization theory. This interest stems from the belief that organizations have symbolic aspects that affect organizational behaviour (Pondy et al. 1983). Standard organizational phenomena such as decision making or power, as well as previously ignored phenomena such as legends, stories, and myths or collective rituals, have been analysed for symbolic content. Underlying this research, however, are various assumptions about the nature of the meaning of the term 'symbolic'.

The majority of writers have assumed that symbols perform an expressive function and are used in a type of action they call 'symbolic action', which they contrast with 'substantive action' (Pfeffer 1981). Substantive action is assumed to result from decisions taken in regard to objective criteria such as external constraint and power-dependence relations, while symbolic action is used to develop 'shared meanings' to enhance commitment and compliance (Pfeffer 1981). Hence, these writers have limited symbolic analysis to organizational phenomena in which expression plays an obvious role, such as leadership (Pondy 1978) or communication (Peters 1978). Symbols are seen as models *for* reality, as instruments to motivate or direct people toward actions that will achieve substantive results. Thus, this approach – the management-as-symbolic-action approach – assumes that 'organizational culture' is a causal factor in organizational change and should be controlled by the management of symbols (Beer 1980; Tichy, 1983).

There is, however, a fundamental problem with the dichotomy between substantive action and the symbolic action which makes it, and the conclusions drawn from it, extremely misleading: 'substantive reality' cannot be known independent of the language or other symbolic medium in which it is represented (Ricoeur 1974). Symbols are never just models for reality; they are also models *of* reality (Geertz 1973a). It is true that symbols are used as blueprints to model organizational, environmental, social and psychological processes, so that the processes can be grasped and manipulated; but, as the symbol is shaped to grasp and manipulate these processes, it also shapes these processes. Whether one wishes to understand managerial behaviour or environmental trends, one needs a symbolic structure capable of distinguishing, analysing, and ordering experience. The assumption of an objective social world underlying Pfeffer's concept of 'substantive action' is invalid in the study of human social behaviour, because symbols are integral to the existence of the social world (Cassirer 1946).

By contributing to the creation of the social world, symbols make purely rational action, based on calculations in an environment independent of the decision maker, impossible. All action must be partially subjective or value-laden. The behaviour of a management group is partially influenced by its tendencies and traditions (Mintzberg 1978), and the decision making of individual managers is primarily influenced by his or her past experience

(Schwartz and Davis 1981). All decision-making and organizational behaviour must be investigated in terms of the subjective or non-rational
(though not irrational), social and historical influences that affect it. These
influences are maintained in the symbolic forms – memories, plans, roles,
and group relations – that individuals use to orient themselves in the world.

Symbols are inseparably bound up with the ongoing stream of human
social activity and human social activity is inseparably bound up with
symbols. It can be seen, then, that symbols are not entities that can be
isolated, but become meaningful only through their relations with other
symbols in social activity. They develop their meaning over time as they are
used in social interaction (Pettigrew 1979), and are maintained collectively
through interaction (Van Maanen 1977). Therefore, the meaning of symbols
can only be understood by focusing on both the specific social activity in
which they are used and the historically-developed *system* of symbolic
relations of which they are a part (Geertz 1973b).

The management-as-symbolic-action theorists do not attempt to study
symbols in terms of their meaning, but, on the contrary, as action – 'symbolic
action' – which they define as action having no substantive or material effect
(Pfeffer 1981). The concept of 'symbolic action' is used to explain (and
predict) the effect non-substantive action has on phenomena like 'attitudes',
'sentiments', and 'perceptions' (Pfeffer 1981). Thus, 'symbolic action' is the
same as 'substantive action' except that, instead of causing changes in the
material world, is causes changes in a mental one. The problem with this
approach is that symbols are of a different logical type than actions, and
cannot be understood by the same explanatory framework (Ryle 1949). For
example, to say that a company president eating lunch with factory workers
to improve factory morale is acting symbolically, is not to refer to a second
set of actions he is taking in addition to his eating, drinking, and talking, but
to refer to their *meaning*. Symbols do not exist like actions – they are not
happenings – and cannot be understood as causal agents.

Symbols are *dispositions* to action. They do not cause action, but shape it
by inducing a certain set of moods and motivations (tendencies, capacities,
skills, habits, and so forth) in the actor (Geertz 1973a). Dispositions,
capacities, skills, and so on are what Ryle (1949) has called 'inference
tickets'; they admit to a certain variety of reactions and behaviours. To say
that someone is moody or motivated is not to say that the person will act in
this or that way. It is to say that he or she will *probably* act in one of a certain
number of ways. The study of culture is not, then, the search to determine
what effect 'symbolic action' has on 'attitudes', but the explication of social
action in terms of the system of shared symbolic constructs that tend to give
rise to certain behaviours in certain situations.

The conclusions that we have reached – that all actions have symbolic
aspects, all actions are value-laden, symbols are only meaningful in terms of
their relations to other symbols, and symbols are dispositions to action, not
causes of it – suggest a reframing of the way we understand culture. Culture
is *context*. It is the system of symbols that people use to give meaning and

order to their actions and the actions of others; action is meaningful only in terms of the symbolic context in which it is interpreted. By positing action as action in context, we open to investigation both the model-for *and* the model-of aspects of symbols, since the focus is no longer on the relationship between 'symbolic action' and its effect, but on understanding social action in terms of its symbolic meaning.

This approach – what I will call the culture-as-context approach – by bringing both the model-for and model-of aspects of symbols into the concept of culture, alters the way we understand the relationship between culture and organizational change. The management-as-symbolic-action approach, as we have seen, assumes culture is a causal variable that – ultimately – by causing changes in 'attitudes', effects organizational change. I have shown that this approach focuses on the model-for aspect of symbols while overlooking the model-of aspect. Weick (1979) has cogently pointed out the problem that results from assuming symbols have only a guidance function: *goal-interpreted* behaviour is explained as if it is *goal-directed* behaviour. Thus, it can be seen that the management-as-symbolic-action approach to cultural analysis is actually an *obstacle* to change because it denies its own involvement in conceiving the change process and thus tends continually to repeat it.

The culture-as-context approach solves this problem by going beyond goal-directed explanations of change and examining the symbolic forms – concepts, theories, plans, and goals – that are used to determine what *is* changing or what *should* be changed. We can understand organizational change more effectively only if we bring into analysis the capacities and inclinations of those dreaming up the goals and changes in the first place. The culture-as-context approach accomplishes this task by taking into account both the result desired for the future, which the 'model-for' symbol embodies, and the repetition of the past, which the 'model-of' symbol describes (Ricoeur 1970). Thus, the organizational change process can be analysed in terms of what motivates managerial action, and also what more diffuse habits and dispositions manifest themselves in certain thoughts about, and actions toward, the change process.

The Cultural Context of the Telephone Company

If one were to ask a telephone manager, especially a high-ranking one, what the company culture was, his reply would be spontaneous: 'It's a culture of service'. By this he or she would mean that the telephone company was dedicated to serving its customers, shareholders, and employees. The telephone system was established as a legally-protected monopoly designed to provide the greatest number of people with the best possible telephone service, at the lowest possible price. This ensured that all but extremely poor people would be able to afford a telephone. It was made possible by a cross-subsidization of revenue from business users to residence users. In addition, shareholders received a 'fair return' for their capital investment and the security of owning one of the most stable and reliable stocks on the stock exchange. Finally, the organization designed to accomplish these objectives was dedicated to the welfare of its employees. It not only provided extensive employee benefit and development programmes, but also maintained a no-layoff policy – almost without exception – throughout this century.

The culture of service thus presented, as bureaucratic organizations go, a familial organization. It cared about and took care of its constituents. For the employees who wanted employment security and appreciated the non-competitive, communal spirit of the company mission, the culture of service was an attractive environment. But this familial ethic was not enough to cover all the needs of an *economic* organization.

Not only did the telephone company have to *promise* good public service; it had to *deliver* it (deliver it in the spirit of community service). Thus public perceptions of telephone service were taken very seriously by top management because without public support the legal monopoly would collapse. To ensure good service, the management had developed an extensive system of statistically-measured task categories. The system was used to measure and thus monitor everything from the number of telephones installed per day to the politeness of operators answering service calls. The managers who were best able to maintain superior results in these competitively-compiled task categories were most valued by the company and promoted to positions of power and status.

The fact that the statistical categories defined managerial tasks narrowly meant that the type of management style that could succeed was also defined narrowly. It was a style that emphasized control over the variables of operations above all else. This emphasis on control was successful because innovation was the responsibility of Bell Laboratories, and because the monopoly terms of trade meant that the rate of organizational change was not spurred by reactions to, and anticipation of, competitors; thus, managerial adaptability and creativity were less essential. Successful managers who had gained power looked for similar characteristics in subordinates, and subordinates attempted to conform to these characteristics in the hope of winning promotions (Feldman 1986a). Within this structure, by these means, and with this rationale, conformity as a pattern of behaviour became the norm.

As time passed, standards developed that were collectively maintained and defined the meaning of conformity. But these standards went beyond the need to achieve statistical results. They included criteria for racial and ethnic preferences, a tendency to promote male managers, and a demand for behaviour that indicated deference to superiors (Feldman 1986b). In addition, there were extensive rules for relations between superiors and subordinates which demanded subordinates to respect, admire, and conform socially to superiors (Feldman 1985).

To account for these strong demands for racial, sexual, ethnic, and behavioural conformity, we must look back to the culture of service. This familial type of organization attracted people who valued security over risk, and stability over ambition. When some of these people received promotions to positions of power – promotions they had earned through conformity to certain behavioural styles – they used this power to increase their personal security. Their need for security, however, was not just occupational or economic, but also psychological (Feldman 1985). Indeed, their wish for a familial type of organization was born out of strong dependency needs. It was a wish to be taken care of, and to be monitored and controlled. When they gained positions where their task was to control others, their unconscious needs to be controlled had to be suppressed. This suppression of their own needs to be controlled was accomplished by increasing their demands for control over others. The result was little delegation of authority and much control over behaviour (Feldman 1985). In this way, the culture of control was maintained and perpetuated. Thus, unwittingly, managers created – and re-created – an organizational reality which evaluated, rewarded and punished individual behaviour in accordance with a set of homogenizing standards.

We must recognize one further point about the culture of control. The literature on organization theory has long realized that there is a natural tendency for fear and conflict to develop between staff groups and line groups. In this telephone company, the natural tendency for conflict between staff and line had been exacerbated by a lack of integration between the two groups in the development of the organizational structure (Feldman 1986b). In addition, the staff group was *not* measured statistically and, it was commonly said, received all the line personnel who did not meet line-operating standards. Thus, there were both organizational and career differences between the two groups.

In 1981, when this operating company began to prepare for divestiture, it was the staff group that monitored and interpreted the incoming changes. The line group, of course, was more inclined to routine activities (Dalton 1959). Historically, the staff had had little power, given that the organization was measured by operational statistics and revenue – both of which were primarily line responsibilities. As the external environment began to change, however, AT&T relied upon the staff groups in the operating companies to implement its goal of making changes evenly across the whole telephone system. By controlling the information and plans provided by AT&T, the staff group, in this operating company, was able to increase its influence in the decision-making process (Pfeffer and Salancik 1978). The *culture* of control was not weakened because of this change in the distribution of power, but the increasing power of the staff group, relative to the line group, made the tendency that both groups had to demand conformity problematical for the company's efforts at managing the organizational changes resulting from the deregulation of the Bell System.

Cultural Analysis of Three Transition Team Meetings

In this section we will examine three transition team meetings to determine
the effect cultural influences had on the efforts of this team to create
organizational change. The transition team was set up by the chief executive
officer (CEO) in accordance with directions he had received at the Bell
System President's Conference in May 1981. The staff AVP of corporate
planning was made the committee chairman. The first transition team
meeting was held on 29 June 1981 and began at 8 a.m. in a third-floor
conference room. Present were six other staff AVPs, one staff division head,
and seven staff district-level managers who made up a subcommittee that
was supervised by the chairman. In this meeting the transition team was to
hear the subcommittee's report on its research into how the company should
be split into regulated and competitive organizations.

During the first hour of the meeting, a district head presented the plan that
the subcommittee had devised for the split. At 9.13 a.m., a line AVP (Jones)
arrived. His late arrival was probably due to a last-minute decision to attend
the meeting and a call to see his boss, the senior vice president (who was in
charge of all line operations), to find out his position on the newly-
developing role of the transition team in the divestiture planning process.
The committee chairman brought him coffee; there were five or six 'hello's'.
The district head who was giving the presentation started to review what he
had said and a staff AVP brought Jones a copy of the 'assumptions sheet'
that had guided the subcommittee's research. Jones was generally considered the most powerful AVP in the company; he was the highest-paid
AVP, and his geographic area had consistently achieved the best statistical
results for telephone service in the company.

Less than 10 minutes after he arrived, Jones stopped the presentation to
object to a point being made. A staff AVP then backed him up by saying,
'Me, too', and added jokingly, '[even though] I hate to be with Jones'. Jones
then quipped, 'This will be the first time'. This exchange reflected the
changes in self-interest of both line and staff and the as-yet-unclear form the
results of this transition would take. Traditionally, the two groups had been
in conflict over most staff proposals. Now, however, AT&T and the CEO
had made it clear that the line would have to make some changes and the
staff would play a role in determining those changes. This was a situation in
which both groups knew they would have to cooperate, but were not sure
how to do so or how much cooperation would be required.

The subcommittee members' presentations continued until the staff AVP
for public relations questioned the proposed splitting up of the geographical
areas. Jones added that it had been done incorrectly and that 'we will have to
break the geographical areas up according to who is in charge'. The AVP for
public relations then said, 'There are other criteria for breaking these things
up'. Others in the room chuckled. The points being brought up by these two
AVPs reflected their specialized interests and not the overall objectives of
the transition team. This was a reflex action in the culture of control.

Superiors received cooperation, but peers were seen as competitors and, in some cases, enemies. The reason for this is that the culture of control encourages domination over people and things; it does not encourage the recognition of other groups, as independent and legitimate organizations. Cooperation between groups certainly can occur, but such joint efforts are somewhat tenuous since they are based primarily on mutual need, not on mutual trust. The culture of control developed in an era when multidisciplinary work was not essential. The problem in the current situation was, now that multidisciplinary decision making was essential, the need to control one's own functional interests still guided interpersonal relations.

The next part of the presentation began with an examination of a chart of Jones' geographic area. A staff AVP jokingly said, 'Skip this'. Another staff AVP remarked, 'Oh, I thought we would never get to this', then turned to Jones to say, 'Wake up'. Implicit in these jokes are the contextual issues that were dominating the minds of these managers. To say 'Wake up' to Jones during an analysis of his own geographic area implied the opposite of the well-known fact that Jones had built his career by being extremely alert to all factors that affected his organization. The use of irony was a way of emphasizing Jones' propensity to control (and expressing anxiety about it). In addition, by suggesting that Jones had been asleep, the staff managers were expressing their belief that Jones had no concern for anything but his own organizational interests. Then by pretending to have to wake up Jones, the staff managers were perhaps suggesting that they wished he *would* fall asleep, or at least relax his tendency to put control before cooperation.

The presentation continued for a while, until Jones stopped it to say he was confused. A staff AVP said that the decision just made had been taken in anticipation of what would probably be said in the soon-to-be-released AT&T guidelines for restructuring. Jones responded, 'the senior vice president (SVP) told us at dinner on Thursday night how we will do it. We might as well wait for the SVP to announce it. Basically, the SVP is saying that many of these things have [already] been decided.' This remark by Jones demonstrated two things. First, it was common knowledge that Jones and the SVP were close friends; it was not unusual for Jones to have superior information. Second, the SVP's primary responsibility was supervision of the line. Most of the staff reported to the CEO, who also, however, had always strongly supported the line. With these comments, Jones was attempting to say that nothing had changed; that the line would continue to dominate decision making in the future. In this way, he was hoping to discourage the staff from participating in the changes to come.

It was not long before Jones' comments began to prove false. At 11.19 a.m. a staff VP arrived unexpectedly. This was a most unusual event. It was a sure sign that the line managers' control over decision making was no longer being fully enforced by the ultimate powers of the SVP (and CEO), since the staff VP's presence meant that he was not being stopped from openly pursuing staff interests. Shortly after, at 11.32, a second line AVP arrived. Towards the end of the meeting, the chairman announced that the line AVPs would be joining the committee. This in itself was most unusual because the line managers had never before bothered to attend staff meetings; they had just ignored staff demands and fought them in front of the final authority of the CEO. The meeting ended with the newly-arrived line AVP questioning the subcommittee's plans and saying, 'No way'.

This first transition team meeting demonstrated a number of issues. One, the dominating role of the line was being challenged by the growing power of the staff. Two, the line and staff groups had never faced common external forces of this magnitude before, and did not have a tradition of cooperative relations upon which to base a joint effort to manage these forces. Three, the situation was so new and the uncertainty of its outcome so great, both groups attempted little more than to position themselves advantageously *vis-à-vis* each other.

The next transition team meeting was held on 8 July. Participants formed an expanded version of the transition team because this meeting was called by the SVP to clarify the transition team's mission. It was held on the eighteenth floor in the officers' conference room. Present were the SVP, two staff VPs, the one line VP, all five line AVPs, ten staff AVPs, and the seven managers who made up the subcommittee. The meeting was started by the SVP. He had just returned from a meeting at AT&T and had brought the AT&T guidelines for restructuring with him. Early in the discussion he said that the guidelines could be disagreed with and, in fact, 'thrown away if we like'. This somewhat ambiguous statement left room for the line managers to remain in control or at least for them to control the changes to come.

As the chairman was about to explain the purpose of the transition team, he noted, 'We will have to spread the cost of the charts [the subcommittee used charts for their presentations] around the various budgets'. His small corporate planning budget could not cover it; he joked, 'We are conscious of budgets in staff'. There was laughter. In response to this, the line VP quipped, 'You are conscious of how to get rid of budgets'. The laughter was louder. This joke reflected the tension, emanating from the central issue, that existed between the line and the staff. The staff managers wanted the line managers to give up control of some part of their organization and, the joke implied, the staff were more qualified to operate those parts. The line's counter-joke stated that the staff managers were devious and did not earn what they received.

These views of the current situation were all influenced by, or in reaction to, the culture of control. The line managers felt that the staff managers did not earn what they received because staff did not demonstrate superiority by controlling resources to win advantageous statistical results. The staff AVP, in his remark about budget-consciousness, was implicitly referring to the new code of management: sensitivity to unit price and unit cost. The statistical measurement system (and the culture of control) demanded only an awareness of gross cost, and thus did not really cultivate much of an awareness of cost at all. By emphasizing a greater sensitivity to budgets, the chairman's remark suggested that the staff managers were the representatives of the new market-oriented mentality.

The meeting continued with a subcommittee member's review of the planning in progress for the creation of the new organization, an organization that would be unregulated and able to compete in the market-place. After listening to this presentation for a brief time, the line VP remarked that he was bothered by the emphasis on 'pretty, beautiful structure' and by his sense that the planning was 'not oriented toward making the most efficient operating organization'. He suggested that the transition team focus on 'operating-efficiency questions rather than a balanced-geography approach'. There was some disagreement about the probable results of such an approach. A line AVP recently assigned to a staff position, backing up the line VP, then said, 'Our competition will be operating differently. We are operating just like we always do. We are not thinking about our long-term survival. We can't afford to listen to AT&T'. The SVP responded, 'But we don't want to torpedo our service'. The line VP then said, 'I agree with [the AVP]. We can charge for premium service. We should go further into this. If we did what the System suggests we would have a screwed-up company instead of the fine running company we do have.'

This argument about not following AT&T was several years old at this company and, in fact, eventually led to this company *not* turning residence telephone service over to staff control in 1978, as did the rest of the Bell System. In this situation, the line were implying (by saying not to follow AT&T) that changes should be made by the line, and that the staff – whose primary job was to interface between AT&T and the line – were not needed and should not be allowed any control. The culture of control promoted such opinions by creating a world-view in which cooperation (and the interdependence that it fostered) was feared. Fear of interdependence was the natural result of the need to control. The line AVP's arguments that they should not work closely with AT&T was an attempt to disguise the real issue – which was the struggle for control between the line and staff groups – because no matter who directed the divestiture in this operating company, the interconnection with AT&T was essential, primary, and pervasive. Thus, line managers were simply attempting, by trying to sound more market-driven than the staff, to bypass the staff and deal more directly with AT&T. Since they could not *control* AT&T directly and stop divestiture, they were attempting to control AT&T's local representatives – the staff – and stop them from participating in the change process.

As the meeting progressed, there was much debate over the accuracy and validity of the assumptions being made in the planning for the reorganization. The line managers continuously complained that decisions could not be made without the collection of additional data. This meant, of course, that the line had to supply the data. The chairman stated that he would wait to hear from the line before going ahead with the planning. To this a line AVP responded, 'Until you hear from us, nothing will happen – is this what you're saying?'. Everybody laughed. He added, 'Don't wait by the phone', and then made the gesture of pulling the cord out of the phone.

This interchange provided us with a major insight into the role culture plays in the process of organizational change. When a telephone *manager* mentioned a telephone and telephone wires, he was doing more than discussing a communication system. He was indicating a style of management that was premised on the control of subordinates (and the satisfaction of dependency needs). By telling the chairman not to 'wait by the phone' and pretending to pull the cord out of a telephone, this line AVP was signalling that the culture of control was still intact and the line was still dominating the decision making. But, as we have seen, his presence at this very meeting was a sign that the line was no longer in full control (typically the line managers ignored staff meetings). Indeed, his biggest worry was that the staff managers would disconnect *their* phones and go ahead with changes without considering the needs of the line managers. Thus, this line AVP's joke also expressed, on a deeper level, the anxiety the line managers were experiencing over their loss of power and the future redesigning of their organizations.

Controlling their organizations and controlling their dependency needs were related issues. Culture not only provides a model for action; it also provides a framework for legitimizing that action. When the routines of organizational life change, not only is the model-for-reality aspect of culture called into question, but so is the moral and emotional context that the model of reality provides. This can lead to defensive behaviour. As will be shown below, this line AVP's suggestion of sabotage was real, but it was symbolically displaced on to actual telephone service from its real object: the staff's efforts to participate in the change process.

The third transition team meeting was held the next day. Only the formal members of the team, the AVPs, were present and again, as at the first meeting, they met in a third-floor conference room. Now that the SVP had seen the AT&T guidelines and endorsed the work of the transition team, the team members had to develop detailed plans for separation of the company into two organizations. Present at this meeting were two line AVPs, five staff AVPs, three division heads (sitting in for AVPs who were unable to attend), and one district-level manager who was the chairman's assistant.

The chairman opened the meeting saying that the SVP 'was pleased with [the line VP's] attitude yesterday morning about moving fast on reorganization'. To this a line AVP quickly reacted: '[But this company] is starting from a different point from other Bell companies.' This opening exchange points out the different strategies the line and staff managers were developing to win control over the planning for the reorganization: the chairman wanted to move fast on reorganization because this implied following the AT&T guidelines and would lead to increased staff control; the line manager emphasized the uniqueness of this operating company because this implied the inappropriateness of the AT&T guidelines and required that they be reformulated. The more they were reformulated, the more opportunity the line had to win control over the planning process. That this was the line's intention is shown in the next comment, made by a line manager. In response to the chairman's remarks about moving fast on reorganization, a line AVP stated, 'I can't commit on reorganization until I see those guidelines'. Formally, up to this point, only the SVP and certain staff AVPs had been permitted to have copies of the AT&T guidelines. This line AVP, however, had already secretly obtained a copy of the guidelines and had gone over them. Thus his statement was a deception and his behaviour calculated to thwart the chairman's control of the meeting.

This episode is a good example of how culture is involved in organizational change. The line manager was inclined to control whatever affected his work. He was put in a situation where he was losing control over his organization and losing the power to do anything about it. What happened was not a change in his disposition to control, but an exercise of this disposition through deception and secrecy. In other words, a decrease in power did not lead to cultural change, but his cultural disposition led him to secrecy to expand his possible field of activity to make up for his loss of power.

To be sure, not only had this line AVP secretly seen the guidelines, but he had secretly had breakfast on the morning of this meeting with the staff AVP for customer service, to work out a common strategy to advance their common interests. This meeting was paralleled by the talk that the other line AVP had had with the line VP. In this way, the line group worked out a secret strategy to manipulate the transition team and a secret coalition to implement it. As we shall see, this secret activity, in effect, restructured and redirected the transition team.

The meeting continued with the line AVP suggesting the assignment of tasks. The customer service AVP added, 'Let's also point out functions that are problems.' A short exchange took place and then a disagreement broke out.

The public relations AVP began, 'My observation is that some of you do not really believe that we're going to make the break. [The line AVPs] are trying to get this set up, but some others are still going to be in bed with each other.'

The chairman responded, 'This committee deals with the transition not with post-transition.'

A marketing AVP said, 'The transition is to set up the dotted line organization.'

The chairman replied, 'We are here trying to determine the adjustments that must be made, but you [public relations AVP] can remind us from time to time so we don't unconsciously slip into [our pre-deregulation jargon].'

The customer service AVP quipped, 'I have to step out. I must have swallowed something.'

A line AVP said, 'If we're going to move it March 1, 1982, we should be prepared by October 1, 1981.'

The public relations AVP remarked, 'The only assumption we can make is that March 1 is the day to be two companies.'

The customer service AVP said, 'The output of the assumptions sheet is to guide field people in getting ready for changes.'

The line AVP stated, 'Now that we all agree, let's get on with the list [of assumptions].'

The marketing AVP responded, 'I really doubt that on March 1 we will have a demand sales centre – finding people and training them by that time will be impossible.'

The line AVP angrily replied, 'This group understands what the hell is going to happen.'

The marketing AVP, referring to future directives from AT&T added, 'I'll know more next week about what I will do on this.'

This exchange is important for two reasons. First, two staff AVPs were siding with the line against the committee chairman. The public relations AVP's remark about some people being 'in bed with each other' suggested that some managers were not prepared to change, but that the line managers were prepared to change and thus should be allowed to take a position of leadership. The chairman tried to agree that there was a tendency toward pre-deregulation thinking so that he would not be seen as being guilty of it, but this attempt was rejected by the customer service AVP in his remark that he had swallowed something and had to be excused to rid himself of it. Thus, the AVP public relations and the AVP customer service were working with the line AVPs to isolate the committee chairman.

Second, since this collusion had been agreed upon earlier and handled secretly, the other staff AVPs did not understand what was going on. This is why the marketing AVP kept disagreeing about the dates. He did not know that the discussion was fundamentally a positioning for control of the meeting rather than a serious planning discussion. Later on, the marketing AVP got so lost he remarked, 'This thing is getting bigger than an elephant; when I came in, I thought it was a breadbox.'

As the meeting continued, it seemed to go in circles. Again the task assignment question was brought up, this time by the AVP customer service. The chairman responded, 'I need to receive from each of you [a list of] the activities that you'll be doing.'

A line AVP told the chairman, 'Tell the study group to come up with a PERT chart for next week.'

The chairman replied, 'Why can't individual members just tell me?'.

The line AVP quipped, 'I just want to get out of doing the work.'

The chairman responded, 'The idea of a team is to work together.'

The budget AVP remarked, 'It's a good idea except for the data requests, which will demand too much [manpower].'

The chairman replied, 'You don't need a PERT chart on data, [and on the times when the] data is needed.'

The AVP customer service disagreed, 'Yes you do. We also need a specific schedule showing when we want things to happen.'

The chairman said, 'We want to establish if dates are still good – they need to be re-evaluated.'

The marketing AVP said, 'You may need more than one PERT chart.'

A line AVP recommended, 'Let's wait till we get the list and decide.'

The AVP customer service, agreeing with the line AVP's earlier idea of one PERT chart for the group, interjected, 'It's not a good idea. We need a common approach. Best thing to do is designate a coordinator.'

The chairman asked, 'Who can provide a resource for the coordinating function?'

The line AVP said, 'I'll do it.'

The chairman replied, 'You don't understand' (meaning he wanted a lower level manager for the function who would report to him).

A few comments were made and then the line AVP said, 'Send me the goddamned lists and I'll put them on a PERT chart.'

A little later the chairman remarked, 'Everybody send items to [the line AVP] and he will put them together.'

The three and a half hour meeting came to a close. As the district head walked out of the room, he said, 'This entire meeting was an exercise in futility.'

The meeting thus ended with the head line AVP in charge of collecting and presenting information to the committee. Nothing else had been accomplished! Indeed, much of the meeting was an incoherent discussion, especially for those members who did not know that a subgroup had decided to take control of the meeting away from the chairman. Over the next few months the subgroup increased its control. A district head reported that he had overheard a line AVP tell the staff AVP customer service, 'You're our only guy here. You have to carry the ball.' Eventually, all of the line data that was formally supposed to be sent to the transition team completely bypassed this committee and went to the AVP customer service. Hence, the whole process of planning organizational change was primarily a political process guided by the desire to control.

Control was the motivating passion of the telephone company managers. But control based on power was not a possibility within a changing and uncertain environment. Thus what came about was a compromise decision between the line manager and *some* staff managers to consolidate what control they could. This was done through secrecy. It was the natural result of a culture based on dependency needs, and the need to dominate that the dependency needs stimulated in many individuals occupying positions of power. The compromise decision thwarted the committee's ability to plan for change and, ultimately, limited the organization's ability to make changes because it forced the change process into *informal* channels that purposely excluded the part of the management team that was essential for the implementation of the *formally* planned result. The real result was thus a thwarting and fragmentation of the planning process in the interests of the various actors as they attempted to gain control.

Conclusion

Despite repeated appeals for contextual inquiry and sensitivity to context . . . no one is exactly sure what is being requested or how to produce it. (Weick 1983: 27)

I have defined contextual inquiry as the study of the system of significant symbols that are used by organizational members to give meaning and order to the events and activities they experience. I carried it out by identifying symbolic constructs – goals, ideas, jokes, roles, and expressions of any kind – and tracking down their interrelationships as they were played out in the interactions of managers on a transition team. My contextual analysis demonstrated – through an analysis of the symbolic forms found in the company history, the history of relations between these two groups, and the intentions and feelings of the managers in the current situation – that these actions reflected an inability to trust, a will to control, and a propensity for using secrecy.

By using contextual analysis to explicate the role the system of symbols – the culture – played in the activities of the managers on the transition team, some light was shed on the relevance of culture to the understanding of organizational change. First of all, as we saw, symbols influence action by giving rise to dispositions in the actor, and dispositions are multi-track – they encourage a certain *class* of possible actions. At this telephone company, it had not been standard practice over the years to incapacitate formal committees; but, given what was at stake in the work of the transition team, the line managers adapted their will to control and propensity for secrecy to the situation in a way that was different from their usual practice of ignoring or criticizing staff efforts. Hence, cultures are flexible by nature and permit a certain amount of adaptability without requiring cultural change.

A second point is implied here. It is just as accurate, if not more accurate, to assume that culture is a source of organizational change rather than an obstacle to change. This is so because all ideas for changes must come from the symbol system or be interpreted by it to be understood. The organizational culture is the river of meaning in which any plans for change must be able to swim. For efforts at organizational change to make sense and be accepted, they must not be contrary to the inclinations, or outside the capacities, of the management group. The incapacitating of the transition team was the result of this type of incongruity between plans for change and capacities for change: for the transition team to have been able to carry out its mandate, its members – who were equals in rank and disposed to control (and dependency) – would have had to be inclined to trust and compromise. The team was doomed to failure as long as it was chaired by a peer rather than a superior. If the SVP had chaired the meetings, the category of control that led to deception and secrecy would have led to obedience and commitment. The implementation of organizational change always originates, positively or negatively, in the organizational culture.

Finally, culture is an important force that holds organizations in a given form over time. This is probably the reason why so many writers have seen it as an obstacle to change. But no organization can change totally and fully in its every detail; this is impossible because managers would have no means for judgement without some standards based on past experience. Organizational change is always partial change. Some level of cultural continuity is essential for maintaining cooperative relations, effective leadership styles, and, above all, a sense of order that enables managers to make changes in some aspects of their work life. The literature on 'culture change' is misdirected; it is not changes in the culture that will help organizations change more effectively, but changes in behaviour. Cultural analysis is a means to *understand* this problem.

References

Beer, M. (1980) *Organization Change and Development: A Systems View*. Santa Monica: Goodyear.

Cassirer, E. (1946) *The Myth of the State*. New Haven: Yale University Press.

Dalton, M. (1959) *Men Who Manage*. New York: Wiley.

Feldman, S.P. (1985) 'Culture and conformity: an essay on individual adaptation in centralized bureaucracy', *Human Relations*, 38(20): 341–56.

Feldman, S.P. (1986a) 'Culture, charisma, and the CEO: an essay on the meaning of high office'. *Human Relations*, 39(3): 211–28.

Feldman, S.P. (1986b) *The Culture of Monopoly Management: An Interpretive Study in an American Utility*. New York: Garland.

Geertz, C. (1973a) 'Religion as a cultural system', in C. Geertz (ed.) *The Interpretation of Cultures*. New York: Basic Books. pp. 87–125.

Geertz, C. (1973b) 'Thick description: toward an interpretive theory of culture', in C. Geertz (ed.) *The Interpretation of Cultures*. New York: Basic Books. pp. 3–32.

Mintzberg, H. (1978) 'Patterns in strategy formulation', *Management Science*, 24(9): 934–48.

Peters, T.J. (1978) 'Symbols, patterns and settings: an optimistic case for getting things done', *Organizational Dynamics*, 7: 3–23.

Pettigrew, A. (1979) 'On studying organizational cultures', *Administrative Science Quarterly*, 24(4): 570–81.

Pfeffer, J. (1981) 'Management as symbolic action: the creation and maintenance of organizational paradigms', in L.L. Cummings and B.M. Staw (eds), *Research in Organizational Behavior*, 3. Greenwich, CT: JAI, 1–52.

Pfeffer, J.R. and Salancik, G.R. (1978) *The External Control of Organizations: A Resource Dependence Perspective*. New York: Harper and Row.

Pondy, L.R. (1978) 'Leadership is a language game', in M.W. McCall Jr and M.M. Lombardo (eds), *Leadership: Where Else Can We Go?* Durham, NC: Duke University Press.

Pondy, L., Frost, P., Morgan, G. and Dandridge, T. (1983) *Organizational Symbolism*. Greenwich, CT: JAI.

Ricoeur, P. (1970) *Freud and Philosophy: An Essay on Interpretation*. New Haven: Yale University Press.

Ricoeur, P. (1974) *The Conflict of Interpretations*. Chicago: Northwestern University Press.

Ryle, G. (1949) *The Concept of Mind*. New York: Barnes and Noble.

Schwartz, H. and Davis, S.M. (1981) 'Matching corporate culture and business strategy', *Organizational Dynamics*, 10(1): 30–48.

Tichy, N.M. (1983) *Managing Strategic Change: Technical, Political, and Cultural Dynamics*. New York: Wiley.

Van Maanen, J. (1977) 'Experiencing organization', in J. Van Maanen (ed.), *Organizational Careers: Some New Perspectives*. New York: Wiley. pp. 15–45.

Weick, K.E. (1979) *The Social Psychology of Organizing*. Reading, MA: Addison-Wesley.

Weick, K.E. (1983) 'Organizational communication: toward a research agenda', in L.L. Putnam and M.E. Pacanowsky (eds), *Communication and Organization: An Interpretive Approach*. Beverly Hills: Sage. pp. 13–30.

8

'We are our own Policemen!' – Organizing without Conflict

Stephen Lloyd Smith and Barry Wilkinson

> *NOTE: This case is intended to stimulate discussion. It does not prescribe 'one best way' to manage and it does not proscribe 'wrong' approaches. The case is based on intensive fieldwork; however we have combined features from different companies which we consider to be consistent with a distinctive approach to organization. The case is 'ideal-typical'. We have disguised several details to protect the identity of our sources. The original research has remained unpublished for several years in order to give further protection: most senior respondents will have left the source companies. To readers who feel that they recognize the specific 'company' represented here as 'Sherwoods', we assure them that they are mistaken. The point is that the post-bureaucratic organization described below is recognizable within numerous organizations. Its relentless logic is also clear.*

The world is complicated as a matter of *fact*, argues Weber (1949). What complicates it even more, he writes, is that human association encompasses an infinite range of irreconcilable *values*. Individuals, groups and organizations have difficulty agreeing on what should be done. It is in these contexts that authors such as Bailey (1988) have argued that advances in knowledge about how social systems work have generated a growing appreciation of how difficult they are to change in any desired direction. A growing sense of the depth of social complexity and divergence, has provoked frustration among those who wish to intervene, accompanied by resignation and pessimism about what can be done. It is as if things have become chaotic and intractable – pointers towards a wild, unpredictable, post-modern Dark Age.

But this case study concerns an organization that achieves virtually all its ambitions, on a global scale. That there ever could be such a thing as an 'organization' which has common 'goals' which it 'achieves successfully' is ridiculed by social scientists (Salaman 1979). While we would find difficulty in disagreeing, '*Sherwoods*' is the closest approximation to such an entity – an object lesson in its own terms of how to organize *successfully*. In contrast to Weber and Bailey's pessimistic sense for chaos and intractability, it is the *capabilities* of *Sherwoods'* mode of organization that may worry some readers.

This case usually divides audiences into two opposing camps. Some see *Sherwoods* as a near perfect organization worth emulating – an open, reasoned society in miniature; capitalism without conflict. Others object because, by unusual means, its members are subjected to an unusual degree of control. The organization and the process of organizing have become indistinguishable and the borderline between the organization and its members is difficult to see. Social scientists tend to count among those who worry. But practising managers react much more positively. They welcome Sherwood's palpable success; their optimism is reflected in the generally positive mood of business journals. What causes this polarization between managers and social scientists? Values as much as theory.

Critical social scientists have long drawn theoretical parallels between prisons and modern organizations, most forcefully Foucault (1977), and have no difficulty in explaining high degrees of centralized control which organizations may exert over their members. (See Dandeker 1990; Friedman 1977; Braverman 1974. Also Giddens 1985, 183–4; Bosquet 1971; Pollard 1965; Mellossi and Pavarini 1981 and Rule 1973.) To social scientists, *Sherwoods* may be theoretically troubling because tight control co-exists with a very high degree of autonomy and citizen-like freedom for members. If there is an analogy with penal institutions, it is with the open prison. (See the discussion of Sewell and Wilkinson 1992, below, and Höpfl in Gowler et al. 1993.)

The social scientists find *Sherwoods* theoretically uncanny because it manages to reconcile the value of individual freedom (which Foucault was fond of) with the imperative of collective control (which he mistrusted). On the other hand, managers are perplexed by the social scientists: what's wrong with an organization that is growing, profitable and meets the needs of customers and suppliers?

In this chapter, through a description of *Sherwoods'* managers, their language and descriptions of the organization, we explore what it *is* about the organization that enables it to avoid conflict and to acquire a seamless quality. But we also raise *ought* questions for discussion – is *Sherwoods* a good model to be emulated, and in what senses, 'good'? What values are represented here, and which have been lost? Managers may also be wondering why some social scientists despair of the insuperable messiness of most social systems and yet recoil from effectively problem-free organization where it exists!

Total Control: the 'Is' and the 'Ought'

The researchers were involved with *Sherwoods* for a considerable period of intensive interviewing and observation. Managers often proudly stated that

it was 'no ordinary company you know'. Indeed there are no significant
conflicts of interests, no conflicting practices, 'no secrets' within its
management structure. The organization is complete. There are no 'inside
tracks', certainly no inter-generational conflict between established leaders
and Young Turks. There are no fundamental differences of opinion between
levels and divisions, no plotting, no coups; no strife. The company's external
relationships are also characterized by cooperation, reciprocity and shared
purpose. The company promises, and largely delivers, organization without
conflict.

First the '*ought*'. The reader's moral response, their feelings, about
Sherwoods, will be determined by what they value. This organization is
thoughtful, environmentally and ethically self-conscious, profitable and
highly motivating. It produces useful goods and services to the highest
standards in numerous markets – industry standards which it has set. In
keeping with Japanese practice, *Sherwoods* encourages its suppliers to sell
to direct competitors, in order to strengthen the several highly competitive
industries which it operates in. Problem-solving advice is offered to
suppliers who are in difficulties. It never cuts suppliers out without ample
warning. No decision is taken without careful, reasoned and plausible
justification. The company is the antithesis of 'short-termism'. Excellence is
pursued in a vigorous, systematic, determined and successful way.

If you value these qualities (as managers tend to), then *Sherwoods* is as
close to the ideal firm as it is possible to be. This would be the most obvious
conclusion to draw from the evidence below. Managers can reasonably
claim that 'No one has ever done badly out of *Sherwoods*'. Weber would
have asked, 'What about other values?'

A conservative might be attracted to the order and stability built into
Sherwood's structure – although he or she will be baffled by the lack of a
status hierarchy, the open management system and the absence of coercion
(below). But the value of order and harmony are more of a challenge to at
least three other Western ethical frameworks. *Libertarians* value individual
freedom of thought, creativity, and action; 'entrepreneurial' originality;
free markets in capital and labour. *Social democrats* seek social justice,
through a social contract which strikes a kind of balance between conflicting
interests. *Marxists* still value fraternity and equality above all.

To each of these, *Sherwoods* is problematic. For example, although
Sherwoods insists that members speak their minds, it does not recruit
entrepreneurs and individualists. Individualism is eschewed. *Sherwoods*
rejects professional judgement as an adequate basis for decision making,
seeking *corporate* judgement. And *Sherwoods'* markets are carefully
nurtured and managed. Taken together, there is enough here to make
libertarians uneasy. *Sherwoods* directly contributes to solving many public
problems not discussed here. This might please the anti-state libertarian, but
the social democrat would be suspicious of the claim that what's good for
Sherwoods is good for the public. (Though they'd be hard-pressed to refute
the company's utilitarian claims.) Finally, the company fulfils Gouldner's

vision of 'nightmare Marxism' (Gouldner 1980) – a nightmare, not because the company operates satanic mills but because the company *solves* most of the problems of capitalism within the framework of private social relations. *Sherwoods* is not a crisis-ridden, dehumanizing, crushing, enterprise; it does not beg the need for collectivist control to establish a broader social purpose. *Sherwoods* represents a Marxist nightmare, because it delivers much of what a Marxist would want to have, without first having developed the hoped-for signs of contradiction and cracking which would supposedly send it towards the 'transition to socialism'.

While liberals, social democrats and Marxists will have *different* objections to *Sherwoods'* way of doing business, the overall absence of conflict will perplex all three. A reader who subscribes to any of these three values systems must also, knowingly or unknowingly, adopt one of three corresponding models of how the world works. Despite differing fundamentally, these models of the world all predict (albeit different kinds of) conflict. In other words, if you adopt any combination of the values of liberty, fraternity and equality, then you have to expect and tolerate varying degrees of conflict as inevitable and normal. To a liberal and social democrat, competition and conflict are signs that the system is working as it *ought* to, and for Marxists, that the system is at least operating as predicted. Conflict between individuals, groups, professions, and working- and capitalist classes, is to be expected because these categories presuppose conflicting subjective or objective interests: market rivalry between economic agents; clashes of individuality; professional rivalry and protectionism, tests-of-strength between owners and employees.

There is no need to elaborate these models here. They can be summed up by the truism that 'the pursuit of conflicting interests leads to conflicting pursuits'. This chapter will argue that *Sherwoods* is conflict-free because it takes care of, or redefines conceivable needs and interests – anticipating, representing, pre-empting and, therefore, incorporating them into its strategy. It does much more than mind its own business. By taking care of these interests, it avoids the conflicts which 'underlie' them.

Interest pre-emption secures a good deal of control and stability for the company. This leads us straight into the second main question (an '*is*' – type of question). How is control brought about? This case is significant because it permits an exploration of the most encompassing forms of control. Not control by force or coercive means; not simple instrumental control, nor 'Panoptic' control – the detailed observation of compartmentalized individuals from a central vantage point – Foucault's all-seeing central office. Individuals spend more time observing each other and thinking carefully about their next step, than they spend being observed from the centre.

Nor is this case about control secured by winning commitment by granting *individual* responsible autonomy. Here individuals exercise their autonomy within the limits imposed by a clearly *shared*, evolving consensus about what to do. At *Sherwoods*, nothing of importance is left to individuals. On the contrary, this case concerns the much more effective control secured through inclusion in the process of control itself. No manager is debarred from taking part in decisions on the basis of inadequate seniority. *Sherwoods* is an 'equal status' organization. Inclusion and total involvement mean that control is *total*-itarian yet unobtrusive.

This chapter will focus on how this is brought about, in terms of day-to-day practice. What distinguishes *Sherwoods* is its thoroughgoing management culture and symbolism. 'Culture' is used here in the sense of a shared everyday ideology, not the unconvincing imagery contrived by senior managers to captivate subordinates. The culture of an organization is its *broadly accepted* 'way of doing things around here'. The open culture at *Sherwoods*, though centrally inspired, is successful because it is enacted at all managerial levels. As a manager said, although it is difficult for an individual to pinpoint where a decision had been taken, nevertheless everybody felt 'involved all the time in everything'.

Control and Consent

Sherwoods is a wholly-owned European subsidiary of a global multi-product firm. It turns over more than £800m per year and is capital intensive. This private corporation has tended to avoid traumatic restructuring. Like many Japanese companies, *Sherwoods* has a very 'flat hierarchy'. Participation is not simply welcomed by the owners, it is expected. Status differences are minimized and all managers, workers and the owners clock in and share common facilities. Openness was identified as the key reason for the absence of departmental and generational conspiracies. 'Subversive discussions cannot go on behind closed doors', explained a manager. Open manage-ment and equal status are apparent in managerial work. *Ad hoc* impromptu discussion is pervasive, formality absent.

Owners make unannounced visits to the plants and wander around under the protective anonymity of the company uniform. Appointments to the top four management 'sectors' have to be owner-approved 'at least by repu-tation', while Sector 3's and above are 'personally known to the owners'. The owners are noted for being direct to a degree that would not be permitted among their managers. They 'break off conversations abruptly' . . . 'jangle keys and loose change in their pockets'. European managers observe that '[the owners] . . . don't have the trappings of wealth and all the profits get ploughed back in. They don't even pay themselves as much as others in the organization.' They are 'workaholic'. Fifteen minutes into a lunch break they'll exclaim 'Right, let's get back to work!'. 'They're a hundred per cent devoted to the business' and 'they clearly enjoy it – the sense of power.' 'They are not playboys.' 'They'll drive [cars] hired from Hertz rather than Rolls-Royces.' They stay in cheap hotels. 'Methodism gone mad.'

The owners have a Western approach to asset performance ('beating the hell out of your assets'), but have a Japanese preference for long-term growth and low dividends. As a result, said the personnel director, ' . . everybody was keen to see the company grow'. The nominal (reinvested) rate of return stood at nearly 30 per cent per annum (*sic.*) at the time of research. Variance from financial targets elicits feverish activity to 'get them right'. Low returns in one week could mean a salary cut of up to 60 per cent for senior managers; 'at a stroke, . . . it tended to get people focusing their attention . . . married with [the idea] that "we're all in the same boat, so let's all pull together".' There is 'meticulous attention to cash and credit control'.

Twenty-four hour, seven-day, four-shift operation was introduced in 1964. Automated production systems have been consistently among the world's fastest. The company was quick to contract out 'peripheral' functions. Managers share their determination to keep plant utilization as high as is possible, short of jeopardizing 'competitiveness and growth'. This demand for uninterrupted utilization contributes to *Sherwoods'* phobia about unions. High returns also demand critically low levels of buffer stocks, some synchronous supply of raw materials and the minimum of work-in-progress, demanding in turn very careful scrutiny of suppliers and distributors. With barely an hour's worth of some raw materials in stock, constant re-supply is critical. Any failures by suppliers and distributors would have rapid and drastic consequences. Managers must exert progressively more 'up stream and downstream control'. Now familiar as just-in-time (JIT) manufacturing, and total quality management (TQM), *Sherwoods* have spent 30 years ensuring continuity of supply. Excepting planned maintenance, machine cleaning, and one or two days each year for holidays, production has continued uninterrupted, seven days per week, since the early sixties.

Distributors and suppliers are monitored to the extent that *Sherwoods* intervenes in financial, organizational, and technical matters. Attentiveness and vigilance lead to 'a tendency to overreact, but we don't get caught'. Pretty well everything is under review.

Suppliers' product and process innovations have been instigated by *Sherwoods'*, who have also had an influence on appointments to major suppliers' senior management. This derives partly from *Sherwoods'* adoption of JIT manufacture. But the absence of 'internal boundaries' associated with open management also reflects in the externally unbounded nature of the organization.

> We're good at manufacturing and marketing, so we leave distribution to others . . Its very difficult for us not to run their show . . . we do investigate contractors in great detail, including their management structure and strength. Many of our suppliers think we know more about them than they do! In some cases we've asked them to put up the prices! We have had suppliers ask us for help, and we've stuck an accountant in and it's worked. It gives us a very strong position.

One supplier admitted to having conceded dual management of his company to *Sherwoods*. He offered a somewhat defensive justification, making stilted use of *Sherwoods* distinctive terminology. In dealing with other firms he preferred to purchase purely on the basis of narrow short-term commercial criteria. But the relationship with *Sherwoods* 'is different'. Two *Sherwoods* Sector 5 managers were observed negotiating (I'm okay, you're okay fashion) with this supplier's managing director and Board (representing a large multi-national branch-plant). Shirt-sleeved, informal, but frank, *Sherwoods* applied 'free speech' and 'equal status' to the older, conservative directors. (The negotiation had been 'role-played' in advance.) *Sherwoods'* stamina was evident. The suppliers' impediments of status distinction and stiff protocol seemed to slow them down against *Sherwoods'* self-styled 'Olympic runners'. At the close, the directors asked *Sherwoods* to dictate a checklist of what they had agreed. Speaking slowly, patiently repeating, so that the directors could write them down, *Sherwoods'* middle managers included the reminder that the suppliers had agreed to replace their works manager.

'Good Relations' are constantly sought after and maintained. Managers can provide ready off-the-cuff accounts of the company's approach. Thus,

> One of the messages we give out might be on the assonance of industry, the public and the legislature, helping each other along the road . . . [It's a case of an] *altruistic ulterior* motive . . . [We've] always tried to be . . . considerate. (emphasis added)

A global attitude survey tested some 6,000 managers' understanding of the philosophy to ensure that it has been absorbed by all divisions, 'using the language of today'. In practice, 'good relations' is found to be a plausible principle and it has been widely invoked 'to manage a [wide range] of vagaries' – in very imaginative ways.

Control and Consent: Knocking the Corners off Shopfloor Politics

In the early sixties there were attempts to unionize *Sherwoods'* European plants. There was a series of spontaneous walkouts. *Sherwoods* sought to avoid confrontation. Before the unions could capitalize on unrest and launch official recruitment drives, company-run consultative systems were in place. This undermined unionization because union activists tended to get elected to the committees. Concessions were made, giving credibility to the new system.

Once on the committees, the activists were entrusted with 'top secret information', not to be divulged to the shopfloor. This had a disarming effect. Trust was engendered, while the sanction of dismissal for 'unauthorized disclosure' remained. Having regained the initiative, the company was able to alter the shopfloor mood and avoid unionization.

The committee system was still in place for widespread consultation during several rounds of high automation in the mid-1980s. Management has retained consistent control of each investment round, averting clashes with the shopfloor. Committee agendas and terms of reference were set by management, and by this time employee representatives were more likely to have been nominated according to their 'likely contribution' than elected from the shopfloor. *Sherwoods* succeeded in cutting workforces, offering privileged grades and job enrichment to remaining workers, effecting several hundred job-losses over a ten-year period, substantially without opposition.

Job enrichment and semi-autonomous group working gave the shopfloor responsibility for functions which formerly belonged to technicians and supervisors. A notice-board display at the smallest of five UK plants indicated that inter-work-group competition placed Red Shift (the 'Shit Hot Shift') at the top, not only in terms of absenteeism (zero days lost over two years) and production (quality and quantity), but also at the top of local inter-factory sports leagues.

Workers are not encouraged to be deferential. During a research visit an inspection cover blew off a feed line. While one worker closed the valve, a second roundly criticized the plant manager for not having ensured that maintenance was carried out properly as previously agreed; the manager 'owned-up' straightaway and apologized. Workers gathered, telling the manager that his apologies were not really good enough: it should not have been allowed to happen; he'd been 'warned before'.

Vigilant work-group 'coordinators' are testing the degree of autonomy that any group can safely be allowed to have. The effect should be subtle: '. . . if he [the work group coordinator] uses it properly, he can control the group without actually seeming to do so'. A concern persists: 'The key problem is – do they have more short-term loyalty to the [work] group or to the company?' Nevertheless the company has preserved managerial authority, prevented unionization, and raised worker morale and productivity. Managers are justified in arguing that they have been successful. With the decline in shopfloor volatility, interest in the consultative committees declined, replaced with monthly 'wash-down meetings'.

Control and Consent: Knocking the Corners off Managerial Politics

Much of the thoroughness of the organization, and the prime focus of this chapter, has to do with the way it 'knocks the corners off' its managers. As with the shopfloor, openness brings control.

An individual's capacity to cooperate openly is established at the outset. (Most managerial recruits are graduates and postgraduates, a good proportion being from old universities.) For appointments at Sector 5 (there are six sectors) the personnel department consults widely to establish characteristics that colleagues wish to see in an appointee. A circular is drawn up on which comments are invited from several interested managers in all departments. An open decision is made on the agreed characteristics and an appropriate interview schedule is drawn up.

The 'assessment centre' is tested in advance to establish the significance of each conceivable answer to each question. Candidates are 'put through the sheep dip'. The results of the customized questionnaire are factorized to identify the subject's dominant styles and eccentric answers. In group exercises opinions close to, and deviating from, the consensus are also collected. The recruitment manager argues that the company has developed this method as far as any in Europe.

However, information on candidate characteristics 'is not used more than twelve months afterwards', he explained, 'because after that time the organization is beginning to make a personality, and people will change enormously'. Through the procedures they tended to 'get people who are similar to yourself, and you finish up by creating the people you have rapport with'. Under open management, it should be noted, rapport is essential. New managers are trained in negotiating skills through courses lasting between one and six days. These include the use of video for the analysis of performances. Under an open management regime, negotiating skills are indispensable because all tasks involve negotiating with other managers.

Control and Consent: Lateral Careers

Individual ambition is harnessed in a variety of ways; this is attempted by all organizations, of course, but not usually achieved so fully, nor without significant clashes and conflicts. At *Sherwoods*, task groups are constantly broken and remade because the company encourages managers to take novel, *ad hoc* career pathways (though again, this is not unique to *Sherwoods*). An increasingly important part of 'knocking the corners off' is to promote across functions, especially at higher levels. Senior managers are put through, and *seek*, radical changes of function. Transfers between functions, for example between marketing, commercial, personnel and manufacturing functions are common. They are a condition for senior promotions. Consequently, senior managers and directors do not face subversive professional allegiances. Instead, managers have a career interest in job switching. The personnel director explained why they had increased managerial rotation:

> I felt we needed to encourage businessmen, and as we talked it through in the Strategy Meetings, we decided people should have opportunities with other jobs: there'd be less risk in promoting that manager. We have told people, "you'll have to get multi-disciplined and the earlier you do it the better . . ."

Broad cross-divisional experience helps to 'knock the corners off' individuals, and divisional rivalries. Patronage is abolished. Managers are detached from their subordinates and strive towards the wider organizational purpose. Cooperation and competitiveness have been welded together, while individualism and professional allegiance are held in check. A manager pointed out, 'this company can't afford entrepreneurs, the wildcat'. He added, 'I don't like specialists, they're dangerous.' The managing director saw the threat thus:

> . . . the people below you are more expert than you – so from time to time you have to act against expert advice. When a senior manager says that he's the expert, then I know he's not really a manager . . . The . . . company breeds people who

will react to a situation with a long-run view. They like certain types of individual. Hard-nosed bastards don't get on.

He had been presented with 'expert' marketing advice on prices, that is *professional* advice, he emphasized. He had rejected this out of hand, without examining its merits. He stressed that decisions needed to be taken across divisional boundaries, so that all gains and penalties could be thoroughly examined. For instance, an increase in demand should only be stimulated if the purchasing, production and distribution implications could all be handled, and only if the personnel department generated the appropriate level of workforce incentive. Decisions had to be coherent and compatible in every sense. Individual expert advice was unlikely to meet this requirement, he explained; therefore, professional decision making was ruled out.

Said another manager:

> . . . people compete in this outfit – you're not going to get on if you haven't a competitive drive. There is the danger of by wanting to be an achiever, going against the company's ends. But you can see in the attitude survey that there's a lot of loyalty to the company . . . there was the legend of [one of the owners] 'God Himself', who kicked down a door because he wanted more frantic interrelating.

While 'people aggressively measure themselves against other people', to be promoted 'you all have to help each other out'.

The involvement of managers in reasoned decisions on their own fate also contributes to consent. It is not unusual for organizations to employ review procedures, but *Sherwoods'* are unusually well developed and taken to their logical conclusion. As elsewhere, 'measurement criteria' for well-defined 'effectiveness areas' (job descriptions) are specified in terms of corporate management objectives. Each element of the 'scaler's' report is subdivided into more detailed parts. The manager, at the beginning of the appraisal periods, 'sits down' with his scaler to codify his tasks for the year ahead. At the end of the year, manager and scaler reckon up the credits and debits. Each manager is a guardian for the sector below. None of this is novel.

However the system also operates in reverse: junior managers are free to evaluate the performance of their nominal superiors – right up to board level. They have recast directors' job descriptions and openly initiated 'sideways moves' by directors with their full participation and consent. Openness thus means that there are no sinecures here: appraisal clearly operates upwards, downwards and sideways, reinforcing departmental and vertical coherence.

The scalar process extends to managers who 'separate' from the company altogether. Managers are keen to point to amicable separations, which they support 'good-relations'-fashion, with business advice and generous start-up loans. Managers are not 'sacked'.

The sense in which *Sherwoods* is an open organization should now be apparent. It should be clear that openness and control are compatible; control at *Sherwoods* operates on the basis of openness. The corner-stone of the system is 'free speech', which 'knocks corners off politics'. As one manager pointed out: 'We have *open* conflict all the time. There's no *subversive* conflict.' Another explained:

> 'We can criticize each other without fear : we're our own policemen. I can talk to the MD when I want to. That sort of access is probably the most advantageous thing of all.'

As pointed out earlier, the owners are anxious to foster 'frantic interrelating', this being expressed in open plan offices. But local managers have elaborated on this. For example, through 'TTs':

> We set Team Talks as opposed to 'boss and guy'. It knocks all the corners off politics. We've done TT's for years. Having to justify your objectives openly is a very cleansing process – you can't say I'm doing it 'cos I hate that bastard over there! At any time at least half a dozen are going on . . .

Another manager suggested that the pace of work among the 'Olympic runners' contributed to this abolition of managerial politics. Speaking quickly, as if to emphasise the point, he explained:

> . . . conflicts get ground up on this, they aren't really allowed to exist. Efficiency . . ., you just get on with it. And in that situation you've not really got time . . . [draws breath] . . . Conflict is burnt out by the situation itself. Conflicts have no time to flourish, and of course you can talk to people.

Managers were often at a loss to explain where authority for particular decisions lay, let alone recall who had inspired them. Decisions, then, are organic and spontaneous, rather than contrived and imposed. As another manager said, 'When something changes, everybody will be thinking that way in any case. The whole mentality will be tilted in that direction.'

The intensity of *Sherwoods'* organizational life is not immediately apparent; indeed managers appear composed and relaxed. However, there is a great deal of collective movement here. A useful analogy might be the progress of a major river: there is massive, cumulative, unobtrusive momentum.

It was clear that *Sherwoods* managers are consummate negotiators. Over the period of observation, no raised voices were ever noted; instead there was quiet and polite 'consultation'. Respondents were often interrupted by offers of help on the internal telephone system; sometimes these addressed problems that the recipient was not aware of.

Although individualism is not welcomed here, *individuality* is recognized. Personalities are meticulously accounted for: 'Knowing who you are as a personality is very important,' said one manager, adding, 'the company spends a lot of time on developing inter-personal skills.'

It seems that open management is successful because managers enjoy the *presence* of their own *selves* 'at work' within it. Managers are, therefore, not alienated in any conventional sense. But the system is nevertheless *absorbing*. This is not easy to describe. The system absorbs the individual in proportion to the individual's absorption of the system.

Equality is essential in an organization based on task sharing and cooperation. Status hierarchies may mark differences in 'office' (position), while the status of persons remains equal. This may be connected to the Puritan view that status hierarchies are this-worldly and profane, that hierarchies have no real standing in the next world, and that souls are equal. It is probable that puritanism enters the owners' thinking.

Although a small minority, a couple of managers did confess that their involvement remained partial. For them a degree of superficiality was necessary in order to maintain harmonious relations. The training officer put it this way:

> We teach for internal negotiating among managers. You become someone who is seen to be helpful and work in a team. It's a kind of calculated thing, helpfulness. Sometimes you catch yourself asking the same 'friendly question' twice.

Some thought that superficiality obviated inter-functional differences. Lower level managers do need to possess some specialist (professional) skills and have 'specialist personalities'. For example: 'Commercial will try to develop the impression that they are hard to do business with; Personnel makes the guy feel good in himself; R & D, now they are *very serious.*' (original ironic emphasis).

'Frantic interrelating' may demand that some managers adopt different apparent personalities when dealing with lower specialists. For instance, a systems analyst, whose work brings him into contact with many departments says, 'We peddle our mathematical skills, but with soft shoes on. We pride ourselves on knowing when not to use it.' He explained he resorted to conscious use of the 'OK Corral' (You okay/me okay).

To the extent that a minority was conscious of using deliberate techniques, then their absorption into the organization remained incomplete. Total absorption by an organization would be marked by losing sight of the way it worked – as in religious cults for example. But there is one much more revealing exception.

The research departments employ highly qualified engineers and technicians. The technical demands of their work precludes job rotation with other functions. The result is that a quite separate organizational culture has developed, with a different language. As one engineer put it, 'Open Plan? I'm just not that sort of person!'; 'Don't get taken in by all this stuff' and 'I'm here because of golden handcuffs . . . they pay me too well!' It was an engineer who called it 'Methodism gone mad'.

Summary and Discussion: Non-organization

The central feature of this organization is that it is both an open system and yet achieves unusually complete control. There is little scope for privacy. Managers have been active in bringing this about. 'We are our *own* policemen' (emphasis added). They are not passive 'cogs in a machine'. The owners don't want them to behave mechanically. Anti-bureaucratic, relatively undifferentiated, this is not an *organ*-ization of discrete parts.

This degree of control is exceptional: the institutionalization of cooperation; the exorcism of politics through 'cleansing' 'free speech', job rotation between functions for managers – 'safer promotions', and through keeping the characteristics of new recruits within known and agreed parameters – the 'sheep dip'. *Sherwoods* is a somewhat *total*-itarian system, not in a coercive sense, but strictly because, engineers excepted, it is *total*. Several of its officers reported that when they first came, they thought *Sherwoods* 'a bit funny', but that they 'see it as natural now'.

The accepted lack of privacy precludes serious dissent. Criticism is encouraged, but only within bounds. Excepting the unchallenged, strategic rules on asset utilization, open management and good relations, day-to-day restrictions are set by the evolving collective conscience of the organization itself. Control does not have a specific location. Everybody is 'central' but each has several others within their gaze, and everybody is clearly observed by many others. Each is central both as an agent and in terms of the encircling attention of co-agents.

Attentiveness is probably the best summary of the way *Sherwoods* works. In any organization there are dividing lines and points of censure. But few would devote the attention that *Sherwoods* gives to happy 'separations', or to the obsessive degree of quality and supply control. Subtle scrutiny keeps managers alert.

The language is interesting; there is a mixture of semi-military and semi-religious symbols. Military symbols include workforce 'de-briefings' and 'wash-down meetings' (decontamination?); in external relations they 'hit the right people', 'identify our allies' and keep a 'low profile' as necessary. The sales staff constitute a 'field force'; the company induction film is 'shown to the troops', and so on. These gung-ho terms are used in many organizations. but the frequency of military and religious usage marks *Sherwoods* out.

Quasi-religious terms such as the 'cleansing process', 'mission', 'separation', the 'good news' about business, the 'sheep dip' (baptism), are also part of the everyday vocabulary. Is it reasonable to think of 'equal status' in terms of religious equality – 'Methodism gone mad' before 'God Himself'. Could it be that because religious and military commands are forceful imperatives, that they lend themselves to the language of control?

Is *Sherwoods* an anomaly? Sewell and Wilkinson have argued that *visibility* is an essential feature of JIT/TQM systems. Just-in-time removes buffer stocks, exposes bottlenecks and weaknesses. Defects cannot be hidden. 'At the UK Nissan plant' Sewell argues, 'surveillance includes a "Neighbourhood-Watch System" (described by a manager as a system for "employee peer surveillance" . . . at [Peugeot] there is even less ambiguity . . . at its [Ryton Plant] the shop-floor is divided up into specific zones explicitly labelled "Surveillance Areas"' (Sewell and Wilkinson 1992: 280; see also Slaughter 1987). Electronic surveillance of the performance of work-teams – an effective centralized, real-time filing system – further underlines the 'peer pressure being brought to bear on individuals within the team . . . In other words', Sewell continues, 'JIT/TQM regimes . . . put the collective ingenuity of labour to work on behalf of capital' (Sewell and Wilkinson 1992: 281).

Sherwoods' collectivism (and in-corporating behaviour) is typical of Japanese management, based on mutual 'interest structuring' within and beyond the business. And like archetypal Japanese firms, it has 'flat hierarchies' and a quiescent workforce. Although *Sherwoods* is worth comparing with Japanese-style management, there are differences. *Sherwood's* emphasis on good relations and its reluctance to borrow were evolved in order to minimize the influence of governments and banks; whereas comparable Japanese firms maintain long-standing and deep relations with their bankers and with the national government (via MITI).

To what extent has it been, or could it be, copied? There is an intellectual push towards this model: recent thinking in management theory aims to encourage much of what *Sherwoods* has already achieved – to invest meaning in business; to confer spirituality on the organization; to generate a mission (for cases, see *Dragon*, the journal of the Standing Conference on Corporate Culture and Symbolism). Like *Sherwoods*, several academics advocate the deliberate management of organizational cultures (for example Denison 1990; Barney 1986; Kilmann et al. 1985). Others have, like *Sherwoods*, shown sensitivity for what Berg termed 'emotional structures' in work and organizations (Berg 1979; Evans and Blase 1984). Company attempts to elicit 'deep-acting', authenticity and personal commitment from their workforce have been noted (discussed critically by Hochschild 1983). There is, therefore, an intellectual shift which acknowledges, and mostly favours many of the *tendencies* found at Sherwoods. There is disagreement on whether or not these tendencies might have thrown up distinctly new, 'post-Fordist', arrangements (see Piore and Sabel 1984, and Sabel's various recent works; also see the debate in Gilbert et al. 1992). But *Sherwoods* surely deserves classifying as a *post-bureaucratic* form of industrial organization.

What features would have to be taken into account in forecasting the extent to which *Sherwoods* might be copied? Wider social systems? In corporatist societies such as Japan, which has set itself, and realized, a series of collectively-agreed social transformations and global economic objectives – total, coherent systems of managerial control, like *Sherwood's*, make sense. But in, say, the UK a strong mid-Victorian separation between the public and the private, and an English sense of propriety and social distance, renders a management philosophy which equates the status of the worker, the manager and owner, and equates private aims with the public good as *Sherwoods* does, will be treated cautiously. We have argued that individualism is incompatible with this type of organization – as the scepticism of *Sherwoods'* engineers indicated.

Financial structures? How much does *Sherwoods'* long-standing and distinctive management system and culture depend on the company's financial stability in private hands? It could be argued that the short-term paybacks demanded by typical institutional shareholders in large manufacturing firms, cause regular structural upheavals which militate against stable management systems of any kind – let alone 'total' systems like *Sherwoods*.

Yet *Sherwoods'* commercial success, the fact that the parent company has reproduced similar systems in the USA, Western and Eastern Europe, in Latin America, East Asia and in the Antipodes, in urban and in rural settings, and, perhaps, the general spread of JIT/TQM, each suggest the scope for a coherent alternative to conventional bureaucratic organization.

References

Bailey, J. (1988) *Pessimism*. London: Routledge.

Barney, J.B. (1986) 'Organisational Culture: Can it be a source of sustained competitive advantage?', in *Academy of Management Review*, 11(3).

Berg, P-O. (1979) *Emotional Structures in Organisations*. Lund: Studentlitteratur.

Bosquet, M. (1971) 'The Prison Factory', *New Left Review*, 67: 23–34.

Braverman, H. (1974) *Labour and Monopoly Capital: The Degradation of Work in the Twentieth Century*. New York and London: Monthly Review Press.

Dandeker, C. (1990) *Surveillance, Power and Modernity*. Cambridge: Polity Press.

Denison, D.R. (1990) *Corporate Culture and Organisational Effectiveness*. New York: Chichester.

Evans, M.K. and Blase, J.J. (1984) 'The Moral Perspective: The Life Insurance Agent as Guardian of the Family Ethic'. Paper to the First Standing Conference on Organisational Symbolism and Corporate Culture, Lund, Sweden, June.

Foucault, M. (1977) *Discipline and Punish: the Birth of the Prison*. London: Allen Lane.

Friedman, A. (1977) *Capital and Labour: Class Struggle at Work and Monopoly Capitalism*. London: Macmillan.

Giddens, A. (1985) *The Nation-State and Violence*. Cambridge: Polity Press.

Gilbert, N. Burrows, R. and Pollert, A. (eds) (1992) *Fordism and Flexibility: Divisions and Change*. Basingstoke: Macmillan.

Gouldner, A. (1980) *The Two Marxisms: Contradictions and Anomalies in the Development of Theory*. Basingstoke: Macmillan.

Gowler, D., Legge, K. and Clegg, C., (eds) (2nd edn) (1993) *Case Studies in Organisational Behaviour and Human Resource Management*. London: Paul Chapman.

Hochschild, A.R. (1983) *The Managed Heart: Commercialisation of Human Feeling*. University of California Press.

Kilmann, R.H., Saxton, M.J. and Serpa, R. (eds) (1985) *Gaining Control of the Corporate Culture*. San Francisco: Jossey-Bass.

Mellossi, D. and Pavarini, M. (1981) *The Prison and the Factory*. London: Macmillan.

Piore, M.J. and Sabel, C.F. (1984) *The Second Industrial Divide*. New York: Basic Books.

Pollard, S. (1965) *The Genesis of Modern Management*. London: Arnold.

Rule, J.B. (1973) *Private Lives and Public Surveillance*. London: Allen and Lane.

Salaman, G. (1979) *Work Resistance and Control*. London: Longman.

Sewell, G. and Wilkinson, B. (1992) 'Someone to Watch Over Me: Surveillance, Discipline and the Just-in-Time Labour Process', *Sociology*, 26(2): 271–89.

Slaughter, J. (1987) 'The Team Concept in the US Auto Industry: Implications for Unions'. Paper to the ERU Conference on the Japanisation of British Industry, Cardiff, 20–22 September.

Weber, M. (1949) *The Methodology of the Social Sciences*. New York: Free Press of Glencoe.

PART 4

CONSUMING AND CONSTRUCTING IDENTITY

9

Marketing, or the Anthropology of Consumption

Robert Grafton Small

In societies like our own, where organizations and markets shape each other, and industrially generated goods and services are the means and bases of ordinary existence, any problem of management or structure may be similarly widespread in its significance – and for the same reasons – as consumer well-being. Not that the two are easily, or even reasonably, separated, given the implicit permeability and interpenetration of organizational boundaries and common analytical categories in cultures where any sense of community is unthinkable outside the mass production of order and the ordering of mass production. These processes of interplay and exchange are, however, not usually considered across their normal range, either by analysts of consumer behaviour or by the individual consumers whose unsatisfied desires and unspent incomes habitually underpin this trade, in the market-place and in all the attendant industries designed, built and managed on commercial terms.

A New Approach to Demand

Traditional theorists of marketing such as Gist (1971) and Kotler (1985) construct their analyses of organizational or group behaviour on the basis of 'commendable' decisions made for reasons of profit or some other economic variable and not 'emotional' choices which draw their small worth from aspects of design or the psychology of ownership. Lip service may be paid to disciplines like anthropology or sociology, yet no real effort is ever made to discuss either marketing managers, or the society they seek to serve, in anything approaching these terms. The importance of this criticism is

underwritten by, but not restricted to, Douglas and Isherwood's work on
the understanding of consumer behaviour demonstrated by marketing
professionals (1980: 177).

Douglas and Isherwood argue that while the consumption criterion used
by market researchers might yield a good idea of what social class is like if
it were used systematically, such a definition of social class could not then
be used to explain consumption behaviour. Nevertheless, the authors
maintain, this circular explanation of consumer behaviour is often heard.
In recognizing the potential of market research, Douglas and Isherwood
accept the importance of consumption as a societal habit yet make no
allowances for the marketing function, which is stripped of its pretensions
and treated as the practice of applied economics. Their reasoning is
devastatingly simple. They claim demand theory to be at the centre – even
the origins – of economics as a discipline, yet 200 years of thought on the
subject have produced little to show *why* people want goods.

Sahlins sees this ignorance as the result of an inherent deficiency in
economic theories of consumption (1976: 166–7). He feels that in judging
the creation and movement of goods by nothing more than pecuniary
qualities, or exchange values, the cultural codes of concrete properties
which govern 'utility' are overlooked and what is actually produced
remains necessarily inexplicable. According to Sahlins, a concentration on
exchange values allows production to be seen as no more than the
precipitate of an enlightened rationality and an objectively-achieved
economic structure, rather than a social and cultural design of persons and
goods.

Sahlins' critique offers a fair indication of the methodological demands
resulting from an investigation of the management of consumption for,
clearly, marketing may no longer be considered as an occupation which, as
Wilensky and Lebeaux suggest, is practised almost totally in an institutional setting (1965: 8). Admittedly the parallel argument, that such an
evaluation has therefore to be set in both societal and cultural terms, is not
without its own difficulties. The following brief case in illustration of this
would also justify Anderson's claim (1982) that marketing theorists have
never come to terms with the organizational realities of which industrial
relations are just a part.

The implications of this apparent lack of interest can be gathered from a
case which considerably weakens Kotler's (1976: 79) definition of marketing as '*human activity directed at satisfying needs and wants through
exchange processes*'. The incident referred to (Linstead 1984: 21–6)
occurred at a bakery in the North of England where the workers in
question were making fruit mince pies for the early Christmas market:

> the work force frequently *did* show considerable concern for its [the product's]
> quality. They would often fail to pack pies which they considered to be
> sub-standard. Once a pie was made, the policy according to supervision was
> 'pack as much as we can get away with', although quality control had other ideas.
> When confused about what to pack and what not to pack, and finding the

criterion of whether they would like to purchase the goods themselves in such a condition of no help, [and] caught between supervision and quality control, they resorted to the management for arbitration. 'Who pays your wages?' said Jack [the Production Manager], 'Me or Quality?'

While the relationship between marketing, industrial relations, and production management may well be less than equitable, it is also apparent that each of these managerial disciplines is, in some way, intended to control the creation and movement of goods. However, the bakery workers represent a more curious imbalance in the cultural design of persons and produce for, although they have some sense of themselves as both producers and consumers of mince pies, they can be shown to have little or no control over the production of goods that are supposedly directed at satisfying their own needs and wants.

These circumstances are clearly beyond 'rational' economic decision making on at least two grounds. First, the idea of the *solitary* consumer as the basis of economic consumption is shown to be spurious in the extreme as this is obviously *communal* decision making. Secondly, it is equally apparent that consumption goes on before and long after the market-place transaction has finished.

Anthropology: the New Approach

Given factors such as these, Douglas and Isherwood (1980) argue for an anthropological definition of consumption which applies equally to industrial and tribal societies, perhaps based on the fate of material objects after their sale or those aspects of consumption that are voluntary rather than compelled. Significantly, Douglas and Isherwood also point out that anthropology assumes goods are needed for making cultural categories visible and stable, as well as providing subsistence. Furthermore, they claim, every anthropologist accounts for a tribe by studying the material parts of a culture. As Lévi-Strauss notes, commodities are goods for thinking (1976: 21).

The following echo of this insight comes from a Northern factory which is perhaps best-known for the construction of rolling chassis for lorries and buses (Grafton-Small 1985). A machinist, who specialized in the making of crankshafts, was astonished to hear the quality control department describe the tolerances on his work as 'all over the place, too bloody big one day, too small the next'. The machinist had his own gauges and callipers which were checked at least twice a day against those of the quality control department and still the rejection rate ran at between one in twenty and one in thirty pieces of work. The puzzled machinist eventually visited the quality control department where he explained his position. He then suggested that the master callipers might themselves be checked. The chill provoked by this impudence became icy when the machinist made reference to a sticker on the gauges which said, quite simply, 'to be checked: 3rd May'. It was, by then, late August. The problem was finally resolved by the Works Manager. He felt compelled to give the machinist a severe warning because he would accept neither the strictures of the quality control department nor any share of the blame for the poor goods being made. The machinist was obviously a 'troublemaker'. That all the gauges and callipers in the quality control department were then replaced was, of course, purely coincidental; while this apparently unscheduled refurbishment may have been a chance occurrence, no one offered anything approaching an apology to the machinist.

The incident is important for a number of reasons. It shows that, in contemporary society, everyday culture is in part negotiated through the medium of work; that understandings of goods and tools such as machinery are continually redefined in terms of each other; and, finally, that any attempt to assess consumption and consumers in terms of their own culture is bound to include these considerations. It is also clear from this incident that whatever the meaning or value of a product, it is *inherently unstable* and difficult to grasp – it flows and drifts. Meaning or value, say Douglas and Isherwood, is fixed by negotiated and agreed rituals and rationalities. This rationality makes sense of the environment to the point where time and space are socially defined – witness the disputed gauges and the overdue calibration – and the goods therein are anchored to human, hence social, purposes. Above all, it must be stressed that the value of goods comes from exchange which means social structures and values are inseparable. Similarly, no human being and therefore no consumer exists except in the terms of his or her own culture.

A New Approach: the Broad Implications

Nevertheless, as the mince pies and the crankshafts show, there are imbalances within these determinations that reflect the nature of contemporary society by showing some to be more capable than others of assigning values to products. This line of argument can be usefully developed on two fronts. The first, as Sahlins is quick to point out, is the way in which the importance of work, as a measure of an individual's contribution to society, is culturally determined (1974: 51–2). Logically, the second development concerns the distribution of whatever has been produced by these efforts.

Ramond (1974) reasons that because anthropologists themselves have not yet assimilated their own prodigious fieldwork, any hypotheses for marketing will have to come by analogy with specific anthropological cases. Mauss is far bolder (1974: 3). He states that markets are a human phenomenon familiar to every known society, whether 'primitive' or 'developed', and fundamental to morality and economy as well as social life. This alone raises serious doubts about Gist's notion of marketing as a necessary development of 'sophisticated' economies (1971: 55). Mauss also suggests that the North American Indian's 'potlach', a gathering which involves feasting and competing for social status by giving gifts or 'shaking hands in a material way', is not exactly alien to our own society.

If Mauss, or indeed Ramond, is justified in approaching consumption in this way, the concept of economic rationality is further undermined. It says nothing anywhere about any general objective of the individual whereas anthropology assumes that making sense of the world involves interpreting the world as sensible, and that consumption goods are not merely messages but the system of sensibility itself. Consider, then, the bakery workers and their mince pies when Eco (1979: 21) shows how three fundamental cultural phenomena – the economic exchange of goods, the kinship element in social institutions, and the use of objects to transform relations between people and nature – may be seen as *communicative* on an individual and collective basis.

Any such understanding has a number of severe repercussions, including the disappearance of the Cartesian dichotomy between physical and psychic experience which McLuhan (McLuhan and Fiore 1967: 63) embodies in his view of electronics and technology as extensions of our central nervous systems. So, in industrial societies, buses built around the exemplary crankshafts exist primarily to provide a schedule of mass-produced speed and movement without similar sensations of work, effort or disturbance. We acknowledge and reinforce this reordering of our being by machine – and more – every time we stand at a bus stop, yet neither the everyday expectations and obligations of public transport nor the networks of employment and investment behind the provision of each vehicle can readily be inferred from the stop or the range of possibilities we assume when purchasing a ticket. Thus, once it is accepted that all goods carry meaning but no one item does so by itself, it becomes apparent that consumers' understanding of goods must lie *in the relations between all the goods available to them*. Moreover, ignoring the falsely abstract individual and concentrating on society as a whole is still notably problematical for there is a range of analytical techniques to consider.

These techniques, or methodologies, can be broadly described as falling into three basic categories: *phenomenology*, which assumes the world is socially constructed by individual actions and interactions; *ethnomethodology*, which presupposes the social nature of reality and concentrates on the formulation of acceptable interpretations and behaviour; and *structuralism*, which focuses upon the social processing of knowledge and thereby transcends any approach which begins with the individual. All of these techniques are alike in that they assume meaning to be embedded and never easily picked up from the surface of a communication or an item. Current circumstances are taken to be similarly dependent upon 'prior' or established patterns and cultural rules emerge accordingly, as a possible pattern of meanings inherited from the immediate past which also enables the fulfilment of contemporary interpretable needs.

In turn, these appetites develop their own significance, once allowance is made for the apparently contradictory tendencies in contemporary society toward organizational fragmentation (Lyotard 1984; Bauman 1992) and order based on the celebration of difference rather than uniformity, meaning multiplicities of subcultures (Hebdige 1979), and the development of consumption accordingly. Indeed, this pervasive and knowing use of goods in deliberately skilful yet arcane ways represents a further set of challenges to any prospective inquirer. Bearing in mind the traditional, largely academic concerns – with anthropologists and similar investigators 'going native' in circumstances where cultural boundaries are both indistinct and a major topic of interest – the pursuit of 'objectivity' or a 'neutral' viewpoint is itself surely somewhat perverse, especially when all concerned are ultimately members of the same social order. In the case of the machinist, for example, the debate over meaning may concern everything from ethical issues (like those of the bakery or the instance of a crisp [potato chip] factory to be discussed below) to interpretations of industrial process, which the analyst is aware of, while excluding our deeper preconceptions about people and nature implicit in the unquestioning acceptance of mass-produced buses as means of transport.

Market researchers make crude attempts to exploit this relationship but the question remains: *how can economic theory incorporate implicit knowledge?* Douglas and Isherwood (1980) suggest ignoring the explicit function of goods and looking at the way these goods are used to classify the world. So, for example, the consumption of mass-produced rather than home-made mince pies is not only an explicit celebration of a certain sort of Christmas, but also a tacit acknowledgement of changes in contemporary understandings of domesticity and marriage. Thus, women are no longer expected, or perhaps no longer able, to stay at home since they too must go out to work – in places such as the bakery. This is a vital step in clarifying theories of demand, for although intelligible as individuals, consumers are more readily appreciated in terms of the company they keep and the assumptions implicit in the goods they trade. The resultant culture may be appreciated on the basis of at least two criteria: the extent of these assumptions or prior patterns and the degree of their acceptance or integration.

In the finite social world, these implicit meanings act as a means of mutual reinforcement which allows any mass-produced item to be seen as part of an information system and, equally, to be an important means of gaining or maintaining control over ways in which the world is interpreted (Grafton-Small 1985). On this basis, the concerns of the pastry-makers and the machinist may be seen as a direct reflection of the division of labour (Grafton-Small and Linstead 1985). Even so, in advocating an anthropology of consumption, certain points must be understood clearly. First, any 'rational' or socially and culturally acceptable individual must always seek to make sense of the world in terms of his or her own understanding, a process which requires other people to affirm and stabilize their mutual interpretation.

Secondly, these social constructions of reality depend upon goods as a medium for consensus. Consider the incidents involving the mince pies and the buses. While their production and their quality may well be disputed, no one at the bakery or the machine shop is seriously suggesting that society should abandon either industrially-baked pastries as a form of food or buses as a form of transport. Thirdly, as the same disputes also demonstrated, the parties to these negotiations were not equal; some were clearly more powerful than others and this meant that their understanding of goods tended to hold sway. Indeed, the question of power is vital to the attraction and assertion of meanings of goods in general, for consumers will always be involved in negotiations like these whenever they consider a product or a purchase. The interplay of social structure and industrial activity has one other significant implication. It is now apparent that characteristics such as product quality can no longer be assessed in absolute terms. The cases concerning the mince pies and the crankshafts have shown that worthy, if not superior, understandings of a given product may be dismissed for reasons far beyond those of mere economic rationality.

In sum, shared culture means exchanging goods – a process which involves the infiltration, usurpation and protection of social systems and interpretative schemes – for, ultimately, consumption is about the holding and focusing of power. In cultural terms, the less powerful have lower access to, and less opportunity of, exploiting a narrower range of goods and therefore fewer implicit possibilities. Braverman, for one, is not surprised (1974: 14). He believes that the pressures of poverty, unemployment and want have not been eliminated, but rather that these have been supplemented by a discontent which cannot be touched by providing more prosperity and jobs because these are the very things that produced the discontent in the first place.

There are grounds for this, according to Douglas and Isherwood (1980: 176–83), who proclaim the importance of trading in everyday goods as a means of defining a given community and maintaining its internal divisions. Mishan (1969: 28–32) agrees that the bases of consumer society, namely the exercise of individual choice and the pursuit of personal well-being, are encoded in a social and symbolic order very much akin to the one unearthed by Wolfe (1982: 80), but Mishan differs by claiming the order is misconceived. With the poor and the powerless again in mind, Mishan reasons (1969: 67) that if an ever-expanding industrial economy were really to the benefit of all those who participate in it, more would surely be done to distribute a part of the resultant wealth to people at the bottom of the heap, wherever they might be.

His, and their, pre-emptive disappointment in the prospect of 'trickle-down economics' may be explained to some extent by Douglas and Isherwood's (1980: 93–4) assertion that, in communities like our own, the rich and the poor may coexist and even, on occasion, share the same goods, yet in practice the two populations manage their various understandings of the world in dramatically different ways. Moreover, members of these and all the intervening social strata commonly use whatever goods they buy or reject as means of excluding one another, just as surely as the same trade signals their own belonging to a given group or culture. In more immediate terms, Bauman (1992: 111–12) believes that instead of engaging the rest of society in the role of producers, as was historically the case, capital tends to engage them in the role of consumers. Thus the recent long-running UK recession, manifested in massive and stable unemployment, is not a latter-day edition of the 1930s, the suffering of the new poor being unmatched by the tribulations of their richer contemporaries. These two nations do nevertheless coexist because of the interplay between 'seduction' and 'repression' as means of reproducing social control and integration.

In brief, 'seduction' is grounded in life-skills which cannot be employed effectively without commercial mediation and 'repression' acknowledges a growing penetration of the 'private' sphere by normative regulations pushed to the extreme – hence a loss of individual power and autonomy in an increasingly-comprehensive, market-centred world. Equally, as practised consumers, we understand there is a third population (the destitute) concerned in these affairs, yet remarkably – given their obvious physical presence – they are defined by exclusion. If our commonsensical restructuring of society and the law are a matter of power in the market-place, the destitute must be unequal partners in any agreement, be it straight coercion or ever-so-seductive.

As we have seen at the industrial bakery, and will again in discussing a Merseyside crisp factory, the desire for satisfying consumer goods is mediated not only by income, though these commonplace foodstuffs are hardly expensive, but by other deeper-lying factors. The point here is that markets are themselves socially constituted responses to effective demand, and exist solely as forms and forums of exchange. Consequently, access to trade on an individual basis reflects and reinforces other inequalities – the fruit pie workers discovering to their own surprise how their immediate concerns as would-be consumers could so easily be overturned by their chronic needs for employment and community. Equally, the crisp-friers 'filching for friendship' may be understood as a locally-determined counter to both the constraints of the labour market and the wider mores implicit in any resultant 'legitimate' trade.

Legitimacy and economy in turn, have various interpretations according to the buyers and sellers involved yet, as O'Shaughnessy (1988: 12) explains, from within a more traditional view of exchange, the pace and scope of these processes of redefinition are notoriously skewed in favour of whoever dominates the market – which consumers rarely do for long. It follows, too, as the unemployed learn to their cost and the poor tend to discover if their wants are at all unusual, that desire alone or with little means is not enough to justify inclusion in the traffic of daily commerce, so these people are excluded as a matter of course or else driven to increasingly marginal forms of trade.

While this issue is considered elsewhere in terms of everyday exchange (Grafton-Small 1993), the ethical undertow is significant. In effect, those of us who can continue as consumers do so knowing the propriety of our culture makes such a 'design of persons and goods' unavoidable. The same is true for the wider, much-heralded environmental costs of, for example, the motor industry and all its attendant capital investments in roads, services and jobs. When, as is currently the case, the UK economy is not performing entirely as we might wish, even the government is concerned to revitalize trade by increasing sales of, hence our commitment to, these selfsame goods and services. The moral imperatives of our social structure and its maintenance mean such a course is not only predictable, given our history, but unquestionable.

These resolutions of apparently conflicting interests are utterly character-istic of societies like our own that depend on industrial artefacts, interwoven with designs of persons and goods which owe their form to unconventional notions of trade and the market-place. For instance, Henry (1979: 102), in a study of 'pilferage' and theft from organizations, finds circumstances that can be taken to indicate the use of produce to define both legitimate society and behaviour as well as the contrary. Simply put, the manufacture of goods at a specified rate, price and quantity represents a major part of any system of mass consumption and those who trade their labour do so for the means to continue as consumers, albeit meagrely. Consequently, each item of production which is made to managerial requirements is an underwriting of the given order and an indication of employees' complicity in their own belittlement. Henry (1979: 98) argues that the 'hidden economy' is not hierarchical, like the legitimate market-based culture, but stratified, so 'pilferage' is restricted by social grouping, as recognized equals trade with each other.

This is, above all, an exchange of gifts signifying friendship and not the search for profit, so existing patterns of community and kinship are accepted and built upon. Such a reading of unofficial trade is reinforced by the view, among 'pilferers', that a certain amount of extra items or value from work is 'fair' or part of the wage bargain – an unwritten but assumed form of 'perks'. While perhaps representing a less than ideal form of behaviour, 'pilferage' also seems to be outside the normal understandings of deviancy maintained at a Merseyside crisp factory well-known for its range of products. Conversation with one of the managers (Grafton-Small 1985) showed that certain flavours suffered disproportionately from 'pilferage', senior execu-tives being of the opinion that the relevant shifts must be 'completely bent'. It was later decided, as sales returns of new brands came in from all over the country, that the shopfloor had conducted a little 'in-house' market research and everyone wanted the same flavours. The shifts concerned with their manufacture were simply catering for as many as possible. Some of the warehousemen were also being less than rigorous.

Some weeks later, when working on a short contract frying potatoes for a rival company whose plant had burned down, a friend from the Merseyside factory declared that the crisps in question were not worth stealing. So they were left alone. This may be taken as an unwillingness to give away something of no value, though the well-established networks of trade and reciprocity implicit in the previous long-running, hence legitimated, shop-floor sampling procedures and the shortness of the commercial contract, suggest the lack of value is relative rather than absolute. Moreover, the risks and the produce involved do not justify the social and organizational disruptions of opening and closing the factory's informal trading systems to accommodate these alien but hardly unknown goods. It might also be a matter of an outside contract getting special supervisory attention. Deservedly so, as deviant groups form, among other things, an escape mechanism for those who only appear to acknowledge social norms by transgressing them.

A case in point (Taylor 1986: 20–1) involves Les, a professional criminal with 'a terrible antipathy' to Frankie Vaughan, the cabaret singer.

> Anyway, Les went along to see Frankie Vaughan at the Talk of the Town – the club which used to stand on the same site as the new Hippodrome club, at the corner of Charing Cross Road and Leicester Square. He wasn't there however, to bone up on the lyrics of 'Green Door' or 'Give me the Moonlight', but to work out a plan. He noticed on his visit that during the famous 'Moonlight' number Frankie Vaughan came down off the stage and walked along shaking hands with all the punters sitting at tables by the stage. All you had to do to get a handshake was to be near the front and put out your hand. That was good enough for Les. Next night he was back again. Ringside seat. Champagne. But instead of the ice-bucket staying at the table, it went down at the side of Les' chair, and throughout the second half of Frankie's act – 20 mintues – Les sat stoically with his naked right hand buried up to the wrist in packed ice. Come the 'Moonlight' number and the star, microphone in left hand, took his customary stroll. Across the stage, down the steps, round the front of the auditorium.
>   'Give me a shady nook', he warbled, learning over to shake hands with the delighted customers. 'And leave the rest to me' – and there was Les on his feet in front of him, face beaming with pleasure, right hand eagerly extended. 'Give me a shady . . . Aaargh . . . nook . . .' And then it was back on stage for the last number, which had to be sung to an audience which must have seemed to consist of little else but Les's broad, expansive, victorious smile.

While Les' criminality may be seen as an adherence to another, equally coherent kinship group engineered through a parallel form of trade, his willingness to deviate from the social standards implied by the 'Talk of the Town' is indeed remarkable. The club, the behaviour of the 'star attraction', and even the seating arrangements are all reflections of the understanding that those who give of themselves as well as of their money shall be rewarded for the implicit significance of their additional contribution to the furtherance of a commonly-agreed entertainment. Les not only ignores the corollary, that those who disagree do not trade in this way, but chooses exactly the same form of trade as medium for his explicitly antipathetical comment on the significance of this communal 'bricolage' and, by implication, the community of 'honest bricoleurs' (Lévi-Strauss, 1976).

Thus majority opinions are shown to be so as contrary understandings are made explicit and minority tastes are presented in a way which allows a recognition of dissenters. The important point is that socially-constructed and tolerated deviancy mirrors society at large, and criminal theft from organizations is – like legitimate trade – for profit to support its own hierarchies (Hobbs 1989). 'Pilferage' may be argued as contrary to this order in that those who transgress group understandings of 'fairness' for reasons of profit are heavily sanctioned for having brought their social system into disrepute. The punishment involved is generally one of exposure to the legitimate trading hierarchies, leading to either dismissal or prosecution. The criminal 'pilferer' has offended not only the morality of his immediate social circle but also embarrassed the host organization.

The managers of the latter are demonstrably reluctant to clamp down on 'pilfering' within their businesses for as long as it is a self-regulating practice. That there is 'pilferage' at every level of commercial hierarchies, with concomitant notions of 'fairness' or appropriate worth, may go some way to explaining the anger raised by attempts to reduce 'pilferage' to below these limits. Those under investigation are being slighted in that such an evaluation states fairly clearly their inability to manage friendships, make personal judgements, or justify trust. There are, too, the imbalances of power (Perrow 1970: 59; Clegg 1975: 46) through which, for managers, 'pilferage' may be codified as tax deductible perquisites and so legitimate in a way which serves to underwrite the continuing 'pilferage' by their subordinates. This is not to deny that managers also indulge in more traditional forms of 'pilferage'. As Davis dryly observes (1973: 172), the negotiation of legitimacy would appear to form an important part of any means of distributing products.

We all recognize as much from our habitual dealings with each other, and with the world in general, just as we appreciate the interplays of goods and morality which not only enable our everyday lives but also emerge reinforced from our complete immersion in consumption as a means of maintaining our entire social fabric. So it is that the present UK government can seem to condone the sale of arms and weapons technology to Iraq, among many – all to the massive benefit of British industry, meaning ourselves – yet come to grief solely when these munitions are used in actual terms rather than as metaphors of well-regulated commercial order. This may indeed be the darker side of the wealth and the possibilities created by industrialized life in market-based societies, though, as recent UK recessions demonstrate, there are others. It is worth remembering, then, that we as consumers can neither escape the ambiguities of our own culture nor take any active part in it without exercising forms of power and moral judgement over each other, forms which surely demand we each be responsible for the ethics of our communal exchange.

References

Anderson, P. (1982) 'Marketing, Strategic Planning and the Theory of the Firm', *Journal of Marketing*, 46, Spring, 15–26.
Bauman, Z. (1992) *Intimations of Postmodernity*. London: Routledge.

Braverman, H. (1974) *Labor and Monopoly Capital*. New York: Monthly Review Press.
Clegg, S. (1975) *Power, Rule and Domination*. London: Routledge & Kegan Paul.
Davis, J. (1973) 'Forms and Norms: The Economy of Social Relations', *Man*, 8: 159–76.
Douglas, M. and Isherwood, B. (1980) *The World of Goods: Towards an Anthropology of Consumption*. Harmondsworth: Penguin.
Eco, U. (1979) *A Theory of Semiotics*. Bloomington: Midland Books/Indiana University Press.
Gist, R.R. (1971) *Marketing and Society: A Conceptual Introduction*. New York: Holt Rinehart Winston.
Grafton-Small, R. (1985) 'Marketing Managers: The Evocation and Structure of Socially Negotiated Meaning', PhD thesis, Sheffield City Polytechnic (now Sheffield Hallam University).
Grafton Small, R. (1993) 'Morality and the Marketplace: An Everyday Story of Consumer Ethics', *European Journal of Marketing Symposium*, Warwick, July.
Grafton-Small, R. and Linstead, S.A. (1985) 'Bricks and Bricolage: Deconstructing Corporate Image in Stone and Story', *Dragon*, 1(1): 8–27.
Hebdige, D. (1979) *Subculture: the meaning of style*. London: Methuen.
Henry, S. (1979) *The Hidden Economy*. Oxford: Martin Robertson.
Hobbs, D. (1989) *Doing the Business*. Oxford: Oxford University Press.
Kotler, P. (1976) *Marketing Management: Analysis, Planning and Control*. (3rd edn) Englewood Cliffs: Prentice-Hall.
Kotler, P. (1980) *Marketing Management: Analysis, Planning and Control*. (4th edn) Englewood Cliffs: Prentice-Hall.
Kotler, P. (1985) *Marketing Management: Analysis, Planning and Control*. (5th edn) Englewood Cliffs: Prentice-Hall.
Lévi-Strauss, C. (1976) *The Savage Mind*. London: Weidenfeld & Nicolson.
Linstead, S.A. (1984) 'The Bloody Worm: Problems in the Production of a Consulting Report', *Personnel Review*, 13(1): 21–6.
Lyotard, J.F. (1984) *The Postmodern Condition*. Manchester University Press.
McLuhan, M. and Fiore, Q. (1967) *The Medium is the Massage*. Harmondsworth: Penguin.
Mauss, M. (1974) *The Gift: Forms and Functions of Exchange in Archaic Societies*. London: Routledge & Kegan Paul.
Mishan, E. (1969) *The Costs of Economic Growth*. Harmondsworth: Penguin.
O'Shaughnessy, J. (1988) *Competitive Marketing: A Strategic Approach*. London: Unwin Hyman.
Perrow, C. (1970) 'Departmental Power', in M.N. Zald (ed.) *Power in Organizations*. Nashville: Vanderbilt University Press. pp. 59–89.
Ramond, C. (1974) *The Art of Using Science in Marketing*. New York: Harper and Row.
Sahlins, M. (1974) *Stone Age Economics*. London: Tavistock Publications.
Sahlins, M. (1976) *Culture and Practical Reason*. Chicago: University of Chicago Press.
Taylor, L. (1986) *The Underworld*. London: Counterpoint, Unwin Paperbacks.
Wilensky, H.L. and Lebeaux, C.N. (1965) *Industrial Society and Society Welfare*. Toronto: Free Press/Collier Macmillan.
Wolfe, T. (1982) *From Bauhaus to Our House*. London: Jonathan Cape.

10

Autobiographical Acts and Organizational Identities

Barbara Czarniawska-Joerges

The legitimacy crisis of the welfare state, especially acute in Sweden and called by outside observers 'the demise of the Swedish model', has very palpable consequences for many public administration organizations. It is perhaps most visible in that constellation of public organizations which for years served as the symbol of the welfare state: the social insurance offices. The ways in which insurance offices experience and try to cope with the crisis is the subject of this chapter. An assumed analogy between the notions of personal identity and organizational identities permits the exploration of the legitimacy crisis in terms of an identity crisis. Following this, the construction of individual identity, understood as a modern institution, is conceptualized in terms of autobiographical acts. In this light, the multiple autopresentations constructed within the insurance constellation can be seen as a case of an autobiography 'written' by a collective actor. These autobiographical acts involve a creative re-writing of the history adapted to a purpose at hand, a skilful use of rhetorical devices, an internal fight over the right to write the final version of common history and other power games which both dynamize and debilitate the ongoing quest for identity.

The Narrative of the Self: On Individual and Organizational Identities

For some time the notion of individual identity has attracted much attention in the social sciences, but it has recently been problematized by the conception of it as a modern institution, a phenomenon situated in time and place (MacIntyre, 1981; Meyer, 1986). Such a perspective stands in contrast to essentialist definitions of identity as a 'true self' which can be exhibited or hidden, but which has fixed properties that can be demonstrated and described from the 'outside'. This latter understanding of identity, exemplified by many authors within psychology and sociology, has also found its way into organization studies (see, for example, Albert and Whetten 1985; Dutton and Dukerich 1991; Alvesson and Björkman 1992).

A non-essentialist definition would have it that identity is achieved

through actual performances. People do not exhibit personal characteristics, they perform them according to a code specific for a time and a place.
Close to Goffman's concept of the self (Goffman 1959), this definition goes
further in refusing the idea of static, formal and ritualized 'roles' to take on;
roles are created when performed. Such a way of conceiving of individual
identity reaches back, most likely, to George H. Mead's negation of the
dualism of 'self-society' (Baldwin 1986; Bruner 1990). It comes to its full expression in the conception of the *relational self*, as elaborated in Gergen's
notion of the 'saturated self' (1991) and Davies and Harré's (1991) discussion of *positioning*: the self is produced in actual conversations – past and
present. The notion of the relational self rejects the romantic perspective of
the actor and the positivist perspective of the structure in order to claim that
both actors (that is, their identities) and structures are constructed and reconstructed in action, which, in turn influenced by past performances, is
always prone to change – even if by virtue of simple error.[1]

But how are individual identities performed? After all, it is dangerously
easy to replace the essentialism of 'actors' and 'structures' with that of
'action', and arrive at a concept of action which 'speaks for itself' telling the
true identity of the individual to whoever witnesses it. As Giddens (1991: 76)
points out, 'self-identity . . . presumes a narrative: the narrative of the self is
made explicit'. Bruner (1990: 109) introduces the notion of 'Self as story
teller'. Thus, within a repertoire accessible within a given temporal and spa-
tial context, actors tell stories and spectators evaluate them according to the
(performative) criteria of the autobiographic genre (on how a modern identity is narrated, see Meyer 1986; Brown 1989; Giddens 1991).

Within those assumed rules of the genre also lies a legitimate twist of the
plot which came into being in the nineteenth century – although then limited
to biographies of upper class women – and which by the time of late modernity had become a 'natural' part of human existence: an 'identity crisis' (Giddens 1991). An individual re-making her or his identity still has to follow
what is perceived as a correct storyline in a given type of autobiography and
yet create the impression of a profound change. The story must remain the
same, or at least recognizable, since continuity is an important textual strategy of the modern identity (Brown 1989; Davies and Harré 1991), but the
spectators must still be impressed by change.

A caveat must be given here: identity narratives come not only as
coherent stories of an explicitly autobiographical kind (indicated by the pro-
noun 'I' or 'we'). Before a familiar audience, and especially in the context of
an organization, many rhetorical performances aimed at identity creation
are autobiographical only implicitly. One can tell 'the true story of oneself'
only so many times, but all utterances involve an element of positioning (or
could be read as such) – that is, establishing one's identity *vis-à-vis* others or
imposing it on others within a given storyline. As Davies and Harré point
out, people tend to organize conversations around two parallel modes of expression: 'the "logic" of the ostensible topic and the story lines which are
embedded in fragments of the participants' autobiographies' (1991: 48).

There is one more step to be taken before we can see how this is done: I shall have to defend the analogy between individual and organizational identities, an analogy which is often taken for granted (Czarniawska-Joerges 1994). Actually, there are very good reasons why this is so. In the first place, the notion of the individual is an institutional myth developed within rational theories of choice, and so close to the core of organizational analysis (Meyer et al. 1987). As a result, organizations are anthropomorphized to reinforce the impression of accountability central to modern culture (Douglas 1992; Gowler and Legge, Chapter 2 in this volume) and, I may add, to the notion of narrated identities. Individuality as an institution belongs with two other modern institutions: the state and the market. The invention of the 'legal person', which makes organizations accountable both as citizens and as consumers and producers, is a necessary link between the three and is reflected in everyday language.

Thus organizations (actors emerging from interlocking patterns of action) narrate their identity to the spectators which, in late modernity, are other organizations. What are legitimate narration rules; that is, which narratives gain acceptance?

Modern Identity

What is 'an identity'? must be the opening question. According to Vytautas Kavolis (quoted by R.H. Brown 1989), the concept of identity encompasses three elements:

- an overall *coherence* between the individual's experience and the way this experience is expressed;
- a memory – on the part of the individual and others – of a *continuity* in the course of the individual's life; and
- a conscious but not excessive *commitment* to the manner in which the individual understands and deals with his or her 'self'.

Kavolis evokes the concepts of opinion, memory and self-awareness, thus emphasizing that it is not the identity as an essence but the impression of an identity which a self-narrative achieves or fails to achieve. Hence the peculiarity of modern identity: although it is formulated in and through interactions, the impression that it aims to achieve is that it is individual – that is, independent of other people's reactions. If we contrast modern identity with, for example, that typical of heroic societies, we notice that the latter was predicated on the basis of the individual's relations with the community, and not, as with modern identity, on the basis of the individual's own life history (MacIntyre 1990).

There are further specifications of a modern identity which make it differ from any other: *self-respect*, *efficiency*, *autonomy* (internal locus of control in psychological terms) and *flexibility*, that is, the absence of a long-term commitment to one particular object (Meyer 1986). These can again be contrasted with, for example, traditional Roman virtues: *pietas* (reverence for the past), *gravitas* (bearing the sacred weight of the past), *dignitas* (a manner worthy of one's task and station) and *constantia* (the faithfulness to tradition: Pitkin 1984). Where modern identity conceives of self as a project, traditional identity compares the self to an already existing blueprint.

If it is useful to treat identity as a narrative, or, more properly speaking, a continuous process of narration where both the narrator and audience formulate, edit, applaud and refuse various elements of the constantly-produced narrative, then the most appropriate literary *genre* is that of autobiography. The analogy lies obviously in the fact that autobiography is a self-narrative of identity but also in autobiography's claim to facticity. Autobiography belongs to literature, but not to fiction.[2]

This is an analogy which works both ways: Elisabeth W. Bruss (1976) presents autobiographies as an institutional way of creating personal identities, thus proposing to see text as action, much as I propose to see action as text:

> All reading (or writing) involves us in choice: we choose to pursue a style or a subject matter, to struggle with or against a design. We also choose, as passive as it all may seem, to take part in an interaction, and it is here that generic labels have their use. The genre does not tell us the style or the construction of a text as much as how we should expect to 'take' that style or mode of construction – what force it should have for us. And this force is derived from a kind of action that text is taken to be. Surrounding any text are implicit contextual conditions, participants involved in transmitting and receiving it, and the nature of these implicit conditions and the roles of the participants affects the status of the information contained in the text. (Bruss 1976: 4)

Genre is a system of action which has become institutionalized and it is recognizable by repetition; its meaning stems from its place within symbolic systems making up literature and culture (and therefore is diacritical, like that of other signs). In the same sense as we characterize modern identity only by contrasting it with non-modern identities, we may see autobiography as a genre acquiring specificity by difference from other genres. Again, we detect an analogy and a connection. A societal institution – individual identity – is similar to but also helped by a literary institution: a genre called autobiography.

This conjecture stems also from observation that modern identity and autobiography emerged at about the same time. Although what Elisabeth Bruss calls 'autobiographical acts' existed as early as the sixteenth and seventeenth centuries, they were considered at the same level as private letters, 'memoirs' and not literature. 'Biography' became a known term after 1680, but 'autobiography' was not coined in England until 1809 (Bruss 1976). After that date the genre began to develop both in relation to, and in difference from, other contemporary genres. And so, for example, the realist novel borrowed from autobiography the strategy of introducing the narrator as a direct observer (the first-hand experience). On the other hand, autobiography discovered that there exist other modes of self-narration than a straightforward one (Lejeune 1989). This growing sophistication apart, it must be pointed out that there are two characteristics of modern identity which make autobiography the most appropriate analogy – its individual and not community-based character, and its orientation towards the future and not the past.

Textual Strategies

Within one and the same genre several textual strategies are accessible (Harari 1979). These can be characterized, for example by the role that is given in text to three personages typical of the genre: an author, a narrator, a character. I shall illustrate these with examples relating to the construction of organizational identity.

One typical strategy is that of an omnipresent author, who claims the responsibility both for the acts reported in the text (and supposedly taking place in 'reality') and for the text itself. This strategy is often taken by the founders and the leaders of big corporations. The text and the world in the text have the same creator and, by the same token, create the author's identity. One could claim that this is the most pure form of autobiography as identity creation, where a person, an organization, and a text all become one (Lejeune 1989). By no means is it, however, the most popular one.

An introduction of a narrator is a common device. There is a person who tells the story, but the story could have been authored by somebody else, although it may be the narrator acting within the text in the role of an author. The distance created gives more room for manipulation: the narrator can praise the author in a way the author could not praise him or herself, but also can distance him or herself if necessary. 'The Self as narrator not only recounts, but justifies' (Bruner 1990: 121). In terms of organizational identity, this strategy opens up many possibilities. A narrator can be, for example, a PR officer who is telling a story of a mighty author – a founder, a CEO. Alternatively, the narrator may be only a sample of a collective author – an organization.

The strategy that is most complex and, therefore, gives most room to a skilful writer is one that introduces a character. Here the possibilities of distancing, identification, and self-reflection are limitless. There is a hierarchy of knowledge: the author knows most and the character least. It is reversed in terms of freedom: the character can be wild but the author must be responsible. The narrator, as the reflexive one, always knows more than the character but can be, temporarily, ignorant of the author's knowledge ('At that time I did not know that the marketing group had already formulated a plan' or even 'that, soon enough, I will come across crucial information in the matter').

The three can be one but they can also separate or form dyadic alliances if needed. In *A Portrait of the Artist as a Young Man*, the mature James Joyce is the narrator, the young James Joyce is the character, while James Joyce, the author, comments on both of them. In such a triad, the narrator is the rhetorician, the character the actor, while the author takes the moral blame or praise – depending on the doings of the other two. Gore Vidal often uses this strategy (for example, in *Julian*). There is an old narrator, a young character, whereas the authorship lies with 'fate' or some divinity, depending on the period of the tale. It can lead to most interesting complications, as illustrated by Eco in his 'A Portrait of the Elder as a Young Pliny' (1990).

Pliny the Younger, in his old age, authors a letter to Tacitus, informing him of his wish to share the true story of the death of his uncle, Roman general and scientist, Pliny the Elder, during the eruption of Vesuvius AD 79. He proceeds to do so by introducing a narrator, who is a young version of himself, telling a story where both young Pliny the Younger and Pliny the Elder are characters. A critical reader, or at least a reader instructed by Eco, soon notices that the narrator has knowledge that he could not have had at the time, knowledge which, in fact, only the old Pliny the Younger as an author can have.

Why, then, did he not tell the story straight – that is, as an old author narrating from memory? Because then Tacitus could become suspicious as to the authenticity of the story, seeing it as cooked or invented by the author – which, of course, it is! This paradoxicality is not unusual: it reveals that narrators are commonly characters created by the author and given special status (reflexive) to increase their credibility.

These *actorial shifting operations* (Latour 1988) are actually easier to perform when creating an organizational identity because of its assumed collective character. Additionally, while the shifting of personal identity might sin against the coherence or continuity requirement or call into doubt the reality claim, narrating organizational identities sails clear from all these dangers. There can be several and different authors (for example, top executives); the narrators can distance themselves at their will, and there is a variety of characters accessible without the danger of producing a schizophrenic impression.

One point should be emphasized, a point at which organizational identity and personal identity are at their closest and at their furthest: an organization cannot legitimately claim autism or a defective 'other-perception' (Bruss 1976). Organizational identity makes sense in relation to the institutions of market and state, and one of them must 'understand it'. By the same token, there is a closeness between autobiography and organizational identity greater than in cases of personal identities. Autobiographies are always apologetic in character, even if the means of achieving an apologetic effect can be very complex and paradoxical. An autobiography can tell a story of wrongs and errors, but it must lead to an exemplary solution. So does organizational identity: it must always be exemplary. While individual persons can spin tales of maladjustment and neuroses, a happy ending is a must for autobiographies of organizations.

What happens if they fail to arrive at a happy ending? Several kinds of failure are possible. One is that particular autobiographies and organizational identities fail within the context of existing institutions, for example when the public refused to accept Exxon's story of the oil pollution caused by the wreck of the *Exxon Valdes* or that of Nestlé concerning their powdered milk exports to Africa. But when failures are more frequent than successes, we may be dealing with failure of an institution: 'autobiography could simply become obsolete if its defining features, such as individual identity, cease to be important for a particular culture' (Bruss 1976: 15). A literary evolution consists of audience demanding new works and new works demanding an audience. Is this not the case for institutional evolution in general? In the present chapter, we shall have an opportunity to see individual failures and to speculate whether institutional transformations are in the offing.

Before we move further, an important caveat must be made. Speaking about 'organizational autobiographies' might imply an association of something final and closed – a 'history of the company', perhaps, written every half-century or so. No doubt such official autobiographies are important, but they might be more fruitfully compared to obituaries rather than to autobiographies, which are 'lives under construction'. The focus of this chapter is on what Bruss calls 'autobiographical acts' and what Bruner, on the personal level, describes as 'an account of what one thinks one did in what settings in what ways for what felt reasons' (1990: 119). We may paraphrase it as an account of what one thinks 'organization' did; where 'one' is a narrator and 'organization' is a character or an author. Such *organizational autobiographical acts* occur constantly in organizational life, but perhaps with special frequency and premeditation in times of challenges and turbulence.

A Constellation in Distress: Swedish Social Insurance and its Identity Crisis

What follows is a story of attempts to re-write organizational identity, not for one but for several organizations: the units which are involved in the field of social insurance in Sweden and which I call a 'constellation' – a grouping within an organizational field.[3] The material used comes from a wider study of two such constellations (Czarniawska-Joerges forthcoming). Let me then begin with a general introduction to the Swedish public sector and the way my study went about describing some of its parts.

The Nature of the Distress

The Swedish Parliament makes decisions which are executed by the majority or coalition government, and further by central agencies. These are in other countries called 'government agencies', but in Sweden they are formally separate from the government. The National Social Insurance Board, one of the characters in the present story, is an example of such an agency.

The next administrative level is the county, where one finds the county council, intermediate offices of some central agencies but also, for instance, hospitals and social insurance. The last level are the local governments in municipalities which are, however, autonomous from central government.

At first glance, this seems a perfectly hierarchical system – a typical state bureaucracy. However, the unique Swedish history of an alliance of the king with the peasants (and against the nobility) is also a history of pronounced initiative and self-help at local level. Three major Swedish institutions – local governments, social insurance offices and savings banks – were born at municipal level and functioned in many respects as horizontal unions rather than hierarchical units. The historical sediments are visible in the remaining federative organs, but also in the fact that it is the municipalities which are the main tax collectors, which makes them much more independent than their formal and legal autonomy would suggest.

The fate of the local actors turned out differently. Local governments remained local and autonomous, although their association does not play the role of a federal government, as in Switzerland for example. Rather, it represents the interests of the local governments as opposed to central government and other organizations; it also distributes information and advice. The savings banks remained a federative organization until recently when, following the fashionable urge to become more 'business-like', they adopted a traditional corporate structure (Forssell 1989). The resources for social insurance became centralized and their administration given to a government agency, but insurance offices, moved up from municipality to county level, remained legally autonomous.

Thus the constellation of organizations under study is composed of the National Social Insurance Board, the Swedish Association of Local Authorities, and social insurance offices at the county level. Social insurance covers medical care, rehabilitation in case of work accidents, and so on for all the citizens of Sweden. Although the resources are administered centrally by a National Social Insurance Board, the activity is carried out by County Social Insurance Offices. The popular movement origins of social insurance are still sedimented in its former federative organ, the Association of Social Insurance Offices, which at the time of the study was not involved in any direct activity connected to insurance, concentrating on the offices themselves (spreading internal information, presenting insurance offices to the public, organizing continuous education, editing a journal, and so on).

A changed political climate in Sweden resulted in a proposed bill to transfer the duty of paying for the first two weeks of sick leave from the social insurance office to the employer. The proposal, dubbed as 'employer's admission', put social insurance offices into a state of panic: after all, dealing with short-time sick leaves had been their main occupation since the advent of the social insurance system in Sweden. According to rough calculations, the change would diminish insurance offices' operations by 25–30 percent –

3,500 to 4,000 employee/years, to use the common measure. What would all these people do if no longer needed?

The panic receded when a government investigation on issues of rehabilitation presented its conclusions. The final report stated that long-term illnesses had increased both in number and in duration, and, in order to diminish the subsequent societal costs, an extensive rehabilitation programme must be activated. The sectors seen as central to this process and expected to collaborate in the Rehabilitation Programme were the social insurance system, labour market actors, and institutions responsible for industrial welfare and medical services. More specifically, social insurance offices were given the responsibility to initiate the cooperation and to coordinate the necessary resources at the county level. The way to construction of a new identity was open. Unsurprisingly, the first step was to re-write the history of social insurance, and this event is the focus of the following interpretation. The material was compiled from observations, interviews, official documents, and other inscriptions of 'autobiographical acts' during the 14 months of the study (for more on method, see Czarniawska-Joerges 1992).

Textual Strategies: The Stock of Actors

As reflected in the chapter title, there is no one autobiography: there are many autobiographical acts, formal and informal, which contradict each other, try to dominate or subvert, and so on. Accordingly, different textual strategies are used. As, however, it is still supposed to be a common autobiography, its central elements must be at least recognizable. Therefore, it is possible to take the stock of actors and see which roles are there to be cast.

There are three categories of narrator: the first is my interlocutors, presenting their versions in a conversation with me, to support one or another story or argument. Often they will strengthen their argument by quoting one of the other categories: writers within social insurance who wrote PR brochures or official histories, and researchers who took the initiative or were invited to study the history of social insurance.

There are basically three central (and collective) characters: the National Social Insurance Board (NSIB), the Association of Social Insurance Offices (ASIO) and County Social Insurance Offices (CSIO). There are, of course, many other characters within the organization field: the representatives of the employees, the Ministry of Social Affairs, and so on, but they are the public and the judges of autobiographical acts.

The role of an author is the most controversial. Historically, and there is complete agreement here, this role was taken by a 'popular movement'. The disagreement – as usual – concerns the present. Some claim that the State has overtaken the authorial role and all other versions are just sentimentality and nostalgia; some others claim that the State has such ambitions, but they are abominable and one must put an end to it; still some others maintain that the original author is still at work. Let us look at different versions and then confront them in a present day's battle for influence.

The ASIO Story

ASIO has almost a monopoly on the autobiographies of Swedish social insurance because it is their task to produce the majority of PR brochures. So here is a concise history of the Swedish social insurance as presented in a glossy brochure called 'Association of Social Insurance Offices. A Presentation'. I translate this history *in extenso* so that, in what follows, I can concentrate on comments and interpretations, and avoid repetition of dates and events.

> The Association was formed in August 1907.
> At the dawn of the twentieth century, sickness pay-offices were the biggest popular movement in Sweden. The formation of a country-wide organization was important not only because a uniform and effective sickness pay-office movement was needed, but also in order to attract public attention to the idea of universal and obligatory insurance against ill health.
> At the beginning there were around 1,000 voluntary, small pay-offices which dealt with infirmities and funerals. Half of them had less than 100 members and their finances were very modest. When the Association came into being, it began the difficult task of organizing and changing structures so that the present-day effective insurance offices could materialize.
> In 1931 a decree recognized sickness pay-offices, which enabled a rationalization of work and led to a better allowance.
> In 1955, obligatory social insurance was introduced. The whole nation was insured and benefits became much better. The recognized offices were changed into common sickness pay-offices.
> In 1962 their name was changed to insurance offices. The appellation 'sickness pay-office' vanished because offices now took care of many other matters – for example, the national old-age pension and national supplementary pension schemes. Since then the offices obtained many new areas of responsibility. During the 1970s these included, for example, payment of allowance advances, dental insurance, work-related disablement insurance and parental insurance. The latter has been expanded in several stages.

The historical presentation begins with a date when the Association was formed but there is no mention whatsoever of even the existence of NSIB. Clearly, the author was and is the popular will, and the two main characters are the offices and their Association. There is no mention of the present crisis, although on other pages (the brochure has eight) there is a list of wishes for the future which includes, among other things, the development of rehabilitation activities.

Personal accounts reflect many more tensions and uncertainties, but the general line is the same. Here is the story as rendered by an executive of the Association:

> The coming into existence of common insurance has its roots in the support which people wanted to have in the first place in cases of infirmity. It originated with guilds, whose members came together to be able to face sickness and infirmity

rather than to be in the hands of fate. This development grew all over the country, and there was always this tendency to cooperate, first at the local level, then at the county level, so that it became clear what advantages came out of such a cooperation. Thus the formation of the Association. Then we witnessed the development of the social security system and the social insurance system, when our Association got quite a different role from, let us say, the Swedish Association of Local Authorities or County Authorities. Today we have social insurance; the NSIB has an important role there as the government's supervisory authority, a leading role within social insurance, if you will, but the Association is formed by the social insurance offices themselves . . .

The offices are autonomous legal persons, they have both local political boards and local social insurance boards which make difficult decisions, very much in accordance with the social insurance tradition as a popular movement. This is also why we consider that we have an advantageous start for this decentralization process which is expected of us: this decentralized attitude permeated our activity since its beginning, this is what our spirit has always been . . . And this tension that accompanies it: the tradition of the popular movement versus the tradition of central authorities, this is also something very characteristic . . .

It is indeed, and not only for the social insurance. This paradox of a very strong tradition of local autonomy and central control permeates everything in the public sector. Some actors, like municipalities, win through it, claiming their decentralized character 'since time immemorial'; some, like state actors, suffer most. The whole issue is debated and twisted, and turned again on the spit of public attention as moved by the mass media.

But declarations alone are not enough; an external ally was found in the person of a historian who, after having studied social insurance in Sweden, came up with three phases: 'solidarity culture' (from the turn of the century until the beginning of prosperity in the 1960s), 'regulation culture' (until now), and 'service culture' (for the future). This was the kind of biography that fitted well with the Association's image: both because it offered an attractive vision of the future, formulated in fashionable 'cultural' terms; and also it made a link between the original culture and the one of the future. Service culture is 'a kind of need-controlled culture, where citizens themselves decide what they really need'.

To be sure, this was not the only version of the history and the future of social insurance in Sweden.

Local Offices

Many people in social insurance offices support the version of the Association in its most important aspects. Here is one voice that emphasizes the popular movement tradition as connected to the workers' movement and opposed to centralized authority:

Social insurance offices, which are legal persons today, originated in recognized sickness pay-offices which were more related to workplaces; every guild had its pay-office whose task it was to save the members' skins, beginning in the nineteenth century. It wasn't until the late 1950s when they were united with the state's office taking care of pensions. So, you see, a people movement tradition was suddenly put together with an administrative tradition, and this battle of

values continues until today: We still feel strongly connected to the workers'
movement and want to be faithful to this idea . . . of serving the common people.
This is why we oppose losing our legal sovereignty and becoming a part of the
state. (Middle County)

Another person presented a history of battles for preserving the offices'
autonomy where the metaphors of identity are very clear. She used a punn-
ing expression which means both 'we became an authority' and 'we were
declared responsible adults'. There was a bitterness to her story, where the
supervisory organ was presented as having deprived insurance offices of
their rights to be a 'person', of their autonomy:

> Don't forget that social insurance offices are not a part of the state, but juridically
> autonomous persons. The fact is, though, that the state budget finances the ad-
> ministration of insurance even if the insurance comes from the employers, but
> there is a state supervisory organ which has the right to prescribe the terms of our
> operations. The end of the 1970s was characterized by a strong centralization and
> it was then that NSIB became our supervisor and started telling us in detail what
> we must do in local offices. They prescribed our operations step by step. But the
> last years have seen a kind of a revolution, there is talk of decentralization and
> deregulation, and consequently we became recognized as being of a sane mind
> again . . . (Middle County, another interlocutor)

Observe the shift in characters. The Author is the same – the popular
movement; the offices are in their place. The Association faded away; a
slightly blurred enemy – the central authority – appeared in the stories.

I was also told that the Association did not always limit itself to writing
about history. Some time before I started my study, the Association openly
questioned NSIB's right to control insurance operations. The main claim
was that the supervisory role concerns the administration of insurance, not
management of insurance offices. The Board made an interpellation to the
government:

> The [Association's] perception did not tally with ours. We think that it is clearly
> said both in the law and in budget bills that NSIB is a management and super-
> vision body for the insurance system and its administration. . . . We have now
> received a very clear answer in the present budget bill which says that NSIB man-
> ages social insurance operations but it did say, also, that we have to take into
> consideration offices' opinions and cooperate with them.

As to the clarity of this, opinions were divided. My interlocutor in Northern County expressed an opinion that the ambiguity remains as it was, only
that the 'Association sings now small and does not dare to take up the
battle again'. He was not very optimistic about future developments,
either:

> The Association is now trying to change its role and to lobby the government and
> the Parliament. They want to represent those interests of the offices which are
> not reflected by the NSIB. I think personally that it is all very frustrating because,
> for us, it simply means many double signals. It would be unjust to blame it on the
> Association; it is how the whole system is organized. To tell you the truth, we

belong to the state. The autonomous standing of the offices is a chimera because we are totally financed by the state.

The last word has not been spoken yet, but it might be interesting to point out that the NSIB are very disappointed with their lack of printing capacity (all PR production is located with the Association). They pointed out many times that the quality of their documents (of which there are thousands of pages – all sent to the offices) is unsatisfactory. In the NSIB's computerization programmes, in contrast, the layout software is given special attention.

NSIB took over the responsibility for training and development which had formerly resided with the Association. If they also succeed in becoming the official narrator, there will be no plural autobiographies anymore.

Tentative Identities in Blurred Organizational Fields

This search for a new identity with old roots can be analysed as a part of a more general attempt to change the public sector in Sweden and to restructure the existing organization fields. The interesting point about this attempt is that the actors are uncertain of their identity, and also that the structures are not given. Not even the NSIB is certain of its identity in the situation where short-term-sick payments will be effected by the employers.

Identities and structures are the result of *structuration* processes. Actors' identities can be created with the help of models and histories, but in practice their relevance is confirmed or rejected in concrete interactions. It is not sufficient to select an attractive identity and then present it. The new (or the old-new) identity must be accepted by the other actors involved, both those who are operating on an established stage with a clear identity (for example, the private sector) and also by others who find themselves in a similar situation. The same applies to structures.

The government's actions have created a new space, a certain amount of freedom, but new rules have not been established. These new rules must be created through action. You can only know what is right or wrong after you have acted (or someone else has). The difference between this process and the trial and error method is that there are no rules to be 'discovered', and no 'referees' who know the answers. When the field has been restructured and the new stage institutionalized, it is highly probable that someone will acquire a new identity as 'referee'. Perhaps it will be the ASIO. This will depend, as usual, both on random factors and on the Association's identity-creation skills.

Although the versions of autobiography differ, they are all created with respect to the rules of a modern identity creation. Coherence, continuity and commitment become the norms to be observed in one's own narration, and the contestable aspects of rival versions. But, in interactions with the world outside, it is efficiency and flexibility which are under scrutiny, thus threatening the other claims – to self-respect and autonomy. Negotiations continue, both inside and outside the constellation, and their crucial point is whether the insurance constellation will be able to produce a believable story of a 'profound change' following the 'identity crisis'.

Processes of this kind obviously involve great risks. On the one hand, the risks are concrete (for example, possible unemployment of many low-qualified women in the offices), while on the other hand, there is considerable risk of public ridicule. The transformation is taking place on stage. The citizens, who want good entertainment without paying too much, are sitting expectantly in the audience along with competitors – who would prefer to see a real fiasco – and press critics – who will be writing their review of what 'actually' happens.

Can any help come from taking the narrative approach? I think so, and in at least two ways. Public sector organizations, like everybody else, are only partly authors of their auto-narrative and the acknowledgement of this fact can widen the understanding of the situation without encouraging fatalism. Second, self-conscious attempts may be made to limit the role of others as authors and expand one's own.

Within this second task, another insight is at hand, encompassed in the difference between a 'search' and a 'quest'. 'Search' has been until now a legitimate term in organization theory, and this might be part of a problem rather than a solution. The notion of 'quest', as used in medieval ballads, did not connote a search for something already adequately defined, like oil or gold.

> It is in the course of the quest and only through encountering and coping with the various particular harms, dangers, temptations and distractions which provide any quest with its episodes and incidents that the goal of the quest is finally to be understood. A quest is always an education both as to the character of that which is sought and in self-knowledge. (MacIntyre 1990: 219)

A search for a new identity, like one for excellence, assumes that such an identity already exists and waits to be discovered. This can be correct only if this new identity is to be authored by somebody else, for example, the private sector. If the public sector wants to remain its own author, then it must embark on a quest – where a new identity will be formed as an autobiography but in accordance with what are legitimate autobiographies of our times. This, however, must be discovered in the process of formulation itself.

References

Albert, S. and Whetten, D. (1985) 'Organizational identity', in L.L. Cummings and B.M. Staw (eds), *Research in Organizational Behavior*. Greenwich, CT: JAI Press. Vol. 7, pp. 263–95.
Alvesson, M. and Björkman, I. (1992) *Organisatorisk identitet*. Lund: Studentlitteratur.
Baldwin, John D. (1986) *George Herbert Mead: A Unifying Theory for Sociology*. Beverly Hills, CA: Sage.
Brown, R.H. (1989) *Social Science as Civic Discourse*. Chicago: University of Chicago Press.
Bruner, J. (1990) *Acts of Meaning*. Cambridge, MA: Harvard University Press.
Bruss, E.W. (1976) *Autobiographical Acts*. Baltimore: Johns Hopkins University Press.
Czarniawska-Joerges, B. (1992) *Exploring Complex Organizations*. Newbury Park: Sage.

Czarniawska-Joerges, B. (1994) 'Narratives of individual organizational identities', in Stan Deetz (ed.), *Communication Yearbook*, 17. Newbury Park, CA: Sage. pp. 193–221.

Czarniawska-Joerges, B. (forthcoming) *Narrating the Organization: Dramas of Institutional Identity*. Chicago: Chicago University Press.

Davies, B. and Harré, R. (1991) 'Positioning: The discursive production of selves', *Journal for the Theory of Social Behaviour*, 20(1): 43–63.

Douglas, Mary (1992) 'Thought style exemplified: the idea of the self', in *Risk and Blame*. London: Routledge. pp. 211–34.

Dutton, J.E. and Dukerich, J.M. (1991) 'Keeping an eye on the mirror: Image and identity in organizational adaptation', *Academy of Management Journal*, 34(3): 517–54.

Eco, U. (1990) *The Limits of Interpretation*. Bloomington, Indiana: University Press.

Forssell, A. (1989) 'How to become modern and businesslike: An attempt to understand the modernization of Swedish Savings Banks', *International Studies of Management and Organization*, 19(3): 32–46.

Gergen K. (1991) *The Saturated Self: Dilemmas of Identity in Contemporary Life*. New York: Basic Books.

Giddens, A. (1991) *Modernity and Self-identity*. Oxford: Polity Press.

Goffman, E. (1959) *The Presentation of Self in Everyday Life*. New York: Doubleday.

Harari, J.V. (ed.) (1979) *Textual Strategies*. Ithaca, NY: Cornell University Press.

Latour, B. (1988) 'A relativistic account of Einstein's relativity', *Social Studies of Science*, 18(1): 3–44.

Lejeune, P. (1989) *On Autobiography*. Minneapolis: University of Minnesota Press.

MacIntyre, A. (1981/1990) *After Virtue*. London: Duckworth.

Meyer, J.W. (1986) 'Myths of socialization and of personality', in T.C. Heller, M. Sosna and D.E. Wellbery (eds), *Reconstructing Individualism*. Stanford, CA: Stanford University Press.

Meyer, John W., Boli, John and Thomas, George M. (1987) 'Ontology and rationalization in the western cultural account', in George M Thomas, John W. Meyer, Francisco O. Ramirez and John Boli (eds) *Institutional Structure: Constituting State, Society and Individual*. Newbury Park: Sage. pp. 12–37.

Pitkin, H. (1984) *Fortune is a Woman*. Berkeley: University of California Press.

Silver, M. and Sabini, J. (1985) 'Feelings and constructions in making a self', in J.K. Gergen and K.E. Davis (eds), *The Social Construction of the Person*. New York: Springer Verlag. pp. 191–201.

Notes

1   This idea of the self as socially constructed – in the interactions between individuals within social worlds relevant for them – usually raises the issue of sincerity. However, as Silver and Sabini convincingly show, 'even sincerity seen as a match between feelings and avowals, requires rules, standards, and even manipulation – the constructed stuff' (1985: 199). What is more, sincerity of self-presentation belongs together with other institutionalized attributes of the modern identity.

2   Needless to say, this distinction is as impossible to maintain in autobiography as everywhere else, but it is the claim that distinguishes a genre, not the complications of the actual praxis.

3   Readers interested in the argument of this chapter might consider collecting all the material concerning the creation of the medical insurance system in the USA – it might make an interesting story in 10 or 20 years' time.

PART 5

CHANGING IDENTITIES

11

Between Managers and the Managed: the Processes of Organizational Transition

Paul Jeffcutt

In the 1960s 'symbolic anthropology' emerged as one of several theoretical movements which challenged older and, to Ortner (1984), 'exhausted' paradigms that had been established in the early development of anthropology as a science of human social organization (see Stocking 1987). 'Symbolic anthropology' explored symbols as the social space in which cultural understanding was interactively contested and formed, challenging established understandings of culture as being located either inside people's heads or as functional derivations of social structure (see Keesing 1974; Ortner 1984). These ideas have shaped a body of work which has been influential both within anthropology and in related areas of the human sciences.

In organization studies (that is, the theory and practice of organization) this influence has particularly been felt through the development of the cross-disciplinary field of organizational culture and symbolism (see Jeffcutt 1993). However, the translation of the work of the two major theorists of 'symbolic anthropology' – Clifford Geertz and Victor Turner – into organization studies does not appear to have occurred in proportions equivalent to their influence in anthropology. Accordingly, while Geertz (1973) became the most widely-cited (and misinterpreted) theoretical source in the early development of the field of organizational culture and symbolism (Ouchi and Wilkins 1985), the work of Turner was comparatively ignored, being most conspicuously cited as a minor methodological influence in an important early paper (Pettigrew 1979).

Although not specifically focused on righting the imbalance, this chapter will consider aspects of the work of Victor Turner in the context of organization studies. Since Turner's work on the process of transition has been particularly influential in anthropology, the chapter will focus on relating his work to contemporary understandings of transition in organization studies. These objectives will be pursued through the consideration of an ethnographic field study of organizational symbolism in which the work of Turner became a significant influence.

The Process of Transition

Turner in one of his later books (1982), considered that his work as a whole had been concerned with the 'anthropology of experience'. This was a focus, which had connected investigations which ranged from ritual and change in African tribal society and medieval religion (1969, 1974) to performance in metropolitan experimental theatre and contemporary politics (1982, 1986). Through this breadth of insightful work in very different contexts, he was developing a major and long-established theme of anthropological concern, the examination of the process of transition in social life. Turner's distinctive contributions to this theme are numerous, but of particular significance are the following:

1 The analysis of the process of transition as a contextualized cultural performance articulated by ritual, ceremony, carnival and story.
2 The understanding of transition as a reflexive, contested and creative process in the restructuring of social order.

To examine the process of transition Turner elaborated and extended an established anthropological analytical frame, that of a rite of passage (Van Gennep 1912), to describe different cycles of social change (see Fig. 11.1).

These elaborations of the process of social change effected a thoroughgoing critique of established anthropological understandings of both transition and cultural performance (for example, Radcliffe-Brown 1952; Gluckman 1965). For Turner, cultural performance was not merely reflecting or maintaining existing social structure, but articulating resources through which social life was made, transformed and remade (that is, in a process of transition). The key phase of this transitional process thus became the central part which Turner described as 'liminal' (that is, betwixt and between). This phase was characterized by uncertainty and ambiguity, in which cultural performance was understood as working with and through this liminality in a reflexive, contested and creative process of remaking the social order.

In organization studies, the massive literature on organizational change and its management has only relatively recently begun to emphasize transitions (see, for example, Johnson 1987). The mainstream of this literature, following Lewin (1951), has been heavily influenced by understandings of organizational change where cultural performance in the process of transition, whether supporting or resisting, typically functioned to maintain or reinforce structural equilibrium (see Trice 1985). Consequently, in organization studies, despite an apparent diversity of strategies for the management of contemporary complexity (see Pascale 1990), mainstream approaches to transition are still dominated by concerns for prescription, linearity and the maintenance of order.

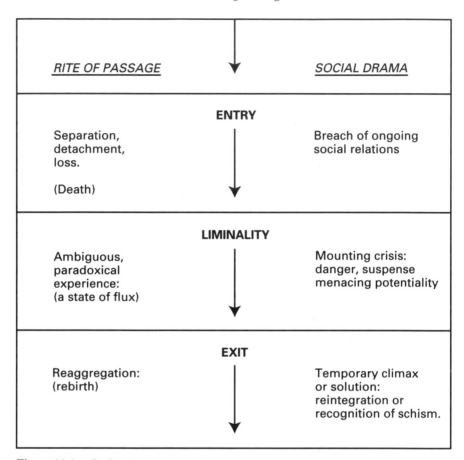

Figure 11.1   *Cycles of social change*
Source: Turner (1974)

In contrast, Turner's important work on transition has been taken up by relatively few organizational researchers. Pettigrew (1979), McLaren (1986) and Feldman (1990) have translated this work into organizational culture and symbolism to examine the longitudinal experience of organizing through 'social drama'. This term has also been employed by Rosen (1985, 1988) in his consideration of specific ceremonial events (for example, an organization's Christmas party), however, his organizational analysis concentrated on symbolic inversion and neglected the four phases of social drama's longitudinal process. It would thus seem more appropriate for Rosen's work to be described as focused on the final phase of a social drama (that is, a rite of renewal or integration), with little explicit consideration of its processual antecedents. Pettigrew (1979) worked in an opposing direction, neglecting the four phases of a social drama in his concern to explore a sequence of social dramas over a long period (41 years) in a particular setting.

This chapter, following Jeffcutt (1989, 1990), will take a middle focus, by considering each of the phases of transition in a particular setting as well as the processual whole. In this way, the productivity of Turner's work on transition will be considered through a field study in which 'rite of passage' and 'social drama' became employed to interpret the interactions of managers and the managed as they worked through interconnected processes of transition. Importantly, these interrelated experiences of organizational transience and transformation were found to be both sustaining and debilitating for all participants.

First, the setting and its participants will be outlined (pseudonyms have been used) as a precursor to examining their transitions. The setting was an industrial city in Northern England and an educational organization which was brought into being by temporary funding from the National Commission (NC), an agency of central government. The purpose of this organization was to provide short-term training for the female adult unemployed of the locale, and it was established during a period of rising unemployment (the mid-1980s). This educational organization, New Opportunities for Women (NOW), was designed, operated and managed by a privately-owned training consultancy company, Meadow Lodge (ML), in collaboration with the regional office of the NC. NOW represented the second such collaboration between these partners, since a year previously they had established another educational organization, the Inner City Programme (ICP), which provided training for the unemployed of the most deprived areas of the city. The ICP had since operated successfully and had also gained renewed funding from the NC for a further year of work, thus providing ML with an operational model and experienced staff from which to develop NOW.

Participants in this organization can be separated into three broad categories – the managed, the managers and the go-between – each of which was identified with particular transitions. Significantly, these transitions were not only interconnected through the setting but were also projected as both integrated and harmonious.

The Managed

Trainees were projected to be transformed from unemployed to employed through the educational and training activities of the programme. The NOW programme was based in a suite of rooms attached to, and rented from, a local public library. Trainees participated in the programme on an open access basis, responding to publicity in local media and in job centres. While on the programme, trainees remained registered as unemployed, receiving benefit and an additional subsistence allowance.

Trainees who undertook the NOW programme ranged from 28 to 57 years old (mean 43), with the majority having been unemployed for between one and three years. A wide background of occupational experience was evident in which office, shop and assembly work predominated. A further significant trainee characteristic was the proportion (75 per cent) who lacked any recognized educational attainment.

The Managers

The NOW programme was projected to be transformed from a temporarily funded 'pilot' programme to a more permanently funded 'renewed' programme through the agency of trainee success in gaining employment. Such organizational success was proposed to be beneficial for all major partners in the programme: the NC would be successfully addressing the needs of a particular segment of the unemployed; ML would be developing its contact with the government agency, its niche in the expanding sector of training the unemployed and gaining further income; and finally, since the training staff of ML were employed on a short-term contracting basis, the success of the programme would develop expertise, enhance experience and provide a dependable source of income (that is, making these trainers more employable).

While trainees were all female, the trainers (those who designed, operated and managed NOW) were predominantly male, younger (mean 35), and had professional or managerial work experience. Trainers had all, at some time, participated in higher education, and had relatively little personal experience of long-term unemployment.

The Researcher

I had been working part-time for ML as a trainer on the ICP while commencing doctoral research in the then relatively 'new' field of organizational culture and symbolism. Shortly before the NOW programme was proposed within ML, I lost access to the field setting in which I had been expecting to conduct fieldwork towards my doctorate. Consequently, the founding of the NOW programme represented an opportunity to overcome this obstacle and to commence a field project focused on the longitudinal process of an organizational culture in a new organization in real-time. However, ML were hostile to the notion of such open-ended research access and an initial bargain was struck with the chief executive of ML whereby I would undertake a limited evaluation of this 'pilot' programme for my employers. Importantly, this bargain also provided the necessary 'front' from which I was able to conduct covert ethnographic fieldwork, and so acquire detailed field data in the setting that would be related to my doctoral thesis.

The Experience of Transition

At the outset, NOW was established as a temporary organization, since it was funded to operate initially for a three-month period and was described by the funding agency as a 'pilot' programme, although what this 'piloting' actually represented, or focused on, remained ambiguous. The planned duration of the programme for a trainee was four weeks, while for trainers this represented three successive trainee cohorts. The NOW programme was organized into three distinct phases which were replicated in a stable pattern over time. An initial period of group work and individual guidance took place at the programme base leading to a period of occupational experience (predominantly 'work sampling' at a local Skillcentre), followed by a further period of group work and individual guidance at the programme base. The operational activities of NOW were bounded by the ceremonial events of a launch meeting and a Christmas party, although NOW's organizational activity extended substantially before and beyond these formal confines. The researcher undertook detailed data collection in the field for 18 months, approximately spanning the period both before and after the operation of the NOW programme.

Trainees

Though trainees were not the discrete homogeneous group, in respect of their 'disadvantage' (in terms of age, work experience, educational attainment, socio-economic group, and so on), that had been assumed by trainers, there was considerable commonality in their experience of passage. Trainee accounts of their transition through the NOW programme exhibited the following character.

The first phase of a 'rite of passage' is one of 'loss', indicating a separation from pre-existing structures and conditions. On joining the programme, trainees described this separation from the mundaneness and limitations of their previous experience in terms of stark contrasts. On the one hand, they described their pre-programme situation as being *dormant* and *unseeing* – they felt 'stale', 'blindfolded', 'asleep', 'lost' – while, on the other hand, their initial experience of the programme was one of *revelation*, articulated by images of 'light' and 'clarity'. However, with this entry into the 'liminal' phase of transition, trainee experience of the programme rapidly became more confused and ambiguous. By the end of the first week, tensions were expressed in terms of *good health* ('a tonic', 'refreshing') and *bad health* ('exhausting', 'draining'); as the programme continued, such paradoxical imagery increased with trainee experience characterized by *disorientation* (for example, trainees felt they were both 'going on' as well as 'slipping back'). Throughout the varied activities of the 'work sampling' phase of the programme, trainee imagery contrasted the 'togetherness' and 'sharing' of the trainee group at the programme base with the 'isolation' and 'depression' (images of 'flatness'/'falling') of being apart from the group. The third phase of a rite of passage is one of 'reaggregation' or 'rebirth', and trainee imagery of their entry into this phase was oppositional in character. While some trainees were 'waking up' and 'simmering down', others were still 'high on a drug', that is, 'addicted' to their liminal experience. This opposition continued up to the point of leaving, when some trainees felt they had 'got something', while others felt as if they had been 'dumped', needing to 'go on' in order to 'get something' from the programme. Beyond the end of the programme, trainee imagery became even more stark and oppositional, with their experience of the programme being summarized as a 'holiday entertainment' then 'going back to before'; or about 'finding yourself' and 'breaking free'.

Importantly, the increasingly oppositional character of trainee transition was closely related to the contradictions of trainer transition. However, there are important tensions which need to be aired in advance of this discussion. With the female experience of unemployment being understood as essentially one of loss of autonomy (Coyle 1984), followed by entrapment in the private and isolated world of unpaid domestic labour (Finnegan 1985), trainee participation in the programme could only represent a transient and partial 'escape' from this domestic world. On the one hand, the programme offered alluring prescriptions of a return to work or learning but without an effective change of status for trainees, who were occupied for a temporary four-week period without any change in their contractual or financial circumstances – conditions which effectively denied them any gaining of autonomy. On the other hand, trainee participation in the programme offered some release from a private domestic world, through the communal experience of 'togetherness' and 'sharing'. Yet this participation was continually mediated by the encroachment of domestic labour, in terms of the double burden of work experienced by employed women (Pollert 1981), and the 'emotional blackmail' of the family in a contest of allegiances between the private and public worlds of trainee experience.

Unsurprisingly, trainees displayed different levels of attachment to the ambiguous transitional processes of the NOW programme. For some, the programme was an entertainment, a *holiday*, before an inevitable return to pre-existing limitations. These trainees achieved a transient escape from their isolation (and oppression) through a collective experience of sharing and potentiality. However, their low investment in the programme's potential outcomes meant little risk of disappointment or gain. Hence the programme represented a holiday, even if this only were 'a change being as good as a rest' – the reformulation of an oppressive social order in a fresh setting. For those trainees with a big investment and a strong attachment to transition, the programme was really about change and *breaking free*. These trainees had 'burnt their bridges' and could not go 'back to before'; thus they had a sense of desperation about needing to go on to get something. Their experience of the programme was not enough to sustain them (like a holiday effect) when they returned, unsupported and isolated, to the oppression of their former lives. The programme was thus a glimpse of a different world that they had to strive alone to rediscover. One trainee in particular, Cathy, was determined enough to pursue this long hard road alone, while others had to return, embittered, to a progressive acceptance of their former lives and restrictions. Thus NOW was, on the one hand, a delicious fairy tale, a fantasized and transient holiday; while on the other, it was a catalyst, a cathartic and traumatic process that exposed needs that were either unrealizable or, if potentially available, had to be realized alone and unsupported.

As Turner (1974) argues, the liminal stage of a rite of passage is replete with ambiguity and paradox. Indeed, the trainee's experience of NOW was certainly characterized by contradictory and competing understandings of their transition. However, a significant contribution to this process of transition and its ambiguity was made by trainers. Not only were cultural performances – training activities – invoked and interpreted differently by different trainers as two antithetic processes of passage were constructed for trainees, but also each of these processes of passage was also internally inconsistent. In such an intensively ambiguous and confusing situation, the one consistent and fresh experience that the programme provided was the formation and interaction of the trainees as a collectivity. A culture of female solidarity was strongly and consistently evident, becoming the motivation and the support to overcome difficulties and problems in participation, as well as the lateral space in which useful learning was both created and discovered. Indeed, as Thompson (1983, 1988) and others argue, the formation of such a women's learning group provides the basis for challenging patriarchy. Although it would seem that while one can indeed take steps to facilitate such an outcome, it is at the same time difficult to prevent such developments spontaneously occurring, even in the most inhospitable of settings.

During the course of the NOW programme, it would seem that trainees did achieve a collective experience which was both supportive and developmental, an experience of 'communitas' (Turner 1974). However, while such trainee progress was apparently what trainers espoused, it would appear that this was achieved more despite, than because of, their ministrations. Committed or not to the various transitions proposed through the programme, trainees all exhibited a strong dependence on their collectivity, sharing an experience of loss as well as fear of the future by the end of the programme. Whether this passage had been an experience of a *holiday*, or a catalyst in a process of *breaking free*, trainees would inevitably be leaving to enter a world in which they would be more isolated and unsupported. From a liminal state of possibility and potentiality, however gendered and domesticated, they would be re-entering a limited and stratified world of disadvantage.

> The programme was a springboard. I'm diving in deep, going where it's dark. I'm going further and needing a bit of support. Some of the others are paddling, some are drying their feet already. (Cathy, a NOW trainee from cohort 3, recorded five weeks after the programme finished.)

Trainers

While the NOW programme was structured by trainers as a process of trainee transition from origins to destinations, the 'pilot' programme as a totality must also be seen as a trainer rite of passage that exhibited three stages (before, during, and after operations), which were both temporally and symbolically different from those of trainee transitions.

As was considered, the founding of the NOW programme represented trainer and trainee rites of passage as harmonious and interdependent, since the trainers' expertise would transform the trainees into 'employables' while the trainees' success in the employment market would mean that the programme's pilot funding would be extended, providing a source of secure employment for trainers with ML. However, in practice, the nature and focus of trainee passage through the programme towards the objective of employment was contested by trainers. Accordingly, two antithetic processes of passage were designed for trainees; their manifestation in the NOW programme was directly related to conflict in the trainers' process of passage, and can be understood with reference to the transitional process of 'social drama' described by Turner (1974). A 'social drama' is a particular rite of passage which arises in conflicts and expresses, as we will see, disharmony in social process, occupying four rather than three phases.

It was observed that the origins of NOW not only contained projections about trainer and trainee transitions, but also portrayed the programme as a derivation of an established 'second chance' education programme within ML – the ICP. The first phase of a 'social drama' is described as a 'breach of regular social relations' (Turner 1974), and this occurred early in the meetings of the NOW programme design team with the initiation of conflict over whether the ICP offered a good or bad example for NOW. The mission for the team from the head of ML was to design NOW as a version of the ICP that was 'shorter, simpler and easier to operate'. Competing interpretations of this objective proposed symbolic inversions (that is, breaches) of the initial derivative relationship between the ICP and NOW – thus NOW became projected as, on the one hand, 'a poor imitation' and, on the other, as 'what the ICP could have been if organised by the right people'.

Following a 'breach' comes a phase of mounting 'crisis', which is characterized by danger, suspense and menacing potential. This phase of escalation according to Turner (1974) is liminal, akin to the central phase of a 'rite of passage', but public rather than secluded and central rather than confined. This 'crisis' phase occupied the whole of the design period of NOW and ran through to the opening of the programme's operations. The phase was characterized by the circulation of stories and rumours extolling or derogating either the ICP or NOW as models for training the long-term unemployed, and was labelled by a participating trainer as the *poisonous grapevine*. Accordingly, shaping the design of NOW were two antithetic processes of passage for trainees, both of which clearly related to differentiations in 'second chance' education (that is, 'return to work' versus 'return to learn', McGivney and Sims 1986). On the one hand, a more prescriptive process was described which was taken to lead fairly directly to a job. The components of this process were: the identification of trainee deficiencies, such as inadequacy in terms of ability and motivation, and the prescription and enactment of remedial activity – predominantly group confidence-building and attitudinal reconstruction, with trainees then exiting this intense transformative process both empowered and redirected into employment. On the other hand, a more exploratory process was described which was taken as the first step on the road to employment, with trainees identified as unknowing – both of their own selves and skills, and how these could be employed – rather than deficient. A process of guided discovery was initiated, including individual assessment, guidance and skills testing, with trainees then continuing this process of discovery and change under their own power in the direction of their own needs (for example, further training towards a particular goal). While these tensions characterize 'second chance' education for the unemployed, they also articulated tensions of derivation within ML, since the ICP had been established under a 'return to work' ethos but had developed into a 'return to learn' programme. However, both of these passages embodied significant restrictions and limitations in respect of the women trainees' origins, transitional activity and destinations.

Whether trainees were conceived of as *deficient* and thus requiring 'prescription', or *unknowing* and thus requiring 'guidance', trainers were assuming trainees to be relatively homogeneous, meaning 'traditionally conditioned' and 'working class'. These transitional models offered distinctive typifications of successful outcomes for trainees: either as bright, confident and motivated individuals who could 'sell fridges to eskimos', or as knowing, realistic and integrated individuals who could 'take steps along their own road'. In either transition, successful functioning for trainees was presented as their learning of *trainer-like* roles which were depicted in both 'male' (the successful salesman) and 'middle class' (the empowered person) terms. Consequently, the passages which trainers constructed for trainees in the NOW programme were both patriarchal and patronizing, being concerned with trainees losing their 'female' employment identities and acquiring 'male' employment identities, while also losing their 'working class' social identities and acquiring 'middle class' social identities. The projected rite of passage of the NOW programme was thus to be initiated by the 'death' of the trainees as 'trainee-like', and to be completed by their 'rebirth' as 'trainer-like'.

This period of 'mounting crisis' was characterized by both accommodations and intensifications. First, both the 'return to work' and the 'return to learn' transitions were incorporated into the final design of NOW, but were separated in the programme structure and curriculum into 'group activities' and 'individual activities'. Secondly, there was an intensifying contest for the allegiance of marginal trainers, 'the in-betweenies', who were simultaneously members of both the ICP and NOW teams. The height of this crisis was reached shortly after the launch of NOW.

The third phase of social drama is described as 'redressive action', a phase in which a social group is at its most 'self conscious' and prepared to act with force (Turner 1974). This phase was characterized by the scapegoating and punishment of 'in-betweenies' who had come to represent particular problems that afflicted each programme, and occurred in parallel in both NOW and the ICP. The redressive action in both settings was initiated at public ceremonials – trainer meetings – and involved the declaration and enforcement of allegiances. This 'taking of sides' resolved some ambiguity for 'in-betweenies' but produced problems of exposure and disaffection when marginal trainers were working in the 'wrong' setting. This redressive action was clarificatory in terms of publicly identifying the allegiances of protagonists, as siding with the ICP or NOW, and concentrating core disputes around approaches to training the long-term unemployed, but did not resolve this conflict. In NOW the conflict was articulated through the enforcement of formally separated trainer work-roles and the termination of the programme review process.

This third phase of 'social drama' appeared to intensify and entrench the conflict between the ICP and NOW, being likened to a *propaganda war* along overt battle lines, and occupying the majority of the operational period of NOW. The conflict between trainers was played out fully through the NOW programme curriculum, with trainee transition as contested terrain in terms of both objectives and process. Trainee behaviour was thus interpreted as an indicator of the success or failure of antithetic processes of passage through the programme. As Turner (1974) observes, the ritual subject's experience of a rite of passage is one of ambiguity and paradox in which social structures are perceived as being in a state of flux. For NOW trainees, this experience was intensified since the cultural performances which articulated this process of passage – the stories, metaphors, myths, taboos, invocations, and so on, which both shaped and comprised training activities – were contradictory and contested by the programme managers, the trainers. Trainees were thus in the position of troops in the propaganda war which described NOW either as a superficial imitation of the ICP which was temporary and complete – the *cosmetic* scenario – or as an innovative and successful departure from the ICP which was preparing for permanence – the *renewal* scenario. Consequently, the operational activities of the NOW programme were characterized by contradictions and inconsistencies which produced painful and paradoxical passages for trainers and trainees alike.

The fourth phase of social drama is one of temporary climax or solution, which has two potential forms. First, the 'reintegration' of the disturbed social group; or secondly, the recognition and legitimization of a 'schism'. This final phase provided a culmination of the redressive action that had been initiated earlier in both the ICP and NOW, and began during the last programme of NOW's pilot period, when it was publicly acknowledged that the 'next' programme would *not* follow for 'at least three months'. The uncertainty and ambiguity of this organizational future opened a phase of the 'social drama' which was replete with symbolic inversion, fuelled by the heightened unreality of the festive season. Revealingly, the last operational act of NOW was to provide a Christmas party for all trainees and trainers from across the three cohorts. In a eulogy, the NOW team leader described the two programmes in diametrically opposite terms, with NOW as representing the 'future' and going 'up and up', and the ICP as representing the 'past', and going 'down and down'. Accordingly, as trainers left the programme base after the end of the party (ostensibly at the point of closure) they cheerily waved goodbye with the valediction 'see you in three months' time'; and loss was offset with a fantasized 'renewal'.

The NOW team next met again some two months after the Christmas party in order to produce a final report. Since the failure of the programme to be renewed could no longer be avoided, the report (designed and written by the team leader) blamed trainee deficiency for their apparent lack of success in the job market; recommending that the long-term female unemployed be preselected and stratified into 'succeeders' and 'failures', determined by their ability to adopt male occupational roles. Furthermore, these two groups needed to be located in two separate programmes, where women would thus be either returning to work as token men (Cockburn 1985), or returning to learn as a social therapy for their disadvantage (Thompson 1988). These recommendations were based on a celebration of 'male' motivations and values with a corresponding derogation of the female.

At the launch of NOW the leader of the training team had projected that 80 per cent of trainees would find work within three months of leaving the programme. Follow-up research with all participants indicated that the 20 per cent of trainees that had gained employment had done so in work which was poorly paid, transient, deskilled and vulnerable. It is here highly debatable whether trainees' employment prospects were significantly altered by their experience of the programme. The turnover in such employment of 'green labour' (that is, 'inexpensive, inexperienced and unorganised', Wickham 1986) was sufficient for such work to be relatively easily available. Moreover, a 20 per cent employment rate was common for 'return to work' courses (Gardiner 1986) with 50 per cent being exceptional, while the projected 80 per cent had not been recorded in any study.

As Turner (1974) has suggested, the final phase of a 'social drama' provides a temporary solution to a process of conflict, representing a reformulation of social order in a setting, at an observable point in a fluid process, akin to the rebirth or reaggregation state of a rite of passage. In terms of the setting we have been considering, it would be far too simplistic to interpret this phase as the vindication of good training over bad, or a better programme of 'second chance' education over worse. Although this outcome fully resolved some trainer allegiances in ML while making others more problematic or marginal, the eventual lack of renewal of NOW posed a question that was never overtly examined during the course of the programme. NOW was initiated as a pilot programme, yet, the ostensible focus of the 'pilot' was unstated, implicit, and somehow submerged in the conflict over the objectives of return to work or to learn. In these conflicts the pilot status of NOW was clearly of significance, being alternatively denied, where the programme was derogated as a short-term 'cosmetic' measure with no longer-term significance, and asserted, where the relevance or effectiveness of the training provided became the key issue (that is, getting jobs) in the programme's 'renewal'. The social drama of trainer transitions would suggest that this piloting of organizational 'models' for the training of the long-term unemployed was located within a struggle for authority, between trainers and programmes inside a training organization, that was largely unrelated to trainees or sponsors.

The 'social drama' between ICP and NOW can thus be interpreted both educationally, as a conflict over quality, and managerially, as a conflict over profitability. As we should recall, the mission of NOW was to follow the ICP but be 'shorter, simpler and easier to operate'; perhaps one should add, with lower costs and better margins. Indeed, in the following year, the model/derivative relationship of these two training programmes was again progressively inverted, as the chief executive of ML began instigating a series of staff and cost-cutting amendments to the ICP that had been 'piloted' in NOW. The outcome was indeed to give the ICP a more instrumental 'return to work' focus and was paralleled by the departure of a number of original team members. Also, the maintenance of a 'close warm relationship' between ML and the regional NC was supported by the continued privatization of national training initiatives, with an increasing redistribution of national training funding from educational institutions to private training agencies and employers (Finn 1987). Meadow Lodge thus represented one of these newly-empowered training organizations and was, consequently, more concerned with short-term profitability than longer-term educational outcomes (Jeffcutt 1988).

The Researcher

Ethnographic fieldwork has a recognized 'rite of passage' for researchers, in which field relations with informants go from detachment through attachment to loss (Van Maanen and Kolb 1985). However, my transition was both complicated and dislocated by additional and unanticipated factors.

I was a 'direct participant' (Rosen 1986) in the setting and through an 'initial bargain' with my employer had adopted a field-role of 'educational evaluator' from which I undertook covert and semi-covert fieldwork with trainers and trainees respectively. My investigations were focused on 'what it meant to be organised' (Smircich 1983) in the NOW setting, and I sought to record, in real-time, the action and interaction of trainers and trainees as they formed and shaped the culture of this new organization.

Field relations with trainers were complicated by two main issues. First, because my data-gathering with them had to be inconspicuous, I was limited to recording activities to which my work role, as an individual activities trainer, or field role, in educational evaluation, could be convincingly extended. In practice, this gave me substantial freedom in terms of access, but required the development of specialist skills of surreptitious data recording. Secondly, because of this covert field role, I had to manage a double-burden of competing activities in parallel – working and/or research-ing. This raised problems of my resources and their limitations (such as energy and focus of attention), as well as of my cycles of attachment to and detachment from either predominantly participating or observing.

This chapter has already considered how trainers experience a 'social drama' in their transition, and as an original member of the ICP team, I brought a strong 'return to learn' ethos to the NOW team. My diaries show my enthusiastic participation in the early struggles of the design of the organization – the 'poisonous grapevine' – where I felt that NOW, like the ICP, had the potential to be developed and improved. However, this progressive attachment to my training role became inverted through the redressive action of the 'propaganda war', where, as the leading 'return to learn' 'in-betweeny', I was scapegoated and punished in the enforcement of the 'return to work' ethos. From this point of suppression, my diaries show a progressive withdrawal of commitment to and energy from my training role, with an equivalent immersion in my researching role in NOW.

Field relations with trainees were also complicated by two main issues. First, my field roles of trainer and evaluator of trainee progress gave me extensive access and enabled both conspicuous and inconspicuous data gathering. In practice, trainees were not only prepared to talk about their experience of the programme, but also had significant stories to tell which placed this experience in a wider context. As Thompson (1983) and Hughes and Littlewood (1986) found, qualitative research relationships with women in 'second chance education' led to their 'unburdening' of the previously unheard.

Secondly, these unexpectedly 'therapeutic' field relations became re-ciprocal and deepened, as I progressively experienced isolation and powerlessness in my training role in NOW. Not only was I aware of our common transcience in NOW, but I developed an increasing sense of identification with trainee 'needs', which I understood as increasingly incapable of being met by such a rigid 'return to work' programme. It is thus important to consider whether this experience represented what is described in ethnography as 'going native', that is, where a participant/observer loses the ability to remain as a scientific observer. Clearly there was an absolute gender barrier to my becoming a 'native' (Warren 1988); however, this barrier was also a relative one in terms of proximity of understanding. I would contend that the isolation and discomfort of my process of passage through the 'social drama' of the programme (feeling 'trapped') correspon-ded to the female experience of unemployment (that is, loss of autonomy, being isolated in domestic work, Coyle 1984). Consequently, proximity, insight and understanding evolved across the gender barrier of our field relations because of mutual recognition of our vulnerability. Thus for the majority of the operational period of NOW I became, through my research role, more trainee-like than trainer-like; though, I could neither 'go native' nor abandon the demands of my trainer-role.

The end of the NOW programme thus came as a relief, in which I was able to escape the discomfort and ambiguity of being a scapegoated 'in-betweeny' and 'reintegrate' myself at the ICP. I spent the next year, while working part-time at the ICP, transcribing and analysing the mass of data I had collected. This, too, was an uncomfortable period in terms of both my research and training activities. On the one hand, I felt 'overwhelmed' by the complexity of these data which I was unable to 'subdue' adequately (B. Turner 1988). Indeed, the more concentratedly and thoroughly I focused on ordering these data, the more opaque and ephemeral they became; the more I sought to uncover a NOW organizational culture, the more diffuse and equivocal such an understanding seemed. On the other hand, in my training work I had a sense of '*déjà vu*', in which 'old' arguments from NOW about the form of 'second-chance' education for the long-term unemployed, were being replayed in a reorganization of the ICP. The outcome was a redefinition of the ICP towards a 'return to work' ethos, resource constraints, and the departure of several original team members (myself included).

This final escape from the field was thus also paralleled by an escape from the complexity of my field data. As a consequence, the initial account of my fieldwork that I then produced both oversimplified and obscured significant aspects of this work in and from the field. In addition, the selection of field data which were interpreted as explicable, as well as the selection of interpretations which offered explanations, supported my denial of my agency in the achievement of NOW's 'failure'.

However, this escape was incomplete since three years later, I commenced a re-immersion in the field data, making 'discoveries' as I reassessed my initial account and joined the struggle to produce a more sophisticated account of my field experience. This re-entry came as a direct result of personal trauma, the death of my wife in a mountaineering accident, and represented part of a painful and confusing process of personal re-examination, reflection and rediscovery. Through this oppressive process of transition, I learnt that the trauma of loss engenders both destruction and creation.

The writing up of my fieldwork into a thesis represented one avenue for working through this comprehensive and continuing 'sea change' in my life. I later discovered that such a process of writing and reflection had been both therapeutic and creative for other unfortunate sufferers of trauma (Aberbach 1989; Keenan 1992). Researcher transition may thus be summarized as immersion in the field, escape from the field, followed by rediscovery and reinterpretation of the field.

Reflecting on Transition

As this summary has indicated, the interrelationship of trainee, trainer and researcher transitions through the NOW setting articulates a complex web of interconnection. Accordingly, the chapter will now focus on important issues that have shaped this deep and broad connectivity.

Trainers/Trainees

The complex transitions which comprised the NOW organization were sought to be managed as a change process characterized by functional equilibrium. As has already been considered, both antithetical trainer positions in the 'social drama' of NOW assumed the harmony and integration of trainers and trainees in transitions which were understood as interdependent and mutually exclusive (that is return to work/return to learn). These conflictual understandings of transition were also joined by their assumption of homogeneity over heterogeneity, and stability over change in a cultural process characterized by shared meaning. Furthermore, both trainer positions constructed privileged roles for themselves in the management of change, while denying ambiguity, provisionality and difference in the process of transition.

However, at the core of these oversimplifications which sought to manage change were a number of false dichotomies through which central themes of the 'social drama' of NOW may be further explored. First, the interdependence and compatibility of 'return to work' or 'return to learn' was denied as these transitions were constructed as separate and antithetical. Secondly, any separation or incompatibility between trainee needs and the remedial transitions which were projected and provided was denied, as these were constructed as interdependent. Trainer 'social drama' may thus be characterized as articulating antithetical but essentially compatible forms of 'role education', which shared common assumptions of trainee 'disadvantage' (Thompson 1983). However, trainees were a heterogeneous rather than homogeneous collectivity who were themselves working through the contradictions of a gendered terrain of which the transitions of NOW formed a part. As has been considered, the ambiguities of this terrain and corresponding differences in trainee needs (for example, a 'break'/'breaking free') were inadequately explored, only partially recognized (if at all), and inadvertently met.

Consequently, through these interconnected transitions, trainer and trainee processes of passage in the NOW setting produced an experience that was more disabling than enabling for all participants. The most significant feature of this experience was its paradoxical nature: on the one hand, those transitions which were projected were also compromised; while on the other, those participants who were most committed to the process of passage, experienced the least satisfactory outcomes. Thus, what was projected for trainer and trainee transitions was also proscribed, through the processes through which these passages interconnected.

Hence, those trainers who believed the effectiveness of the programme would be judged by the transformation of female inadequates into 'token male' employables, enacted domesticating and limiting roles for these trainees. However, those trainees who sought to break free from the 'female' private world of unpaid work and enter the 'male' public world of paid work, encountered a learning experience which, while providing the potential for consciousness raising (female solidarity), yet was enacted through conditions which disabled these emancipatory or liberating influences. So (in a painful paradox), the developmental processes of these trainees, who sought to move on, were handicapped and impeded by the limiting and stratifying training conditions enacted by trainers – thus disabling rather than enabling the very outcomes they sought to achieve.

Parallel paradoxes were also evident; since trainers who believed that the success of the programme lay in the personal development of individual trainees (being transformed from the female 'disadvantaged' to the 'empowered person'), enacted a relatively routinized and restricted guidance curriculum for all trainees as a homogeneous group. However, those trainees who sought to experience the programme as a 'holiday' or a break from their private world of domestic labour, found their 'sharing' and 'togetherness' interrupted by an institutionalized programme of activities which both differentiated and stratified them. Thus the limited and simplified escape of these trainees (symbolized by their acceptance of domestic duties in the programme), represented simplistic and limiting obstacles for trainers who believed that trainee success would be demonstrated by their 'taking steps along their own road'.

The interaction of trainers and trainees in NOW thus became focused on resolving their connected indeterminacy (that is, the transcience of the programme); however, the transitions enacted through their conjunction in the setting, proscribed the very transitions that had been projected as resolutions. Furthermore, the tensions of transcience for the organization's participants, expressed through the dichotomies of 'renewal'/'cosmetic' (trainers), and 'change'/'holiday' (trainees), being unable to be harmonized or resolved, were, through denial and symbolic inversion, rewritten. Hence the outcomes of transition for both trainers and trainees were mutual dissatisfaction, recrimination and scapegoating, as both a discriminatory sexual division of labour (Dex 1985) and the marginalization of educational provision for women (Thompson 1983) became perpetuated.

Researcher/Trainers/Trainees

The complex transitions which articulated the researcher's interrelations with both trainers and trainees were also sought to be managed as a change process characterized by functional equilibrium. For example, the experiential and academic indeterminacy of the NOW setting for the researcher was sought to be resolved by the uncovering of a structure of transition which would be manifest and changing in a relatively predictable pattern. Hence my initial account of fieldwork portrayed NOW as being shaped by a prescriptive and immutable 'cultural legacy' that emerged from a 'founders myth' and acted as a 'vicious circle', which, in the absence of 'turnaround', was maintained until the organizations 'death' (Gagliardi 1986).

However, this representation of the culture of NOW as an institutionalized 'saga' that failed to adapt, understood the trainers' 'social drama' as an inter-managerial dispute over the interpretation of 'core-values' (Schein 1985) and the articulation of a common purpose in the NOW setting. Thus, my initial account reflected my 'managerial' position as a trainer/researcher in the setting, but suppressed the content of my participation (for example, discomfort, vulnerability, struggle) as a marginal and disaffected member of a managerial team.

Furthermore, this initial account both oversimplified and obscured significant aspects of the organizational processes of transition – on the one hand, suppressing the fact that I was unable to reveal organizational data that my initial theorizing had predicted (for example, clearly identifiable temporal and experiential boundaries for NOW); and, on the other hand, obscuring the fact that I was unable to explain much of the organizational data which I had encountered (for example, the ambiguity and paradox which appeared to characterize the cultural processes I had both observed and participated in).

The deconstruction of this initial account, following my escape from the field, provided two significant realizations. First, that in my search for the 'holy grail' of organization (that is, a coherent, integrated and bounded culture), I had uncovered organizing (that is, the articulation of settings through ambiguity, provisionality and difference in symbolic processes). Secondly, that in my search for the unattainable field role of the comprehensive 'observer', I had effectively denied and suppressed the complexity and complicity of my participation in the setting (for example, sabotage and revenge during the 'propaganda war', identification with trainees). Accordingly, the period of 'writing-up' of later accounts of fieldwork was characterized by cycles of 'letting go' of the assumptions that had structured my initial account, a re-entry into the ambiguity and uncertainty of the field that these had served to protect me from, and the generation of an account (informed by the work of Victor Turner) that was more sympathetic and responsive to the complexity of the setting.

Through this ordeal, I succeeded in an academic 'rite of passage' (see Jeffcutt 1989), and became a participant in a move in organization studies whereby the sterile and authoritarian certainties (for example, functional equilibrium) that underpin organization as a 'sociocultural' system became undermined and problematical (see Linstead and Grafton Small 1992). As was observed in the case study, these reorientations had three significant thematics. First, the letting go of the assumption of shared meaning manifest in a setting characterized by unity, led to the interpretation of ambiguous or paradoxical meaning manifest in a setting characterized by division (that is, uniculturalism is thus transformed into multiculturalism, Meek 1988). Secondly, the letting go of the assumption of meaning as relatively stable and predictable over time, led to the interpretation of meaning as in a state

of flux and transformation (culture as resistant to change is thus transformed into culture as continually changing, Smircich 1985). Thirdly, the
position of the organization researcher was also changed from a safely-
detached vantage point from whence relatively fixed descriptions could be
produced, to inextricable involvement and the production of transient
'readings' or accounts (that is, organization development is thus transformed into organizational deconstruction, Cooper and Burrell 1988).

In conclusion, the putting together of these reflections on transition
presents a distinctive understanding of the theory and practice of organization, whereby the processes of organizing become manifest as text and
characterized by tension and transformation in the transactional constitution of subjectivity. As we observed throughout this chapter, the
transactions of the managed and managers, interconnected in often
inadvertent ways, constituted themselves and their terrain through passages which were both debilitating and sustaining. Furthermore, these are
findings which resonate with ethnographic studies of transition, and the
constitution of subjectivity in the complex organizations of modern society
which have also articulated transformative processes characterized by the
tensions of paradox (see, for example, Willis 1977, 1990; McLaren 1986;
Kondo 1990).

Fundamental to such an understanding of this contested and transitional
terrain has been Turner's account of 'liminality', a social process of
ambiguity, paradox and flux, particularly since it links with Cooper's (1986,
1989, 1992) analysis of organization as a problematic process of transforming an intrinsically ambiguous condition into one which is ordered. In this
way transience becomes unresolvedly interconnected with transformation
(see also Jeffcutt 1993, 1994); consequently, between the managers and the
managed of NOW were transacted subjects, terrain and trajectories around
gendered contestations of successful selves. Finally, we should be very
aware that the researcher/trainer was also one of these transitional
subjects.

As has been intimated, through the trauma of loss I entered an intensive
liminality, part of which returned me as a native to the struggle and
vulnerability of NOW. However, beyond the collapsed boundaries between
the public and the private I found understandings which have reframed my
history, both in general and in particular. In academic terms, my ultimate
departure from the field culminated in the production of a 'deconstructive
ethnography' (see also Rose 1990; Linstead 1993). While the characteristic
self-reflexivity of similar accounts has caused controversy (see Rosaldo
1989), these should not be considered as confessional or heroic gestures, but
as artefacts of a participation that is both inevitable and a necessary resource
for understanding. Consequently, the articulation of a struggle to represent
is to exhibit neither indulgence nor truth, but instead to mobilize our
reflexive participation in the pervasive struggles of everyday life (De
Certeau 1984).

References

Aberbach, D. (1989) *Surviving Trauma*. London: Yale University Press.

Cockburn, C. (1985) *Machinery of Dominance*. London: Pluto Press.

Cooper, R. (1986) 'Organisation/Disorganisation', *Social Science Information*, 25(2): 299–335.

Cooper, R. (1989) 'Modernism, Post Modernism and Organisational Analysis 3: the contribution of Jacques Derrida', *Organisation Studies*, 10(4): 479–502.

Cooper, R. (1992) 'Formal Organisation as Representation', in M. Reed and M. Hughes (eds), *Rethinking Organisation*. London: Sage.

Cooper, R. and Burrell, G. (1988) 'Modernism, Post-Modernism and Organisational Analysis', *Organisation Studies*, 9(1): 91–112.

Coyle, A. (1984) *Redundant Women*. London: The Womens Press.

De Certeau, M. (1984) *The Practice of Everyday Life*. Berkeley: University of California Press.

Dex, S. (1985) *The Sexual Division of Work*. Brighton: Harvester Press.

Feldman, S. (1990) 'Stories as Cultural Creativity', *Human Relations*, 43(9): 809–28.

Finn, D. (1987) *Training Without Jobs*. Basingstoke: Macmillan.

Finnegan, R. (1985) 'Working Outside Formal Employment', in R. Deem and G. Salaman (eds), *Work, Culture and Society*. Milton Keynes: Open University Press.

Gagliardi, P. (1986) 'The Creation and Change of Organisational Cultures', *Organisation Studies*, 7(2): 117–34.

Gardiner, J. (1986) 'Working with Women', in K. Ward and R. Taylor (eds), *Adult Education and the Working Class*. Beckenham: Croom Helm.

Geertz, C. (1973) *The Interpretation of Cultures*. New York: Basic Books.

Gluckman, M. (1965) *Custom and Conflict in Africa*. Glencoe: Free Press.

Hassard, J. and Parker, M. (1993) (eds) *Postmodernism and Organisations*. London: Sage.

Hughes, M. and Littlewood, M. (1986) 'Women as Unwaged Learners', Occasional Paper No. 17. Manchester: Centre for Adult and Higher Education, University of Manchester.

Jeffcutt, P. (1988) 'Education and Training: Beyond the Great Debate', *British Journal of Education and Work*, 2(2): 51–9.

Jeffcutt, P.S. (1989) 'Persistence and Change in an Organisation Culture', PhD thesis, School of Education, University of Manchester.

Jeffcutt, P.S. (1990) 'Transitions in a Transient Organisation', in J. Corbett (cd.), *Uneasy Transitions*. Basingstoke: Falmer Press.

Jeffcutt, P.S. (1993) 'From Interpretation to Representation in Organisation Studies', in J. Hassard and M. Parker (eds), *Postmodernism and Orgtanisations*. London: Sage. pp. 225–48.

Jeffcutt, P.S. (1994) 'The Interpretation of Organisation: A Contemporary Analysis and Critique', *The Journal of Management Studies*, 30(2): 225–50.

Johnson, G. (1987) *Strategic Change the Management Process*. Oxford: Blackwell.

Keenan, B. (1992) *An Evil Cradling*. London: Hutchinson.

Keesing, R. (1974) 'Theories of Culture', *Annual Review of Anthropology*, 3, pp. 73–97.

Kondo, D. (1990) *Crafting Selves*. Chicago: University of Chicago Press.

Lewin, K. (1951) *Field Theory in Social Science*. New York: Harper & Row.

Linstead, S. (1993) 'Deconstruction in the Study of Organisations', in J. Hassard and M. Parker (eds), *Postmodernism and Organisations*. London: Sage. pp. 49–70.

Linstead, S. and Grafton Small, R. (1992) 'On Reading Organisational Culture', *Organisation Studies*, 13(3): 331–55.

McGivney, V. and Sims, D. (1986) *Adult Education and the Challenge of Unemployment*. Milton Keynes: Open University Press.

McLaren, P. (1986) *Schooling as a Ritual Performance*. London: Routledge and Kegan Paul.

Meek, V. (1988) 'Organisational Culture: Origins and Weaknesses', *Organisation Studies*, 9(4): 453–73.

Ortner, S. (1984) 'Theory in Anthropology since the Sixties', *Comparative Studies in Society and History*, 26(1): 126–66.

Ouchi, W. and Wilkins, A. (1985) 'Organisational Culture', *Annual Review of Sociology*, 11: 457–83.

Pascale, R. (1990) *Managing on the Edge*. New York: Simon & Schuster.

Pettigrew, A. (1979) 'On Studying Organisational Cultures', *Administrative Science Quarterly*, 24(4): 570–81.

Pollert, A. (1981) *Girls, Wives, Factory Lives*. London: Macmillan.

Radcliffe-Brown, A. (1952) *Structure and Function in Primitive Society*. New York: Free Press.

Rosaldo, R. (1989) *Culture and Truth*. Boston: Beacon Press.

Rose, D. (1990) *Living the Ethnographic Life*. London: Sage.

Rosen, M. (1985) 'Breakfast at Spiros: Dramaturgy and Dominance', *Journal of Management*, 11(2): 31–48.

Rosen, M. (1986) 'Some Notes from the Field', *Dragon*, 1(6): 57–77.

Rosen, M. (1988) 'You asked for it: Christmas at the Bosses Expense', *Journal of Management Studies*, 25(5): 463–81.

Schein, E. (1985) 'How Culture Forms, Develops and Changes', in R. Kilmann, M.J. Saxton and R. Serpa (eds), *Gaining Control of the Corporate Culture*. San Francisco: Jossey Bass.

Smircich, L. (1983) 'Concepts of Culture and Organisational Analysis', *Administrative Science Quarterly*, 28(3): 339–58.

Smircich, L. (1985) 'Is the Concept of Culture a Paradigm for Understanding Organisations and Ourselves?', in P. Frost, L. Moore, M.R. Louis, C.C. Lundberg and J. Martin (eds), *Organisational Culture*. Beverly Hills: Sage.

Stocking, G. (1987) *Victorian Anthropology*. New York: Free Press.

Thompson, J. (1983) *Learning Liberation*. Beckenham: Croom Helm.

Thompson, J. (1988) 'Adult Education and the Womens Movement', in T. Lovett (ed.), *Radical Approaches to Adult Education*. London: Routledge.

Trice, H. (1985) 'Rites and Ceremonials in Organisational Cultures', *Research in the Sociology of Organisations*, 4: 221–70.

Turner, B. (1988) 'Connoisseurship in the Study of Organisational Cultures', in A. Bryman (ed.), *Doing Research in Organisations*. London: Routledge.

Turner, V. (1969) *The Ritual Process*. Chicago: Aldine.

Turner, V. (1974) *Dramas, Fields and Metaphors*. Ithaca: Cornell University Press.

Turner, V. (1982) *From Ritual to Theatre*. New York: Performing Arts Journal Publications.

Turner, V. (1986) *Anthropology of Performance*. New York: Performing Arts Journal Publications.

Van-Gennep, A. (1912/1960) *The Rites of Passage*. London: Routledge and Kegan Paul.

Van Maanen, J. and Kolb, D. (1985) 'The Professional Apprentice', *Research in the Sociology of Organisations*, 4: 1–33.

Warren, C. (1988) *Gender Issues in Field Research*. London: Sage.

Wickham, A. (1986) *Women and Training*. Milton Keynes: Open University Press.

Willis, P. (1977) *Learning to Labour*. Farnborough: Saxon House.

Willis, P. (1990) *Common Culture*. Milton Keynes: Open University Press.

12

Postmodernism Goes Practical

Hugo Letiche

First, I will indicate briefly what postmodernism signifies, in my opinion, for the field of organizational behaviour (OB). The postmodern deconstruction of rationalist practice is, I submit, for OB roughly comparable to building catapults in a glass house! Second, I will develop the theme concretely by describing a consulting situation in an organization which will be called Source. In the case of Source, the Modernist assumptions of management were demonstrably problematized by postmodern consulting. In this chapter, I will try to show what happens when one leaves pure theory behind and tries to do something with postmodernism. Postmodernism, which is out to counter the modernist drive to impose rational order and intellectual closure, risks getting stuck in the cerebral mud of an endless production of clever articles. If so, it would do exactly the reverse of what it claims to want to do, enclosing organizational reality even more in conceptual forms, finished texts and clever metaphors. The aspired-to *scriptible* (*writerly*: accessible to change, unrestricting of thought, ajar to fantasy) openness of thought, demands interaction with practice and a no-holds-barred directness of activity.

Deconstructing Organizational Behaviour

At the moment at which one doubts the epistemological validity of *meta-analysis*, one calls the whole project of organizational behaviour into doubt. This makes the postmodern critique of OB so very radical. What has OB done other than create conceptual models, be they functional, economic, communicative or whatever? OB has developed, taught and applied the concepts which are its text. Its practice is, thus, the socio-text of the invention, instruction and exploitation of specialist texts. In OB, the relationship between models (social science 'knowledge') and action ('management' or consulting) has remained very troubled. It is self-evident in education that research should lead to better schooling and/or learning. In psychology, for instance, new work might improve the quality of (personality) testing or provide additional therapeutic possibilities. But what sort of social practice does OB further? In the remote corner of OB in which I am specialized (management learning), reigning theories have:

- analysed organizational learning as being single loop, double loop, deutero;
- categorized learners into divergers, convergers, assimilators, accommodators;
- developed the learning protocols of action learning.

These concepts from Argyris, Kolb and Revans all share in the same Cartesian assumptions. Each celebrates the power of the knowing subject: *I am* (powerful, effective, a good manager) *in so far as I know*. The stronger the theoretical grip one has on reality, the better. Simple, unreflective analysis (single loop, the use of only one type of learning, the mere solving of puzzles) is inferior to self-aware theoretical sophistication linked to the intellectual power to create reality (deutero learning, the effective use of the entire learning cycle, responding illuminatively to problems). All the theories celebrate the power of thought over context; of concept over circumstance; of abstraction over event. OB is part of the modernist philosophical project, which assumes that social existence ought to be thought-driven. Priority is given to generalization before specifics, theory before experience, rationality before perception. No one shouts *hubris*; (almost) no one challenges the overweening pride of (post-) enlightenment thinking. The shipwreck of the planned, theory-driven society is unanticipated – only in the second half of the twentieth century did the *horror* become starkly evident. Postmodernism describes hyperreality – the chaos modern purpose has made; the illogic which social design has produced; the anarchy generated by hierarchical organizations, the formlessness resulting from strict control and the repression into which rational policies degenerate. The challenge to OB is: *Will practice, led by theory, inevitably lead to some monstrous form of hyperreality?* And, if so – *What is the alternative?*

Histoires and the Hyperreal

In postmodernism, the choice for OB is between *techne* and *praxis*, and it is easily made. Technical discourse *(techne) is* appropriate to the solving of design problems; it is the language of the engineer. Given a determinate end (to build a bridge), plans can be made and action undertaken to achieve a set goal in the most effective possible way. But practical discourse *(praxis)* involves a specific situation where action will (explicitly or not) be guided by social ethics. If one is to do justice to the (relative) unity and complexity of the context, one has to find a balance between principles, goals and possibilities. Only by denying the specificity of the situation can one make OB into *techne*. It is this denial of experiential consciousness which characterizes (for Baudrillard) the hyperreal; a world of epistemological terrorism, wherein management systems are more real than individual choice; and packaging is more significant than actual use. Postmodernism's protest against the postmodern society is rooted in the realization that contemporary choices and actions are not grounded in defensible decisions and that the warrants needed to ground decision making are not easily earned. The world of achievable familiar goals only seems to produce ever more meaningless violence and mindless hyperactivity. OB can remain a modernist collection of metatexts, characterized by the will to create a *Grande Histoire* of organizational existence. By generating a system of coordinates – that is, a theoretical frame to analyse and categorize organizational behaviour – large-scale social existence can be made to seem coherent and interpretable. Modernist *techne* has made sense of organizational reality by over-relying on research techniques, via the incessant fragmentation of issues and through the political, ethical impoverishment of action. Alternatively, OB can (try to) integrate itself into postmodernism by displaying an exemplary openness to experiencing actual contemporary social environments. This openness, Baudrillard predicts, will lead to an encounter with the hyperreal. A world will be revealed where the distinction between the 'real' and the 'imaginary' has ceased to function; where there are no concealed truths or deep-level meanings; and where intellectuals take part in a hysteria of producing and reproducing imagined 'realities' (Baudrillard 1981). Records of these experiences are called *Petites Histoires*: texts wherein relationships are always indeterminate, and wherein the results of interaction are rarely commensurate to the expectations or aspirations of self or other. In fact, none of the crucial terms of identity are certain:

- the distinction between the 'I' (the speaking subject) and the 'me' ('identity', or the idea the 'I' has of itself) may be reversed; perhaps the 'I' is a mere product of social conformity, internalized in childhood, and the 'me' is socially more relevant or fundamental;
- the opposition between 'self' (ego, 'stream of consciousness') and 'other' (super ego, the demanding – even threatening-force of social adjustment) may need about facing; possibly sociogenesis (the ideas, possibilities, feelings made available to the individual by his or her surroundings) is more generative than is individual consciousness (what the person alone can conceive of);
- the priority of 'identity' ('who' one is) and dismissal of *fantasme* (imagination/day dream) may need turning around – the *fantasme* is full of life and possibility while 'identity' is retrospective and leads to reification;
- the preference for 'spontaneous talk' (what the 'person' has to say, authentic speech) above telematic images (information as it is organizationally transmitted) needs re-examination; 'speech' is often formulaic, automatic and rehearsed, while telematics are unstructured, out of control and indeterminate.

Petites Histoires (*micro-narratives*) of organizational existence will be full of 'me' 'other' and '*fantasme*'. While modernist texts discuss 'excellence', 'critical intelligence', and 'business ethics', postmodern texts will reveal the 'incommensurability of individual consciousness and organizational structure', as well as explore the 'psychopolitics of functioning at the telematic work bench'.

Postmodernism Defined?

Postmodernism can be reduced to a mere trend in descriptive sociology (or aesthetics), by asserting that there is 'something out there' called a postmodern society (art) that needs to be studied and analysed. This misses the point. Postmodernism is understood here as an *epistemological* breach in Western thought. The rupture has not come suddenly; its various predictors and attempters have included Nietzsche, Husserl, de Saussure, and Merleau-Ponty. Postmodernism is the name given to the most open examination of what knowing in the contemporary circumstance signifies. It involves writing in the language of practice, in the discourse of concrete (inter)action, which is in contradistinction to the language of the modernist theoretic (which *explains, totalizes* and *orders the discourse of practice*).

Because my goal here is to be concrete and practical, I will make use of (relatively) simple basic definitions, embracing the principle that anything really worth saying can be said (fairly) simply and clearly.

By *deconstruction* I mean: the practice of submitting a (socio-)text) to a maximum of interpretative (violence) rigour, revealing the assumptions, ideas and points of view that resist the reflective assault being unleashed on the text.

By *postmodernism* I mean: an approach to understanding which has forsworn the ambition of meta-analysis, having empirically concluded that gains in conceptual power over reality are socially (historically) repressive; that the modern will for technical power is a (self-) destructive practice; and which has opted for an epistemological pause in theoretical knowing, to permit consciousness to regain an experiential foothold in social reality.

The Case of Source

Description

Source Paris was created from DAS-Paris which was itself a result of a merger between the Dutch-based design service division of a British multinational, and Rhizome, a small but highly regarded creative design agency run by its founder Jasper Rietzanger. DAS (Design and Audio-Visual Services) was hierarchical and conservative, with its Head Office in Arnhem and branches in Bristol, Copenhagen, Dusseldorf, Paris, Mexico, San Francisco and Vienna. Its work included storefronts, letterheads, product packaging and design, catalogues and posters, videos, office furniture and delivery vehicles. Rhizome had three semi-independent studios, a head office in The Hague and very successful satellites in Amsterdam and Rotterdam. The avant-garde reputation of Rhizome was founded on Rietzanger's own trail-blazing style, but in the satellites many of the customs of his head office persisted – weekly wine parties, eccentric practical jokes, chaotic working hours, impoverished management style and so on. The organizational structure was simple and flexible, with designers working on projects and on a variety of tasks. This satellite system was the agreed strategy for growth.

Rhizome was a good place for multi-skilled designers to begin successful careers. DAS was highly specialized and a place for security, stability and routine. The British multinational originally bought into Rhizome to provide a creative addition to its own work, and had intended to buy it up later. But cost cutting led it instead to offer DAS to Rhizome. A new organization, Source, was proposed, with guaranteed design contracts to the multinational for five years, underwritten losses for 18 months, and a guaranteed transfer back of individual staff who could not fit in. Source would be independent; Rhizome would disappear, becoming Source-The Hague.

DAS-Paris had 10 senior positions (managers and specialist directors) and a support staff (technicians, account manager, secretaries) of 40. It adapted designs from DAS Arnhem (who employed 60 designers), and did some independent work for the multinational's French operations. Rhizome appointed designer Boudewijn Hooijmans, a member of its permanent staff from The Hague, as artistic director of Source-Paris to help determine its future. Henri-Marc Cusy, Director of DAS-Paris, stayed on as studio director.

Cusy was pleased at the change. Though he had always worked for the multinational, he had begun to find its culture frustrating. He could not get clear answers to proposals from Arnhem or Bristol. The directors of DAS seemed afraid to make decisions. He had wanted to sell DAS design services to other companies, but was told that top-level approval was needed. He could neither get approval nor clear rejection for his plan. When DAS-Paris designed the new divisional headquarters of a high-tech product group in postmodern style, the press applauded; Arnhem frowned. Cusy was convinced that the new independence was a marvellous opportunity, but he quickly discovered that many DAS employees did not share his enthusiasm. They preferred the safe routines of DAS to the adventure of Source. Unfamiliar clients, new projects, and unforeseen challenges did not appeal. Some staff transferred within the multinational; others found *safe* jobs in other large organizations. Those who remained were not so much committed to Source, as reluctantly willing to accept it. Only a handful of staff were enthusiastic about the change.

Hooijmans took on the Paris challenge because he loved the city and saw this as the only way, in the foreseeable future, to achieve an appointment as senior designer. He knew that he was a solid designer, but was also aware that he was offered the job more because he had studied and worked in France, than because he was artistically a *high flyer*. He knew he was not one of Rhizome's best permanent designers; he was promoted because he'd been the right person, at the right place, at the right moment. But now he did have the chance to excel and to prove himself.

He arrived in Paris expecting a challenge. He'd seen and was impressed by an adventurous series of new advertisements launched by Source-Paris after market research had helped them to identify a market niche. Design services were to be offered to large concerns to help them develop or reassert corporate identity and distinctiveness. One page advertisements were placed in quality French dailies with the slogan: THE SOURCE OF YOUR RENEWAL. Supposedly clients could regain contact with basic principles of action and success, and rediscover key goals, via design-led communication. The advertisements featured business leaders of the past and attracted a lot of attention. The selling line, focusing on corporate strategy rather than aesthetic pleasure (snobbery) or functional sophistication (engineering), seemed to Hooijmans to be a first-rate idea. His first meeting with the Source staff revealed a different side to the new concern:

- they did not have enough assignments;
- there were no new clients;
- they did not know anything about corporate communication or corporate culture;
- their skill and training had not prepared them for the new strategy;
- what the advertisements promised, they did not know how to deliver;
- they had no trust in the new strategy.

He was shocked and upset by the negativism. During his first fortnight at Source, he informally interviewed staff members and discovered that the person's length of experience with DAS determined his or her attitude:

- the *juniors* (0–4 years with DAS) welcomed Source's independence from DAS, but were worried about the new company making good; they often wanted to brush up their skills.
- most *medium-termers* (5–15 years with DAS) abhorred the change, many had already left (40 per cent). A few of those who remained were committed to the new company, many simply had no choice. Most were insecure about their skills, and defensive in their attitude towards Rhizome.
- the seniors (15+ years' experience) had either left Source immediately (30 per cent) or were committed to the new strategy. They were the most ambitious employees, and showed the highest degree of willingness to change and to learn.

Hooijmans had expected a mood of resourcefulness and self-assurance. He had not anticipated that an atmosphere of frustration and ambivalence would predominate in the middle echelons. Realizing that he could never change things alone, he was glad that Cusy proposed to develop a

Table 12.1   *Rhizome and Source*

Rhizome	DAS/Source
Success	Crisis
Democratic management	Hierarchical chain of command
Participatory decision making	Bureaucratic decision making
Task oriented	Role oriented
Flat organization	Pyramid organization
Task rotation	Tasks are set/permanent
Strong informal culture	Weak informal culture
First name basis with colleagues	Contact with colleagues is formal
Open communication between employee and boss	Stereotyped limited communication between boss and employee
Fast career advancement	Little career advancement
Creativity valued	Proficiency in technical skills valued
Rejection of authority	Respect for structure
Designers used to little or no supervision	Designers expect constant supervision
High trust of others in company	Relations in company kept impersonal
Mixed responsibility for commercial and artistic activity	Split responsibility for commercial and artistic activity

management strategy together with him. The two men spent several days away from the office defining their priorities. In order to analyse the situation, they compared Rhizome with Source (see Table 12.1).

It was decided that communication in Source would have to become much more open, within and between all levels. The old practice of going through a long and cumbersome chain of command, in order to get a new idea implemented, would have to go. Source needed to take full advantage of its employees' abilities, skills and imagination. The fewer barriers between people, and the faster one could innovate, the better. Source needed to become more adaptive and flexible; it needed to learn to react effectively to external forces in its environment. Staff would have to feel that management would really listen to their ideas and act upon them. Staff had complained to Hooijmans that they were getting no answers to suggestions or constructive feedback on work done. Evidently, improved managerial responsiveness was needed to replace staff frustration and ambivalence with hard work and commitment. Management would have to make it clear that employees would not be punished for criticism, especially the *juniors*, who did not feel themselves secure enough to speak up.

Too many employees seemed to assume that management should only hear what it *wanted to hear*. Cusy and Hooijmans were aware of their isolation and felt themselves uninformed. They knew that their staff was divided into cliques. Many employees only talked to other members of the same clique, and related exclusively to the middle management attached to that clique. A pioneering Source would need to break through these barriers and encourage staff to work in new (more challenging) combinations.

In order to open communication, Cusy and Hooijmans decided:

- to hold weekly staff briefings to discuss company progress. They would give information from management and receive employee input. A high degree of employee participation would be needed to make these a success
- to spend more time talking to staff to make it more clear what was expected
- to organize social events after working hours to strengthen informal communication and to familiarize employees with direct contact with management
- to increase openness by forming project groups whose *membership* crossed over clique barriers
- to consult staff more in decision making and to solicit staff opinions
- to emphasize, to staff, that Source was a growth company which would be opening new Studios elsewhere in France, offering very attractive opportunities later.

Problems in finding new clients were also reviewed. Hooijmans knew it was expected that this would take several months, but a strategy was needed. Source advertisements promised that design would strengthen corporate identity, stimulate identification with key goals (or values), and improve internal communication. But the artists, designers, and technicians who worked for Source knew nothing at all about these organizational parameters. Cusy and Hooijmans decided to hire two commercial managers, with insight into the new strategy, to market it.

Hooijmans felt that the organizational structure of DAS was inappropriate to Source's goals. The old structure had a director, with a vice-president and controller reporting to him. Below this level were six separate skill divisions – commercial, graphics, photography, advertising, audiovisual and industrial design – all with their own director and team. This structure could never deliver the total service approach required for stimulating corporate renewal. Source was supposed to offer an integrated package of design services, not specialized skills. So a new flexible project-based model was introduced. This had a studio director and artistic director at the head, with two commercial managers and a controller reporting to them. Below this were seven project directors with multidisciplinary project teams.

The project directors had to be recruited from the old section directors, and had no experience of project management or account responsibility. Source's new approach was customer-focused, but DAS had merely provided services with little concern for how they were used by the client. Source had to know *what it did, why, and what the results were*. The project team leaders would have to produce coherent communication strategies for their clients. Hooijmans would monitor the team leaders' abilities and potential to determine who could meet the new organization's demand for social and managerial skills for which the technically-oriented section directors had not been trained. The type of client problem they were used to dealing with was technical – now it would be organizational, and ownership of these complex problems was different from the 'make to order' culture of DAS. Technical authority would need to be replaced by the ability to develop open relationships, to allow one's judgement to be questioned and to lead multidisciplinary teams. Not everyone would adapt successfully.

Six months after Cusy and Hooijmans had decided upon their management strategy, Source-The Hague (ex-Rhizome) sent a management consultant, reputed to be knowledgeable about postmodernism, to interview the management and staff at all Source offices. The consultant was to assess if adaption was proceeding satisfactorily, and to offer advice if problems were identified. To encourage the branches to make maximum use of the consultant, it was agreed that he would only report back to Source-The Hague what was agreed to in the field. His findings, after having interviewed widely in Source Paris, were as follows:

- Panic was breaking out because no new clients had been found. Staff mistrusted the ability of the commercial managers to find clients.
- The project managers were finding it very difficult to adjust to the more organizational and less technical work. Designers complained that little had really changed, the creative role promised them had not emerged.
- Top management had little or no contact with designers, technicians, copywriters, photographers, and so on. Middle management formed a wall, between the staff which actually produced design and Source's top management. The open door participatory management model had not created direct communication between the creative staff and the top.
- Many project managers and members of the creative staff had little confidence in their ability to live up to Source goals.
- Cusy and Hooijmans were spending a lot of time shoring up flagging spirits and trying to motivate an insecure staff. They were constantly defending their strategy and trying to prove to the project managers, over and over again, that the new approach really would work.

Examination of the concrete measures which Cusy and Hooijmans had agreed upon revealed:

- The weekly staff meetings had become monthly. Top management complained of a lack of involvement by staff and were very disappointed in staff participation. Staff complained that no one really listened to them and saw the meetings as just another occasion for top managers to lecture them. Staff involvement was very low: staff blamed the commercial managers for the lack of clients; the project managers for the lack of change; and top management for a lack of vision. According to staff, Source was a rudderless boat steered by a top management who had no idea how to get to where it needed to go.
- The after-hours social events were a flop. Staff complained that they were already away from their families far too long; long commuting time meant that most left home early and got back late. Many did not want informal

contact with colleagues. They claimed that things were just fine now; more intensive contact might produce conflicts and disharmony.

- The new organizational model had been introduced in principle, but in reality the old cliques were still dominant. People ate lunch with clique members, informal communication followed the old lines. Open, project-oriented communication was lacking. The specialists were sticking together; the new culture of generalists was not evolving.
- Only Hooijmans seemed to have taken the open door participatory management style seriously. Cusy still worked behind closed doors. Staff valued Hooijmans' accessibility and openness. They did not believe that Cusy really wanted direct contact or that he was able to unlearn DAS practices.
- The promise of new opportunities linked to growth had been ineffective. The idea that success would lead to a splitting up of the large teams into smaller ones, was not attractive to ex-DAS personnel. They preferred the safety of a large group of like-minded specialists to the adventure of the creative multidisciplinary team. Most saw being transferred to Lille, Lyon or Montpellier as being sent into exile. They wanted to work and live in Paris.

As agreed with Source-Paris' management, no report of findings was made to The Hague.

Speculation

Source's top managers tried to succeed on the basis of a modernist management philosophy. Their plight illustrates the consequences of applying modernist principles in the contemporary situation; the solutions suggested by the consultant (described below) provide a postmodernist alternative.

To use Karl Mannheim's (1972: 173–236) categories: Cusy and Hooijman's management philosophy *was ideological*, a mental fiction which veiled the true nature of Source from both themselves and their employees. No doubt they thought they were promoting a *utopian* Source, an organization driven by aspired goals (wish-dreams), which would transform organizational reality. But the plans were inconsistent with the situation, and doomed to fall short of intended meaning. Source, after all, was created by a forced merger of DAS and Rhizome. The call for openness precluded what many wanted: a return to prior practice. DAS had to change because economic reality did not allow its old ways to continue. Demanding individual freedom and responsibility had, as its background, the lack of any such freedom. Employees had no choice in the *de facto* takeover of DAS by Rhizome. They had no role in formulating the new organizational goals. The idea that design should provide a total organizational communicative service came from market researchers hired to assess Source's chances of success. Rietzanger had accepted the notion, Cusy had championed it. Design staff hardly understood it, having little or no idea how to realize it and fearing its implications. They also had to accept leadership from a foreigner, who was found to be likeable enough but was telling them how to *run* Source in a Dutch manner. The decision to transform the bureaucratic skills-led DAS into a flexible task-led Source had little or no support among the studio staff. It was an imposed decision, which no one could explicitly resist because everyone knew that DAS had been extremely inefficient. But actually accepting the need to change was another thing. The blueprint for change was ideological because, while it seemed to go beyond past situations to define a new way of working, it did not really offer a way out of the status quo. Customarily, the design staff had no commercial responsibility: they had had a passive attitude bordering on indifference to the multinational's core business. Now, design staff complained bitterly that the new commercial managers were not winning new contracts and that the strategy imposed by management was not working. Their level of involvement had not *changed*. Top management's story may have outstripped former practice, but studio reality had not changed. Strategy was still a management issue; designers remained technicians who carried out orders. Management's proposed changes did not occur. No one seemed aware of why the new organizational strategy was getting nowhere. Management did not appear to realize that their professed ideas and normal conduct were incongruent. No change in the values and standards of the designers had taken place. Contrastingly, Rietzanger had become converted to the new Source mission statement as had Cusy and Hooijmans. From the third advertisement onwards, Rietzanger designed the publicity himself. The advertisements became pan-European and appeared in all Source markets. But no one in Source-Paris knew, until it appeared, what the next advert would look like.

For the Source message to get beyond ideology, and burst the bonds of the existing organizational order, it would have had to disrupt the world-view characteristic of DAS. Only if the two 'wish-images' – one directed internally towards organizational openness and the other externally, towards selling a new, total communication, service product – are embodied in actual conduct, will Source become *utopian*.

> . . . a state of mind is utopian when it is incongruous with the state of reality within which it occurs This incongruence is always evident in the fact that such a state of mind in experience, in thought and in practice is oriented towards objects which do not exist in the actual situation. . . . Only those orientations transcending reality will be referred to by us as utopian which, when they pass over into conduct tend to shatter, either partially, or wholly, the order of things prevailing at the time. (Mannheim 1972: 173)

Management had wanted to rid themselves of the DAS culture and to create a new client-focused approach, but their top-down delivery had not succeeded in marshalling the energy or commitment of the employees. They were caught in the contradiction of trying via top-down management directives to reject top-down hierarchical modes of functioning. Ideology, what was *said* about organizational behaviour, had changed. But conduct was the same. Managers tried to make their demands on staff: employees passively deflected responsibility and resisted change.

The organizational ideal set for Source was steeped in modernist thinking. A meta-story of goals, missions, purposes and meanings was established for the new firm. The planners seem to have assumed that if the aspirations were clear, Source would inevitably succeed. In fact, there was no strategic plan for the studio, only a statement of intention. Via the media, Rietzanger ascribed an identity to the new organization; employees learned what they supposedly ought to be doing by following the advertisements in the press. Despite this reversal in text and reality – the advertisements did *not* sell an existing product (service) but announced what product (service) ought to exist – no one seems to have doubted the mission of pursuing organizational clarity and communicative originality via artistic authenticity and design uniqueness. Rietzanger retained his credo of design: *to do something magnificent*. For him, design existed to break out of the commonplace commercial environment of ugliness and conformity, in order to achieve dynamism and individuality. He was convinced that the stereotyped mediocrity of mass-produced, mass-repetition goods cried out to be replaced by *almost personalized products* which reflected the values of the users. Neither were Rietzanger's convictions widely shared, nor was his expressive ability to translate them into action very common. He had determined that Source staff would know their clients personally and would be able to translate clients' values into an appropriate aesthetic code. Source supposedly stood for a *people interested in people* approach, rejecting practices wherein design hacks churn out one similar idea after another, on some sort of assembly line. Source supposedly could offer design which at once provided the client with a unified corporate image, and their customers (clients) with an exciting visual experience. The potential contradiction between collective clarity and a rich individual experience, did not seem to trouble anyone. The interests of all parties could be reconciled: those of the client organization, of designers and of consumers. But the designers who were supposed to achieve these aims did not believe in them. They rejected the idea that consistency could exist between their personal needs or group interactions, and Source's organizational purpose. They resisted social contact with their colleagues outside working hours, they held back on participating in weekly staff briefings, and they disengaged from sharing responsibility for the success of the concern. Thus, while the Source advertisements claimed that the integration of self, group and organization was characteristic of their services, the staff did not accept or believe in any such integration.

Jasper Rietzanger had provided Source with a *Grande Histoire*; a whole list of values, goals and purposes. *Renewal* was proposed as strategy of organizational revitalization. Source would 'elaborate activities intended to refurbish or strengthen existing social structures and thus to improve functioning'. It would help 'people strip off accretions and get back to the essence of what they were at an earlier time and what that implied for what they might become' (Weick 1990: 3). Values can be rearticulated, powerful practice reaffirmed; but Reitzanger, Cusy and Hooijmans wanted to empty Source of the old DAS programming as quickly as possible! There was no re-evaluation of prior practice, no effort at re-discovering a positive sense of continuity, no desire to reconstruct a founding vision. Transformation prevailed: DAS was to be dead, buried and forgotten. Source was to embody a radically different point of view. This pretence that one could start from scratch, as if DAS and Rhizome were not crucial factors, was unrealistic. The idea that a statement of goals could energize and provide guidance for a new organization, was impractical. Goals and ideals were confused with work and reality. Practice is inevitably based more on *circumstance* (clients, staff skills, the nature of commissions) than on *credence* (founding values, claims to a core competence). Instead of stressing concrete, specific problem-solving, the doctrine of renewal and social integration had been posited. A modernist self-interpretation – stressing social cooperation, the ability of the group to profit from individual creativity, and the achievement of shared goals – was propagated. Source had become a metaphor for progress via individual creativity and group cooperation. But staff only wanted to produce just another marketable product. They desperately wanted to be performative, efficiently to create an effective output which would sell. The social *logos* of Source did not interest them very much: they wanted a commercial success.

Breaking the Trance

Cusy and Hooijmans preached a rhetoric of transformation, but had changed precious little. Within DAS, the designers had never accepted business responsibility and had often been commercially irresponsible. Management supposedly had the task of running DAS, the designers merely had to perform professionally the routines appropriate to their skills. Little had changed in the role logic. The designers had begun to complain about Source's lack of clients and its management's lack of strategy. Cusy and Hooijmans, increasingly, became defensive and explained their business plans and corporate strategies in ever greater detail. The more they explained, the more staff complained. Roles were distributed so that the artistic staff could escape all business responsibility and did not have to take any commercial initiatives. Top management (in Holland) realized that a crisis loomed: design employees did not have sufficient confidence in management's leadership or in the organization's future. On the one hand, Cusy and Hooijmans tried very hard to prove their competence: on the other, they strove to re-establish motivation by getting their staff to identify with Source. To win staff loyalty, they understated the amplitude of the commercial crisis and exaggerated the chances of success. The old patterns of interaction prevailed. The directors were powerless when confronted by the employees' role definitions. Prevailing modernist assumptions made the directors easy prey to the bureaucratic past – it was incumbent on management to provide a linear logic leading to business success. By one-sidedly stressing what Source had to mean, the directors did not face up to the commodity rationality of the economic environment. Management was ensnared in goals, plans, opportunities and strategies to the point that the disparity between business facts (that is, no marketable off-the-shelf products, zero new sales, no home-grown new ideas) and theories was seemingly becoming hopeless.

The postmodern consultant advised Source-Paris' management to forget *meaning* and to stress direct surface reality. Source was almost broke; if no new clients were found within six months, layoffs would begin. Ideological rhetoric was counter-productive: it convinced no one and veiled the realities of Source in an idealistic haze. The media blitz might make the new studio known, but contracts would come through direct contacts and hard economic negotiation. Cusy and Hooijmans would have to stop trying to cushion their employees from economic reality. The logic of the market-place determined that only commercial success could guarantee the continued existence of Source. Commercial failure would lead to closure. The employees could pitch-in and increase the chances of finding clients, or they could stand on the sidelines, as worthless spectators. Cusy and Hooijmans had to decide whether to confront staff with the iron logic of business, or to stick to their pseudo-democratic ideology. In reality, the designers were not free to choose company goals or to determine the rules of the corporate game. *Performativity* would reign. Source had cherished a modernist rhetoric, but it had to survive in a concrete, postmodern environment. Rhetoric promising organizational harmony, shared values, and high motivation was overwhelmed by the *hyperreality* of micro-politics, boom and bust economics, and individual isolation. Good design was not going to do away with the struggle for economic existence. A fairly unshakeable principle of *performativity* would judge Source against market criteria: how do its products contribute to the market success of its clients? Neither ethical conviction nor creative spontaneity could save Source. By believing in their own rhetoric, they almost went under. The publicity-led strategy, wherein newspaper advertisements replaced planning, consultation and decision making, illustrates the logic of *hyperreality* taken to extremes. Image overwhelmed substance, belief transcended concrete interaction. Cusy and Hooijmans had looked more to what was supposed to be, than to what actually was. The *Petites Histoires* of the studio – that is, what people thought, did, experienced – had been drowned in gigantic intentions. Source had provided itself with a very *lisible* (readerly) philosophy. What it supposedly did, how people supposedly worked together, and why its goals were important, had all been worked out. But there was no *scriptible* (writerly) text which matched the designers' expressed needs, abilities and hopes. Totalization – the big picture – had predominated; small scenes of concrete action had played little or no role. Management energy had been centred on creating an identity for Source. A contractual open organization with lots of accounts might succeed, but perfect ideas without any sales would only lead to bankruptcy. Source's management by goals and principles was unrealistic, and management had got lost in a meta-story of what Source was supposed to be like.

Modernist *ideology* had merely led to entrapment in inconsistency. The goals were phony goals, the plans were unrealizable. Management was lost in *utopian rhetoric*: promising to forge aesthetic quality, commercial prowess and social rationality into one product. Utopias promise to deliver a meaning which shatters social reality and replaces it with something better. Mere ideology is ineffective: it promises what it cannot deliver. Utopian thought can marshal real commitment – persons are empowered by their conviction in an, as yet, not existing circumstance. Utopian engagement requires a belief in a transcendent vision; commitment to an unproven warrant is required. Ideology is rationally avoidable, Utopia is not. Few people today believe in the possibility of Utopian transcendence. But because transcendence has been abandoned without being replaced with anything else, a crisis in meaning has resulted. The immensity of an inhuman, indifferent world threatens the very sense that significance is possible. Postmodernism embodies the resulting *death-of-utopia* logic. Postmodern society may be a cork floating on the changeability of human affairs, but postmodernists remain nonetheless committed to experiencing/ expressing whatever seems to them to be true about that society. The postmodernist is witness to the postmodern society. She or he holds a position of *lay stoicism*, a radical commitment to individual perception and expression. The postmodernist is often horrified by the postmodern society, but retains a commitment to something (post-Utopian/*death-of-Utopia*) nameless in humanity which justifies continuing to look, observe and report. Some imprecise ethic of loyalty or of responsibility propels the post-modernist to keep watching, thinking and feeling. The observing subject does not know what the (post-Utopian) significance is of whatever is being called (or experienced as) reality. Having de-utopianized perception, we can no longer claim that practice is:

- elucidating common goals in a systematic manner, listening to everyone's opinion, arriving at common problem definitions;
- striving to see as many alternative solutions proposed to problems as is possible;
- insuring that optimum decisions are made by having everyone participate;
- facilitating the process of working together so that everyone listens to one another;
- assuming that the relations between the persons are as important as the task to be completed;
- networking with like-minded managers to create a more open and participatory organization;
- developing the skills and attitudes of the persons who work for you;
- and so on.

Persisting with such claims, now unfounded in transcendent belief, leads easily to (false) ideology. Business school *utopias* – mostly degraded into ideology – describe managers as *empowered strategic leaders*: postmodern deconstruction reveals *a somewhat powerless actor*. Management practice is ephemeral, fragmented and discontinuous; management fails to gain rational control over action or to get activity focused on its purposes. The Source managers tried to find answers to their personnel's *need to know*, and to justify their own *need to control*. The managers identified themselves with the modernist goals of rational insight and order. Their aim, to make Source rationally controllable and socially transparent, was more real than reality. Source, actually, was far less an expression of planned thought and calculated action, than a product of organizational forces which threatened the ordered existence and stability of the design studio. The employees were not receptive to Cusy's and Hooijmans' goals. The relationship between management's participatory social text and actual organizational events was, at best, ambivalent. Management tried desperately to reduce indeterminacy. It selected task objectives and a process model; but organizational practice reduced these into a *simulacrum* (fantasy). Management had slipped into the *hyperreality* of managing by newspaper advertisements.

A postmodern leap into acknowledging the inability to plan rationally and effect change, was management's only chance to throw off the modernist ideological yoke. Management was entrapped in modernist belief, leading to simulated goals of *hyperreality* wherein practice has to be (pseudo-) rationally explained and justified. Management assumed that their relations to design employees had to make organizational sense, and be socially ethical: these assumptions had delivered them into the hands of the participatory management *simulacrum*. When he was set the task, by the management consultant, of reviewing how work relations really were in Rhizome, Hooijmans discovered that colleagues actually did not know each other very well, that discussion was pretty limited, and that Jasper Rietzanger took decisions exactly when and how he pleased. The *simulacra* of openness, participation and shared creativity were a text about an ideal Rhizome. It was never a daily reality. Rietzanger seemingly had not been restrained in his actions by the *simulacrum*, it was not an inhibiting ideology for him. Hooijmans had, when he still worked at Rhizome, experienced the *simulacrum* as a positive ideal which had had an energizing effect on him. He had experienced Rhizome as a place of growth, challenge and opportunity. The *weak utopia* of Rhizome had become an ideological impediment for Source. The vague ideal, which did not impinge too much on routine business, had become a strong ideology, tying management up in knots. Rietzanger had understood that a management *simulacrum* is of value, just as long as it remains weak-belief. Contemporary *death-of-utopia* culture needs a little bit of belief, and a few vague ideals. When Cusy and Hooijmans took the *simulacra* literally they lost touch with circumstance. Their management by modernist principles deteriorated into *hyperreality*.

Pretended Closure

If postmodernism deconstructs the rational management of change, at best into sometimes helpful *simulacra* and at worst into dangerous ideologies, how should we value it?

The managerial 'I' of Hooijmans (his persona as manager) was characterized by modernist rhetoric. His *text* at Source – what he communicated in discussion, in meetings, on paper – centered on what *others* were supposed to do, think, create. His own subjectivity (feeling and experience) was not included in the *text*. In his *text* he continually reiterated the norm of participation, openness, and cooperation; but in the same text, he repressed his (and his colleagues') actual emotions, problems caused by professional particularity and issues of creative idiosyncrasy. His managerial 'I' was defined in terms of an ideology of the (ideal) *others*' behaviour. This 'I' was very poor on autobiography, personal experience, concrete practice. The modernist ideology of management prevailed over what had actually, previously, been seen of management. His choices had become painful:

- either admit that his managerial *I* had failed and accept change, which would amount to a self-abandonment of the modernist managerial ideology; or
- preserve his managerial identity at the cost of becoming institutionally, increasingly ineffective.

By breaking with modernist management ideology, he could open himself to experiencing Source. The factum of the organization's circumstance would then hit him full force; he would have to abandon his defences which shielded him from seeing Source's limitations and contradictions. This *factum* would inevitability lead to the *fatality* (*death-of-Utopia*) of his managerial 'I' (Baudrillard 1981). Abandoning this identity (I), could liberate him to tackle the circumstantial crisis at Source or (if too threatening) could plunge him into confusion and ineffectiveness (regression). The abandonment of modernism can be a potential trauma for the 'I'. But equally, the loss of modernist identity can lead to the discovery of postmodern alternatives: a *death-of-Utopia* stance, open to *factum* accepting the *fatality* of the 'I'-centred logic, could emerge. The loss of modernist assumptions can be enabling or debilitating. *Death-of-Utopia* management centres on the small concrete stories of organizational circumstance. Context-bound *rules* replace modernist *laws* of practice. From the wreckage of overwrought ideology could emerge the concrete hard work needed to organize Source's resources, find clients, and develop realistic products. Postmodernism, for Hooijmans, will certainly be painful. It might rescue him from a managerial cul-de-sac, but nonetheless at the price of an identity crisis. The ideology of managerial control, leadership and purpose, would have to be replaced by the *factum* of shared confusion, dealing with complex messes, and accepting limited hope of success.

For the consultant, postmodernism is a powerful tool of analysis. It allows the consultant to recognize the ideological structure of Source's rhetoric. Furthermore, it frees one from assuming that modernist *truths* are inherent in managerial practice. For the consultant, facilitating a shift from ideological practice to implementing *death-of-utopia* action, is problematic. If the client is overmastered by a sense of inadequacy when stripped of the modernist ideology, ineffective practice can be replaced with the total disintegration of practice. If the commitment to circumstance and to concrete interaction is strong enough, the client will develop a new repertoire of activity grounded in newly-won perceptual realism.

In the case situation, *understanding* was clearly inferior to *seeing*. Modernist writers prioritize their understanding of circumstances. The modernists criticize the postmodernists when the latter *see* capitalist society. I answer stressing that modernists, by putting political *understanding* above description, let ideology prevail. Postmodernists choose to *see*; this is a positive choice because it affirms the will to experience the human situation and a loyalty towards lived circumstance. Ideology, by embracing the dominance of *understanding*, rejects concrete existence and thereby impoverishes interaction. However optimistic the explicit content of an ideology may be, postmodernism accuses it of being inherently pessimistic because it remains a *refusal to see*.

There are at least three first person singular personas in this text. There is an *I* who addresses the reader: this *I* expresses opinions, intentions, ideas. It is a *fantasme* of subjectivity: of willing, feeling, communicating. There is a second *I* hidden behind the first one, which writes. It has constructed the aforementioned outings of subjectivity as so many literary artefacts. This *I* is present, as not-present; it constructs text. If text is to exist, some sort of semiotic puzzling must precede it. Text is at the forefront, semiotic construction in the background. The written artefacted *I*, that is, the *subject* expressed in text, can only exist if the *not-I*, the writing agent, remains potent (which, in effect, means hidden). This *fantasme* of pure subject tells what happens and has outspoken ideas about why it happens. Third, there is a postmodern consultant who seems to communicate with others without mutual interaction. The consultant is awareness, insight, idea; that is, represents the *fantasme of pure perception*. The consultant knows without being known, comments without being commented on, and constructs a reality without being moved, changed or moulded by surroundings. None of the *I*'s is any more *real* than any other. All of them are contextual artefacts. Readers are always endangered by textual entrapment – by being captured by a subjugating fantasme of the *I*. Only by believing the text with disbelief, that is, by combining immediacy with a dose of nominalism, can one at once experience the text as a window to look through and as construct/fantasme. By accepting the instability of the relationships between the various levels of the *I*, one can at once embrace *fantasme* and the best approximation to *realism*.

In attempting the transformation from modernist ideology to post-modernist contextualism, writers such as Baudrillard and Lyotard have used radical self-exploration to reveal a process of self-liberation from ideology to radical circumstantial openness. Their path has been illuminating and has energized thought within organizational behaviour. How to make effective use of postmodernism in practice is the next task.

References

Baudrillard, J. (1981) *Simulacrums et simulation*. Paris: Editions Galilee.
Baudrillard, J. (1983) *Les Strategies Fatales*. Paris: Grasset.
Mannheim, K. (1972) *Ideology and Utopia*. London: Routledge and Kegan Paul.
Weick, K. (1990) 'Obstacles to Renewal', Paper presented to the Academy of Management Sessions, August.

Name Index

Abbott, A. 19
Aberbach, R. 186
Abraham, K. 72
Aktouf, O. 67, 68, 75
Albert, S. (& Whetten, D.) 157
Allaire, Y. 17, 3
Alvesson, M. 14, 15, 17, 20
Alvesson, M. (& Bjorkman, I.) 157
Anderson, P. 146
Atkinson, P. 31

Babcock, B. 32
Backler, F. (& Brown, C.) 14
Bailey, F.G. 33
Bailey, J. 130
Baldwin, J. 158
Barley, S.R. (& Van Maanen, J.) 99
Barney, J.B. 143
Barthes, R. 17, 42, 54
Baudrillard, J. 209
Bauman, Z. 150, 152
Beattie, R. 46
Beckett, S. 51
Beckhard, R. (& Harris, M.) 173
Beer, M. 115
Berg, P.O. 143
Binnie, J.H. 42
Bjorkman, I. (& Alversson, M.) 157
Blase, J.J. (& Evans, M.K.) 143
Bosquet, M. 131
Bourdieu, P. 58, 59, 71
Braverman, H. 131, 151
Brown, R.H. 58, 158, 159
Brown, C. (& Blackler, F.) 14
Bruner, J. 158, 161
Bruss, E.W. 160, 162, 163
Buckley, P.J. (& Casson, M.) 14
Burchell, S. 41
Burrell, G. 18, 19, 108
Burrell, G. (& Cooper, R.) 190

Calàs, M. (& Smircich, L.) 13
Carroll, S.J. (& Gillen, D.J.) 15
Carter, P. 15, 31
Cassirer, E. 115

Casson, M. (& Buckley, P.J.) 14
Chambers, R.J. 42
Chapple, S. 109
Child, J. 58
Clark, C.R. 40)
Clegg, S. 58, 155
Clegg, S. (& Dunkerley, D.) 52
Cleverley, G. 31, 92
Clifford, J. 31, 33
Cockburn, C. 183
Cohen, A.P. 24, 62, 87
Cohen, A.P. (& Comaroff, J.L.) 35
Collinson, D. 31
Colville, I. 42
Comaroff, J.L. (& Cohen, A.P.) 35
Cooke, R.A. (& Tannenbaum, A.S.) 39
Cooper, R. 190
Cooper, R. (& Burrell, G.) 190
Coyle, A. 178, 185
Crick, M. 35
Czarniawska-Joerges, B. 159, 160, 163

Dalton, M. 31, 119
Dandeker, C. 131
Davis, J. 155
Davis, B. (& Harré, R.) 158
Davis, T.R.V. (& Luthans, F.) 34
Davis, S.M. (& Schwartz, H.) 116
De Certeau, M. 20, 190
Denison, D.R. 143
Dex, S. 188
Douglas, M. 16, 31, 32, 35, 38, 41, 81, 83, 159
Douglas, M. (& Isherwood, B.) 146, 150
Drucker, P. 15, 37
Dukerich, J.M. (& Dutton, J.E.) 157
Duncan, H.D. 32
Dunkerley, D. (& Clegg, S.) 52
Dutton, J.E. (& Dukerich, J.M.) 157

Eco, U. 149
Evans, M.K. (& Blase, J.J.) 143

Fairhurst, E. 46
Fayol, H. 15

Subject Index